JUMP WITH JOY

Positive Coaching for Horse and Rider

Sarah Blanchard

WILEY

Wiley Publishing, Inc.

Howell Book House
Published by Wiley Publishing, Inc., Hoboken, New Jersey

Photos courtesy of the author unless otherwise noted.

For general information on our other products and services or to obtain technical support please contact our Customer Care Department within the U.S. at (800) 762-2974, outside the U.S. at (317) 572-3993 or fax (317) 572-4002.

Wiley also publishes its books in a variety of electronic formats. Some content that appears in print may not be available in electronic books. For more information about Wiley products, please visit our web site at www.wiley.com.

Library of Congress Cataloging-in-Publication Data

Blanchard, Sarah.
  Jump with joy : positive coaching for horse and rider / Sarah Blanchard.
    p. cm.
  ISBN 978-0-470-12140-5
  1. Jumping (Horsemanship) I. Title.
  SF309.7.B53 2008
  798.2'5—dc22
                                                    2007044698

Printed in the United States of America

10 9 8 7 6 5 4 3 2 1

Book design by Lissa Auciello-Brogan
Cover design by Wendy Mount

CONTENTS

ACKNOWLEDGMENTS

Many, many people have graciously contributed time, photographs, and general assistance to the creation of this book.

At the top of the list is my husband and principal photographer, Rich Valcourt, who is always ready to master new photography equipment and stand in the blazing sun to take hundreds of photos. Thank you for your love, patience, and support.

Thank you also to photographers Ham Ahlo, Jr., and Pat O'Leary of Kamuela, Hawaii, for their excellent photos. Cynthia DeMeter from Horseplay Equestrian Center in Honalo, Hawaii; Carole Geballe of Hilo, Hawaii; and Chandra Chowanec of Newberry Farm in Columbia, Connecticut, also provided photos.

I'd also like to gratefully acknowledge the help and support of Senior Editor Roxane Cerda, copyeditor Carol Pogoni, and developmental editor Betsy Thorpe at Wiley Publishing, who have enthusiastically helped guide the manuscript through the entire process, from concept to completion.

And a big mahalo (Hawaiian for "thank you") to the riders who graciously allowed me to use photographs of their best and not-so-best moments: Emma Ahlo, Scott Walker, Monique Walls, and Lily Startsman, students at Hawaii Preparatory Academy; Rachel Rechtman and Greta Friesen from Horseplay Equestrian Center; and good friends and students Lisa Johnston, Nancy "Bird" McIver, Lori Campbell, Joanne Costa, and Zahra Shine.

The patient, willing, wonderful horses in these photographs are Leo Bar Nani, Wai'aka, Waiwi, Petunia, Wile E Coyote, Tsatyre, and Taser, along with my own beloved Pandora and the talented eventer Cuhoolain. Without them, there would be no joy in jumping.

INTRODUCTION

A highly successful hunt-seat equitation rider once told me, in all seriousness, that she didn't need to learn how to balance her horse on a hill because "All the Maclay classes are held in the arena, where the ground is always level and the footing is always good. I'm an *equitation* rider, not an eventer."

On another occasion, I watched an upper-level dressage rider fall off when her horse unexpectedly hopped over a log at the edge of her driveway. "I don't do jumping," she explained as she picked herself up. "I'm a *dressage* rider."

The mother of a riding student told me, not long ago, that her daughter wanted to learn how to win the hunt-seat equitation on the flat class, but she shouldn't actually jump because "jumping is dangerous."

How sad! Those people missed a grand opportunity to improve their riding skills, develop a fuller partnership with their horses, and have a lot of fun in the process.

The Natural Approach

I believe that basic jumping should be part of *every* horseman's repertoire, no matter what seat you prefer to ride and regardless of whether you ever intend to compete in jumping. An education in equitation isn't complete until you can balance and control a horse through all his natural movements, in his natural environment.

So perhaps you could say that this book presents a *natural* approach to jumping. What do I mean by this? First, we consider jumping from the horse's point of view as an athlete. We examine the mechanics of the jump and understand why some horses are better athletes than others. Then we see how we can use an experienced horse to develop the rider's skills and balance while supporting the horse's natural efforts. Finally, we close the loop by

1

showing how an experienced rider can use her own confidence, skills, and judgment to develop the skills of a novice horse.

We all love watching those world-class riders and horses who excel at jumping—Olympic contenders, Grand Prix winners, national champions. It takes a lot of money, time, and talent to get to that level, certainly, but there's a whole other world of challenges and satisfaction in jumping that's accessible to almost all riders.

Jumping doesn't have to be expensive or complicated or beyond the reach of any rider with good basic skills and a reliable horse. When jumping is learned through progressive, safe, logical methods, it helps improve balance and strength for both rider and horse. Jumping can build trust, confidence, and a strong sense of teamwork between horse and rider. It helps develop problem-solving abilities and good judgment. Isn't that the essence of good horsemanship?

And jumping is just plain *fun*. Ask any ten-year-old who's just trotted through a grid and popped over her first crossrail, or any rider who's just completed her first successful cross-country round. Meeting the challenge is a pure adrenaline rush.

Who Should Read This Book?

One very important aspect of riding is that you can't do it all by yourself. There's always at least one other athlete involved (the horse), so riding automatically becomes a team endeavor. And everyone (including the horse) is simultaneously a teacher and a student. This book, therefore, offers both the learning and teaching perspectives and asks the reader to wear several hats: rider, coach, course builder, horse trainer, evaluator and constant learner.

So this book is designed for every rider who's moved beyond the novice level and wants to learn to jump, or jump better, or just ride better. It's written for the practical rider who already has a fairly solid grounding in balanced-seat riding, who can do the walk-trot-canter routine, who knows her leads and diagonals and is now looking for something more.

And this book is written for the all-around instructor, the coach who wants to help her students learn to explore the many opportunities available to those who can confidently ride over fences.

It's also designed to help a competent rider start a green horse over jumps, and it can serve as a guide for the first-time buyer looking for a suitable equine partner.

So if you're one of those dedicated backyard riders who is committed to learning and doing things right, but perhaps hasn't had the good fortune to come up through the formal hunt-seat equitation ranks, this book is for you.

If you have a solid grounding in dressage, but now you'd like to jump well enough to ride in a hunter pace or a novice three-phase event, or take that dream vacation in Irish hunt country, this book is for you.

If you're the adult rider who now has the opportunity to ride a good jumper, but maybe not the time or money to commit to a full-blown lesson program, this book is for you.

Or perhaps you're an instructor at a summer camp or general-purpose stable, and all the riders are clamoring for jumping lessons. Or maybe you're the parent of an enthusiastic rider who's just brought her first horse home, and you need to learn how to keep your daughter safe while she uses your lawn furniture to create jumps in the backyard. This book is for you, too.

The joy of jumping can help ordinary riders find extraordinary pleasure in riding. I hope you will ride well, continue learning, and make your horse proud of you.

How Should You Use This Book?

Jump with Joy begins by examining the mechanics of jumping, defining the terminology used in this area of riding and training, and discussing some of the common misconceptions about jumping. The first chapter also explains why some horses are more suited than others for this sport, and outlines the skills that both riders and horses must develop in order to be safe and successful.

All riding, and especially jumping, requires a willing and capable equine partner. So the second chapter answers the questions, "How can I find a talented jumper?" and "How do I know if the horse I have is talented?" You can use this section as an evaluation tool to help you determine if a particular horse is suited for the job—by physical structure, temperament, training, and experience.

Chapter 3 can help you determine if you're ready to begin jumping, and also discusses equipment and the importance of finding the right saddle. Read this chapter to identify gaps in your basic horsemanship education and to be sure that you have the right equipment for jumping.

Using a series of progressive exercises, chapters 4 through 5 focus on introductory lessons to help you create a solid foundation in basic skills on the flat: developing your balance, using your eyes and independent aids, and learning to judge speed, distance, and rhythm. To gain the most from these chapters, you should read the discussion section of each chapter before saddling up and following the exercises in each lesson.

More experienced riders might be tempted to skip over chapters 3 through 5 because the lessons in these chapters are quite basic and don't involve actual jumping. I recommend, however, that you read them thoroughly—regardless of your skill level—and be sure to incorporate these simple exercises into your basic flatwork. At the end of chapter 5 is a useful paragraph to help you answer the question: "Are you ready to move on?"

Chapter 6 will help you begin to develop that all-important feel for strides and distances, through the use of grids and related distances. If you've mastered the skills presented in earlier chapters, the jumping exercises presented here should follow quite naturally. Grid exercises are at the heart of skills development in jumping, so you should plan to spend part of every training session using many of the exercises outlined here.

Chapter 7 builds on the material presented in the previous chapter, by asking you to analyze jumping questions and make more advanced decisions about your path, rhythm, stride length, and speed. You shouldn't tackle the exercises in this chapter until you're thoroughly comfortable with the material presented in previous chapters.

In chapters 8 and 9, the focus shifts from the novice rider to the green horse. Chapter 8 addresses many key questions: When is a young horse ready to begin jumping? What's the right training environment? Which skills need to be developed first? How can you use free-jumping, longeing, and trail riding to develop your horse's abilities? Chapter 9 offers a progressive training program for a green jumper, using many of the exercises presented in previous lessons for novice riders. I also explain how to introduce a young horse to cross-country jumping, and how to anticipate, analyze, and prevent typical green-horse problems.

Chapter 10 discusses the specialized demands of different competitive events, including combined training, field hunters, open jumpers, show-ring hunters, and hunt seat equitation. Here you'll find a useful overview of each field, with useful references so you can find more information about each specialty.

Finally, chapter 11 offers solutions to specific "rider" and "horse" problems. This troubleshooting chapter can be used as a standalone reference. It refers to several of the exercises presented in earlier chapters, so it will be particularly helpful after you've read the rest of the book.

As riders, we are always playing the dual roles of teacher and learner, and we are *always* responsible for our own riding and learning process. This book deliberately blurs the line between coach and rider, so these lessons can be adapted for use by riders, coaches, and on-the-ground assistants. Whether you're playing the role of rider, coach, helpful friend, or concerned parent, I recommend that you read the discussions thoroughly, review each lesson carefully, and then bring this book to your practice field for reference.

Even better, keep an extra copy in the barn, right next to your tape measure, safety helmet, and saddle.

Chapter 1

A HORSE'S TALENT FOR JUMPING

We love horses for their beauty, their kindness, and their generous spirits. We also admire and perhaps envy them for their strength, their pure athleticism, and the joy they find in movement.

One of the most impressive athletic movements a horse can perform is the *jump,* an action that propels a half-ton horse over an obstacle in a smooth, gravity-defying trajectory.

At least, that's how it appears when everything goes well!

All horses are born knowing how to jump, just as all horses are born knowing how to run. Leaping over obstacles is part of the prey animal's defense system, the flight reflex that sends them rapidly forward and away from danger. Some horses, however, find it easier than others to become airborne.

The Mechanics of Jumping

Ever since 1887, when photographer Eadweard Muybridge published his first stop-action photos of a horse and rider trotting, cantering, and jumping (*Animal Locomotion*), we've known exactly how horses propel themselves forward, up, and over an obstacle. Knowing how the horse moves is the first step to understanding why some horses are better jumpers than others, and why some riders find jumping fun and easy while others do not.

THE JUMPING STRIDE

A horse can be said to have four gaits: walk, trot, canter, and jump. The horse's jumping stride can be created from a trot, a canter, or a gallop. It's easiest for the horse to jump from a canter or gallop, because the jumping stride most closely resembles a canter or gallop stride, but the jumping motion is *not* just an "elevated canter stride." (See the sidebar, "For the Coach: Myths You Should Never Repeat," later in this chapter.)

The canter stride has three solid beats. The normal sequence of footfalls for a left-lead canter is (1) right hind; (2) the diagonal pair of left hind and right fore; and (3) left fore, followed by a moment of suspension when all four feet are off the ground.

The gallop stride has the same sequence of footfalls as the canter, but it's a four-beat gait. The diagonal pair (the second beat of the canter) is separated, so the pattern becomes: (1) right hind; (2) left hind; (3) right fore; and (4) left fore, followed by the moment of suspension.

To jump, the horse must create a powerful thrust with both hind feet simultaneously, so the pattern of the canter or gallop stride must be modified. The rhythm changes, also, as the jumping stride separates into two parts, half on the takeoff and half on the landing. And there are *two* moments of suspension in the jump stride: one long suspension as the horse is airborne over the jump, and a second shorter one *after* the front feet touch down and then pick up again on landing.

So the pattern of footfalls for a *jump stride* is: (1) both hind feet planting and pushing, followed by the long suspension over the jump; (2) touchdown by the non-leading fore foot; and (3) touchdown by the leading fore foot, followed by another, briefer, moment of suspension. Then the hind feet land and begin the next canter stride.

If the jump is small and the horse is a little lazy or not very talented, or is approaching from a trot, the two hind feet may not plant and push simultaneously on takeoff. Then we say that the horse is "just stepping" or "just cantering" over the jump.

A tremendous amount of stress is placed on the front legs and feet when the horse lands after a jump. For a brief but critical moment, all his weight and the force of his trajectory is supported on just one front leg. Then the front legs must push up again immediately into the next stride after landing, even before the hind legs have touched down. The importance of landing safely will be discussed under "Descent and Landing, a little later in the chapter.

Length of the Jumping Stride

The horse should cover approximately the same amount of ground in a jumping stride as he does in his canter stride. Any fence 3'6" or higher should have a takeoff and landing area of approximately 6' in front of and 6' beyond the jump, measured from the center of the obstacle. The lower the fence, the more leeway the horse has for a safe takeoff and landing, but the horse should always leave the ground and land at least 5' from the center of the fence. Small horses and ponies traveling in 10' or 11' canter strides can get closer on takeoff and landing, but should never be less than 4' from the fence.

Taking off closer than these distances can create an unsafe jump, in which the horse must *prop and pop*, *deer jump*, dangle a leg, or risk a front-leg knockdown. (See the sidebar, "For the Rider: Jumping Terms.") Taking off more than 6' back from the jump can create a risky (unsafe) jump, unless the horse is very scopey (see the sidebar, "For the Rider: Jumping Terms"), because the horse starts to descend before he's cleared the jump with his hind feet.

When the height of the jump is raised to 5' or above, the horse's trajectory becomes steeper (the angles of ascent and descent are sharper) and the thrust becomes more powerful, but the optimal takeoff distance does *not* need to increase much beyond the stride length of the canter or gallop the horse is already in. A steeplechase racer traveling at 30 mph may produce a leap that stretches 25' from take-off to landing because he's already galloping in 25' strides; but an open jumper covering the ground in 13' strides will jump the same fence in a 13' leap. The open jumper may need to create a very long stride to jump a very wide and low obstacle, but he does not need to create a very long stride to jump a very high fence. In fact, taking off too far in front of a high fence creates a risky situation because the horse may not have the power to thrust both up and sufficiently forward.

BALANCE IN JUMPING

Several rapid shifts in balance occur during a jump so the horse can lift his half-ton mass off the ground, become airborne, land safely, and resume a balanced canter.

These photos show a jump from a canter. One stride away from takeoff, Emma's horse stretches and lowers his head and neck to "load" the front end, so he can then . . .

. . . swing the front end up as he leaves the ground. Notice that the front end must lift off the ground before both hind feet have been planted to push off.

A good jumper pushes off the ground with both hind legs together, and folds front and back legs evenly. This is much easier to do at a canter than at a trot. Compare this to the next series of pictures, which show a horse jumping from a trot.

On landing, the horse must raise his head and neck sharply upward to keep from somersaulting, even as his hindquarters must stay tightly tucked to clear the rail. This is the moment when a too-tight martingale will severely restrict a horse's ability to balance on landing. The stress of landing on the forelegs is clearly illustrated here.

As the horse shifts from a steep vertical descent to a horizontal forward canter in the recovery phase, he gives a powerful forward thrust into the first canter stride after the jump. Emma gets pushed sharply forward and up but maintains her balance, her focus, and her steady rein contact.

Approach and Lift-Off

In jumping, the first major shift in balance occurs on the approach, when the horse lifts his head and neck. To get off the ground safely, the horse must:

1. Look at the fence, to judge where to take off and how high to jump.

2. Shift his weight back to the hindquarters so he can find the right takeoff spot. He needs to complete the final steps of his last canter stride (with

his front feet) about 6' in front of the fence, and then plant his hind feet 6' in front of the fence to begin the jumping stride—in almost the same spot as his front feet lifted off from. To get to that good takeoff spot, he may need to lengthen or shorten the last few canter strides, so he lifts his head and neck to bring his hind legs more deeply under his body.

3. *Lower and stretch* the head and neck in the last stride, and then *raise and swing* the head and neck up in a pendulum motion to get the front end off the ground. The front feet lift off the ground *before* the hind feet "plant and push," and this can happen only when the neck and head are free to elevate.

Riders who move into jumping from dressage or other non-jumping disciplines are often surprised and sometimes distressed to discover that their horses can't stay in a round, on-the-bit frame when jumping. Good balance on the flat is very different from good balance over fences.

The horse's head *has* to come up on the approach to a jump, or he won't be able to see the fence, shift back onto his hindquarters, and lift his front end up and over. (I'm not talking about the horse that flings his head in the air, snatches at the bit, and rushes or runs out. That's a problem, not a natural part of the balancing motion.)

Flight

As soon as the hind feet have pushed off, the horse must stretch his head and neck forward and down to stretch his spine up, out, and over the jump. A good jumper creates a bascule in his back from poll to tail with his spine curving upward to follow the arc of flight. In flight, the horse must have the freedom to use his head and neck so he can remain straight and balanced. If he knocks a rail, his head and neck may have to swing up or to one side to help him recover his balance so he can still land safely.

Small jumps don't demand much of a bascule; all the horse has to do is fold his legs and push off a little. But over a large jump, an athletic horse will create such an extreme bascule that the head and neck may seem to disappear down and out of the rider's sight for a moment, especially if the rider is looking up and ahead like she's supposed to. This creates an unsettling feeling, especially if you're accustomed to relying on the horse's neck for visual and physical cues to help you know what your horse is doing and to maintain your balance.

The biggest challenge for the rider during flight is to *trust the horse and not interfere*. The rider must stay in balance, move with the horse, fold and release, stay off his back, stay off his mouth, and allow the horse to keep them both safe.

Descent and Landing

The descent, landing, and recovery of a jump are just as important as the approach and flight. And the landing often creates the greatest problems with balance, for both horse and rider.

For the Rider: Jumping Terms

- **Bascule:** The convex "rounding up" ("roaching") of the horse's spine as he jumps. An athletic horse will create a noticeable bascule in his neck, back, loins, and hindquarters.

- **Cutting down:** When a horse takes off from a long spot, his trajectory peaks before he reaches the center of the fence, so he has to begin his descent before he's cleared the jump. He has to unfold the front legs and begin reaching for the landing while he's still over the obstacle. The landing is noticeably closer to the fence than the take-off. Also called *diving* or *reaching*.

- **Deer-jumping:** The horse appears to spring off the ground (and land) with all four feet together, like a deer. Not desirable, as it produces a very awkward jump that interrupts the forward rhythm and flow. Difficult for a rider to follow or control, and possibly dangerous.

- **Drifting:** The horse that takes off straight but lands to the right or left of the jump's center line. Often seen in horses that strongly prefer one lead over the other. May indicate unsoundness or a sore back.

- **Flat:** A horse that doesn't arch his neck and back into a bascule over the jump is a "flat" jumper. The flat trajectory is easier for beginning riders to learn on, because there's less spring and thrust than with an athletic, scopey jumper.

- **Dwelling:** A lazy, sour horse may lose momentum at the moment of takeoff and "stall" right when he should be making a greater effort. A lazy horse can also appear to dwell in the air. A horse that "dwells" loses momentum with each jump. The opposite of getting quick and over-jumping.

- **Fifth leg:** Athletic horses that can get themselves out of trouble from an awkward takeoff spot are said to have a *fifth leg*.

- **Hanging a leg:** Front or rear legs dangle loosely, instead of folding neatly over the jump. Very dangerous, as the horse can easily catch a leg in the rails.

- **Hollow:** Goes over a jump with a reverse bascule, meaning his head and tail are up and his back is down, or hollow. This horse can provide a comfortable, non-athletic ride for a novice rider, but he's limited in scope and will have to compensate for his lack of athleticism by folding his legs tightly to clear the rails.

- **Long spot:** The horse takes off farther back from the jump than is ideal, and may have to extend his forelegs as he reaches to clear the jump. Often results in cutting down or a hind-leg knockdown, and a very long spot results in an unsafe "risky fence."

- **Loose form:** The joints of the front and back legs aren't tucked as tightly as they should be. Not dangerous, but the horse must jump a little higher to clear the fence. Commonly seen when a good, experienced jumper is asked to jump a small fence.

- **Lying on one side:** The horse that drops a shoulder and leans to one side in the air is unbalanced and dangerous. Open jumpers in a speed class, trying to turn in the air to save time, will sometimes exhibit this very unsafe jumping form.

- **Over-facing:** When a horse is pushed to jump higher than his level of training, confidence, or talent allows. The temptation is often to test a talented young horse "just to see what he can do," but over-facing a green horse can cause him to lose confidence and begin refusing to jump. It can also jeopardize the safety of horse and rider.

- **Over-jumping:** When the horse takes off at a correct distance but lands considerably farther away from the jump, then he's putting more effort into the jumping stride than is necessary. This is common in green horses that are overly careful; but in an experienced horse, consistent over-jumping is often a sign of anxiety and may also indicate a tendency to rush and bolt.

- **Propping:** When a horse appears to push back from the fence on the last stride in an effort to avoid hitting the rails with his front legs. This usually happens when a horse has gotten too close to a fence on takeoff and shortens the last stride abruptly. An athletic horse will manage the occasional deep spot by rocking back on his hind legs and creating a steep but safe trajectory.

- **Quick-off-the-ground:** The horse's front feet quickly pat the ground together just before takeoff. Often indicates anxiety or a high-strung temperament, and may occur with over-jumping.

- **Risky fence:** When the horse leaves the ground dangerously far in front of the jump, then he's making a major safety error. At best, if he's very athletic, the horse will pull a rail with his hind feet; at worst, he will be unable to clear the obstacle and crash. Also called a *space shot*, this is especially dangerous over a wide (spread) fence.

- **Scopey:** An agile, athletic horse that produces a good bascule by roaching his back over a jump and can easily lengthen stride for a big effort. He can manage high or wide fences easily; however, he's not the best horse for a novice rider to learn on.

- **Short spot:** Also known as a "tight" or "deep" spot, in which the horse gets too close to the fence on take-off. A short spot causes the horse to lose momentum and he may hang a leg or have a front-leg knockdown.

- **Twisting or Flailing:** A horse may twist or "flail" his front or hind legs to one side to avoid touching the rails. This can happen if the horse gets too deep on his takeoff, or if he hasn't jumped quite high enough and is making an effort to avoid touching the rails.

During the descent, as the horse's shoulders move downward and the forelegs unfold, the horse must *raise his head and neck* to counterbalance the pull of gravity, while contracting his back muscles to keep his hind legs folded up and out of the way. If he doesn't raise his neck (or *can't* raise it, because of leg or back soreness, a rider interfering, or a martingale that's too tight), he risks stumbling or somersaulting on landing.

The higher the jump, the steeper the downward trajectory, and the more difficult it is for the horse to land without pitching nose-first into the dirt. A balanced landing requires just as much forward momentum as a takeoff, so the horse must keep going *forward* after the jump.

One exception to this need for continued momentum is when landing in water, because the water creates significant drag on the front legs as they land. If the horse's speed is too great, the mass of his body will simply catapult him forward into a somersault over his stalled front feet. See chapter 9, "Jumping with a Rider," for more information about handling challenges presented by jumping into water.

These photos show a jump from the trot. Two steps out from the jump, Lisa's hands and arms reach forward to allow the stretch of Nani's head and neck.

Jumping small fences from a trot is a good gymnastic exercise, especially for a green horse who might not have learned how to consistently judge take-off spots and make stride adjustments. When jumping from the trot, strides don't matter, only individual steps. The horse can take off from any trot step that brings him to a reasonable take-off spot.

The diagonal pattern of footfalls in the trot means that the two hind feet will not push off simultaneously from the same spot, as they do in the canter. A perfectly competent jumper may look as if she's hanging a front leg, because of the oppositional steps of the trot.

When the horse approaches at a trot, he should land in a canter. On the descent, Nani's front legs unfold as her head and neck stretch forward and down, allowing her hind legs to tuck up.

The landing of the right hind foot begins the first canter stride (on the left lead) after the jump. Lisa has stayed in balance throughout, shifting her center of gravity to stay over Nani's. Both have a lovely focus and balance as they move forward into a steady canter.

For the Coach: Myths You Should Never Repeat

Please don't believe or repeat either of these jumping myths! They're utterly false.

Myth #1: *A horse should take off and land as far out from the jump as the jump is high.*

I never questioned this "general rule" until a thoughtful 12-year-old student asked, "So when I'm jumping a 2' jump, my horse should take off 2' in front and land 2' beyond? But isn't his canter stride 12' long? How do I shorten him down to a 4' stride?"

The answer is, you can't. Please don't try!

The only time this "general rule" applies is when you're jumping 6' fences, because then the horse's 12' stride allows him to take off 6' in front of and land 6' beyond the fence. But most of us *aren't* jumping 6' fences, at least not yet.

Yet trainers are still teaching this myth. I recently saw some frightening consequences of this belief at a local horse show, where the young course designer—a graduate of a respected equestrian studies program!—created a low-hunter course with the fences for a one-stride in-and-out set only *17'* apart. Her reasoning was that, since the fences were only 2'9", the horses would land less than 3' into the combination, canter one 12' stride, and take off slightly less than 3' before the "out" fence. Even the smallest, handiest horses found it a serious struggle, and one large thoroughbred decided that the only way to deal with that combination was to bounce it. Miraculously, no one crashed, but no one had a safe, smooth round, either.

Recovery

In a normal landing, the non-leading front foot touches down first, followed by the leading foot, and then both front feet push off into the second suspension phase. The leading foot takes the most strain from the landing, carrying the entire weight of horse and rider while changing the downward trajectory into a forward one. Then the hind feet land—non-leading foot, followed by leading hind foot—and those hind-foot steps begin the first canter stride after the jump.

When the hind feet land, they have to push strongly to shift the direction of motion from *downward* to *forward* into the first canter stride. To help move his weight forward, his head and neck stretch out and slightly down, swinging

So here's a better rule: *The horse should take off and land equidistant from the center of the jump, so that the jump 'fits under' the length of a regular canter stride.*

There are exceptions to this general rule, of course, especially when you're tackling cross-country jumps such as banks and drops, or big spreads like triple bars and water jumps. See chapter 6 for a more detailed explanation of how the unique nature of an obstacle (height, width, terrain, combination with other obstacles) can affect a horse's takeoff, landing, and trajectory.

Myth #2: *A jump is just a big canter stride, with the horse staying up in the air a little longer during the suspension phase.*

Not true. The leap over an obstacle does *not* happen during the normal suspension phase of the canter stride. If it did, your horse wouldn't be able to jump very high at all, because the last step before the suspension phase in a canter stride is taken by a front foot, and the front feet have little or no thrusting power. The *push* has to come from the hindquarters.

What does this mean to the rider learning to jump? The motion of jumping is very different from merely *cantering a big stride*. The rhythm is different, the thrust is greater, there are *two* suspension phases, and the shifts in balance are different as the horse uses his head, neck, and back to negotiate the takeoff, trajectory, and landing. Jumping places a much greater demand on the rider's ability to balance and control his body.

So we can rewrite this rule to say: *Jumping produces a unique motion, similar to a canter stride but with two moments of suspension.*

out like a pendulum to reach forward into the canter stride. To allow the horse to use his back, head, and neck fully, the rider should be slightly out of the saddle (in a light or three-point seat) all the way through the landing and recovery.

Horses that find it hard to recover their balance on landing—because of poor conformation, interference from the rider, or lack of skills and experience—may show their unhappiness by bucking or bolting on landing, at the very moment that the rider is also most vulnerable to loss of balance. A horse that consistently lands on the same lead—no matter which lead he was on during the approach—may have a weakness or unsoundness in the nonleading front leg.

Chapter 2

FINDING A TALENTED HORSE

Why do some horses jump so willingly and easily for their riders, while others appear reluctant and clumsy? And why do certain horses do well in specific types of competition—jumping at speed, for instance—while others excel at providing a smooth, comfortable motion for the rider?

When you're first learning to jump, you probably won't have much choice in selecting a horse to learn on—if you ride in a regular program at a stable, your instructor has probably assigned you a suitable horse for lessons. But when you're ready to lease or purchase your own horse, it's important to know what attributes to look for in a hunter or jumper. Your riding will be a lot more satisfying and enjoyable if you can find a horse that suits your needs and abilities, and has a good aptitude for jumping. You'll want to find a horse that complements your abilities and skill level. He should be both a capable athlete and a willing partner.

A horse's physical ability is a primary consideration, because horses—like people—aren't likely to enjoy a job they're not particularly good at. With horses and people, athletic ability is usually a result of physical structure plus inherited ability.

Breeders and trainers place a lot of emphasis on both *conformation* (the horse's physical structure) and ancestry, and most horsemen believe that jumping—like speed—is a strongly inherited talent. But producing a top-notch jumper is considerably more complex than just following the old dictum: "Breed the best to the best and hope for the best."

The answers lie in the unique makeup of each horse: a combination of nature (inherited characteristics) plus nurture (physical development and partnership training). The three components for producing a good jumper are:

- *Inherited characteristics*: conformation and natural balance, breed and parentage, and temperament

Inherited Characteristics
Conformation and balance
Breed and parentage
Temperament

Physical Development
Nutrition and health
Skills training
Strength, stamina, agility

Partnership Development
Trust and confidence
Responsiveness
Experience and judgement

Inherited factors play the largest role in creating a great equine athlete, but physical training and the development of a solid horse-human partnership are also critical to success.

- *Physical development*: nutrition and health, skills development, and strength training
- *Partnership development*: trust and confidence, responsiveness, and experience and judgment

All three areas of development are equally important. The best breeding in the world won't compensate for poor nutrition, bad training, lousy shoeing, or a horse's fear of his rider.

Inherited Characteristics

Any task is made easier when you have the right tools, and breeders have spent many generations working to create horses with the right tools for jumping. These *natural tools* refer to the physical and psychological factors that are the products of genetics: conformation, natural balance, size, and a family tendency to excel at and enjoy athletic work.

CONFORMATION AND NATURAL BALANCE

Conformation is, quite simply, bone structure: the arrangement of the skeleton. What we see on the outside is the bone structure, plus the muscles, tendons, and ligaments that create the attachments, and a layer of fat under the skin on top. Training, nutrition, and shoeing can change the outward appearance of the horse to some extent—fat can hide minor defects, bad shoeing can make legs look crooked—but the bones are what the horse was born with. For all practical purposes, you can't change the bones; you can only help or hinder their ability to function.

If you're looking for a horse with natural jumping ability, certain conformation factors are critical. There are variations for the different disciplines—show-ring hunter or equitation horse, open jumper, field hunter, or three-phase eventer—but basic structural components are similar for all good jumpers. (See chapter 10 for a discussion of the different demands of these disciplines.)

Remember that when you judge a horse's conformation, you're not just attempting to find all his faults. The goal is to determine the horse's basic ability to move efficiently, carry a rider easily and safely over fences, and stay sound.

Evaluating conformation is largely a matter of physics, involving an examination of the angles and arcs (joints), the strength of weight-bearing columns (legs), and overall balance (proportions of neck, back, barrel, croup, legs and feet, plus musculature).

First Impressions

Look first at a horse's overall proportions and balance. He should give the appearance of being rectangular—longer than he is tall. His body length (measured from point of shoulder to point of buttock) should be about 10 percent greater than his height at the withers. He should give the impression of strength over the top of the neck, back, and croup. Everything should look as if it belongs together—for example, a short back should be balanced by a moderately short neck, and a large, sturdy body needs large, sturdy legs.

Neck and Head

A long, elegant neck can look lovely on a show-ring hunter, but a horse with a very long neck can be difficult to keep in balance, both on turns and over fences. The neck's length should be proportional to the length of the back, and should not be *ewe-necked* (concave on top with strong muscling along the bottom line). A horse in training should show correct muscle development over the top of the neck, back, and croup. The neck should be set fairly high on the shoulder, not look as if it has grown out of the bottom of his chest.

If you're looking at a yearling or 2-year-old that's growing unevenly, with his hindquarters taller than his withers, he may appear temporarily ewe-necked, with weak topline muscles and an overdeveloped musculature along the underside of the neck. Youngsters that stand rump-high during a rapid growth phase often need to move with their heads very high to offset that unbalanced stature and keep from toppling forward. If the colt's neck isn't set too low on his shoulders, and his parents have good balance (withers higher than the croup), the youngster should mature into good balance as well. But you'll have to be patient and let him grow into that balance before beginning work under saddle.

Do You Need a Pretty Head?

Not so long ago, top-level jumper riders seemed to favor horses with big, ugly heads and lop ears. (Some still do!) In the hunter ring, of course, presentation and appearance matter quite a bit more, so you'll pay more for a horse with a pretty, refined head with small, elegant ears. As long as the head supports good vision and breathing (large eyes and nostrils, wide space between the jaws, wide poll with a clean throatlatch), its size and shape are largely matters of preference.

Shoulders and Front Legs

A good jumper must be able to fold his legs snugly, front and rear. A horse that can't fold his legs easily must make a greater effort, jump higher, and land harder than the horse that can tuck his legs up out of the way. Flexible joints also give the horse more "spring" in his movement, so the legs can act as shock absorbers and the force of landing won't jar his legs and body more than necessary. That makes it easier on the horse *and* the rider.

Look for a long shoulder that slopes at a 45-degree angle from withers to the point of the shoulder. The length of the arm (from point of shoulder to elbow) should measure at least half the length of the shoulder, and the angle of arm to shoulder should be 90 degrees or greater. This shoulder-to-arm configuration creates mobility, reach, and flexibility in the front limbs.

Cannon bones should be wide, straight, and broad when seen from the side. Pasterns should have the same or nearly the same angle as the shoulder, but should not slope *more* than the shoulder as this could indicate possible weakness. Look for large, round feet with wide heels. Legs should appear straight when seen from front or back, the chest should be deep and wide, and the rib cage should be large and well sprung, not flat or narrow when viewed from the front.

Back, Croup, and Hindquarters

The engine is in the hindquarters, so its structure is especially important to generate power and thrust. The *length of the back* (from peak of withers to peak of croup) should be less than 50 percent of the horse's overall body length, as measured from point of shoulder to point of buttock. The withers should be higher than the croup, so the horse gives the impression of being built "uphill." And the highest point of the withers should be farther back along the horse's body than the point of the elbow, which will help keep the saddle back off the shoulders.

A long, sloping croup is desirable. The point of the croup is at the lumbosacral joint: the farther forward this joint is, the more strength the horse will have in his loin muscles and the better able he'll be to "sit down" and create a powerful takeoff. The opposite is the horse with the short, flat "table-top" croup; this conformation makes it harder to coil the loin muscles and bring the hind legs underneath the body.

A long croup usually goes along with a long, sloping hip-to-hock line, and a low stifle is also very good. The stifle should be closer to the ground than the point of the elbow, and the pelvic angle (point of hip to point of buttock) should be at least 15 degrees.

The hocks should be a little higher than the knees, but both knees and hocks should be large, low, and tied in smoothly to the cannon bones.

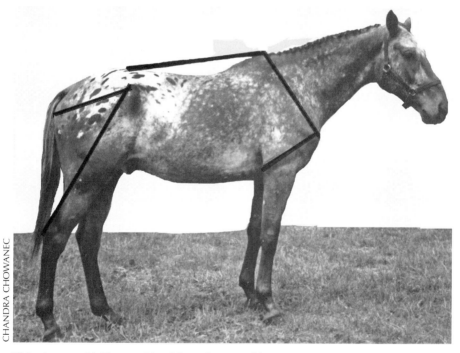

CHANDRA CHOWANEC

This 4-year-old Thoroughbred/Appaloosa gelding wasn't a "pretty" horse, but a quick evaluation of key proportions and angles told us he could jump. He had good shoulder length and slope, a 90-degree shoulder-to-arm angle, withers higher than his croup, a good pelvic angle, and long hip-to-hock length.

CHANDRA CHOWANEC

This is the same horse, during his first season of eventing at novice level. As expected, the nice shoulder produced lots of mobility with absolutely square front legs and excellent balance. And he loved his job!

Does Size Matter?

Fact: It's easier for a large, powerful horse to jump a large fence. Another fact: It's easier for a small, clever horse to change balance, speed, and direction. And the smaller jumper, carrying less weight, may deliver less of a pounding to his legs in this strenuous sport. But the big jumps always look a little more inviting to the rider when seen from the back of a tall horse!

Overall, a horse's height is less important than his takeoff thrust, his length of stride, and his *scope* (ability to lengthen as well as shorten stride). But before judging whether a particular horse's stride and scope will be suitable for a particular type of competition, you need to review the rules and requirements for that discipline.

For example, your horse *must* be comfortable cantering forward in a 12'–13' stride in order to make the distances between related jumps in a standard working hunter or equitation course, because the distances between fences in a 1-stride in-and-out on an indoor course will be set at 24'–26' apart. Equitation classes will require varying stride lengths, so the horses must be responsive *and* scopey. On an outdoor hunter course, the distance for an in-and-out may be set at 26' to 28', so you've got to gallop forward in a big, open, 13'–14' stride. (See chapter 6, "Understanding Strides, Distances, and Grids," for a full discussion of strides and distances.)

Large pony hunters are required to jump in-and-outs set at a 24' distance, which means they must canter in a 12' stride. *Medium pony hunters* work with a 22' distance, so an 11' stride is required.

Open jumpers are expected to be highly adjustable and scopey, shortening and lengthening their strides to range between a tight 23' distance to an open 26' or even a 28' distance in obstacles with several elements. Not surprisingly, the distances get longer in all competitions as the fences get bigger.

Generally, today's winning hunters and equitation horses stand 16 to 17 hands high. Larger shows may offer a *Small Hunter* division, in which only horses under 15.2 hands may compete, or they may split the *Junior Hunter* division for horses under 16 hands or 16 hands and over. Many local shows don't offer separate classes for small hunters, so many riders automatically seek the larger hunter prospects.

In *eventing,* the novice and beginner novice stadium courses are usually based on 11' distances, to accommodate horses and ponies of all sizes and shapes. Novice level demands at least moderate jumping scope, but the bigger horses must learn how to shorten their stride to make it through combinations built on 11' distances. Cross-country and stadium obstacles can be up to 2'11" high and 4'11" wide at the base, which requires a 13' jumping stride. Many talented large ponies and small horses do well on the starter-level, beginner-novice and novice courses, but to be competitive at the upper levels of eventing, you'll want to look at horses that stand 16 hands or more.

Very small increments in height matter most, perhaps, to riders who want to be competitive in the *Pony Hunter* ring, where a half-inch in the pony's height can mean the difference between having to jump 2'6" (the height of jumps for Medium ponies) and 3' (the height of jumps for Large ponies). So pony riders look for the animals that are very close to their division's size limit, but never over. It's to your advantage, for example, to have a Small pony that's precisely 12.2 hands, or a Medium that's precisely 13.2 hands. But if he grows half an inch more, the pony gets bumped up to the larger division!

RICHARD VALCOURT

Bargains can be found if size isn't critical. This 4-year-old Thoroughbred/Quarter Horse mare is just 14.3 hands, but she has the stride of a larger horse. Jumping from a trot, she hasn't snapped her knees up together as quickly as she could from a canter, but her power is evident in her hindquarters and through her back. And her attitude is lovely.

Yes, size matters in some arenas, but not always as much as people think. Many short horses, especially of Connemara-thoroughbred breeding, have become stars in open jumping and eventing. It's important to remember that these successful horses are *short,* not *small.* They tend to *stand over a lot of ground*—meaning their bodies and strides are long for their height—and they can match strides with much bigger horses.

So when you consider size and scope, be realistic about the kind of jumping you intend to do. If your goal is to mount a 200-pound man on a field hunter and follow hounds all day, you'll be looking for a heavyweight hunter, probably a 17-hand thoroughbred-draft combination. If you want your horse to perform well in the open working hunter division on the winter circuit, you'll need substantial size and stride so the horse can make the 4' fences look easy while meeting the distances—but you'll also want refinement and beauty and correct conformation.

And there's always the *worth-his-weight-in-gold category:* The steady, safe, all-around horse who can carry a child around his first beginner-novice cross-country course, do a decent job at the local hunter shows, and take a dozen young riders through their Pony Club levels. If that's the horse you're looking for, then size and scope are much less important than a willing temperament and the capacity to forgive rider errors.

EVALUATING CONFORMATION AND BASIC MOVEMENT

Follow these guidelines to evaluate a prospective horse for conformation:

1. Start by standing back and taking a look at the whole horse from the side. Let your eyes move from front to back, top to bottom. Consider the points of conformation discussed earlier in this chapter.

2. Then examine the horse from front and back, paying close attention to the width of chest and hindquarters, and the straightness of the legs. Essentially, your front and back views should show:

   • *Whether the width of chest and hindquarters are proportionate to the whole horse.* A narrow-chested horse is harder to balance laterally, may not be able to develop good lung capacity, and may have problems with *interfering* (striking his right feet and legs with the left, and vice versa). A very wide-chested horse can be a powerful weight carrier but probably won't show much speed or be very agile. A well-balanced horse's hips are slightly wider than his shoulders. But if the hips are very wide, he'll produce a rolling, side-to-side movement and it will be hard for him to bring his hind legs deep under his body for balance—he'll always travel a little spraddle-legged.

   • *Whether his legs are straight underneath, viewed from both the front and the back.* In front, a straight line extending from the point of shoulder to the ground should pass through the center of the knee, cannon bone, fetlock, and hoof. From the back, a vertical line starting from the point of the buttock should pass through the center of the hock, fetlock, and hoof. (Some very good jumpers are slightly *cow-hocked,* meaning the hocks stand a little inside that vertical line; but the hocks should not appear bow-legged, because this predisposes the horse to hock weaknesses.)

3. Next, watch him move at walk and a brisk trot, from the side and then straight away from and straight back toward you. The legs should travel in a straight path, with no winging out, toeing in, or other gait deviations. The horse should give the appearance of pushing off the ground with energy, and traveling in a balanced, steady manner, with ease and lightness. A hunter or equitation prospect should travel in long, low strides ("daisy-clipping") without excessive knee and hock action. A jumper or eventing prospect can show more loft in his steps, which will indicate a more athletic, springy action. Regardless of the type of horse you're considering, the elevation of the hind feet should match the elevation of the front, and there should be no stumbling, toe-dragging, interference, or trailing hindquarters.

BREEDS WITH BUILT-IN JUMPING ABILITY

Many otherwise wonderful horses do not make good jumpers, simply because that's not part of the breed's mission. Over the years, people have created different breeds to meet different needs, and not every breeder of horses puts jumping at the top of his agenda. Very few talented jumpers, for example, have come from the ranks of naturally gaited horses like Missouri Fox Trotters, Tennessee Walking Horses, Paso Finos, or Peruvian Pasos. Because these horses are bred for smooth intermediate gaits, they often do not trot and their canter tends to be four-beat. A horse that possesses three clean *basic gaits*—an even, four-beat walk with good overstep; an energetic, two-beat trot; and a strong three-beat canter—has the basic mechanics necessary for jumping. The jump is created from the canter, so of the three gaits, the canter is most important.

If you're starting out with an empty barn and a healthy budget, look first among the various warm-blood breeds, the thoroughbreds and thoroughbred crosses, or the pony breeds, such as the Connemara and Welsh, that have been bred specifically for jumping talent.

Look for families within those breeds that have excelled in jumping, and you'll be off to a good start. Many excellent hunters and open jumpers have also come from the ranks of race-bred thoroughbreds—but retraining an off-the-track thoroughbred presents a unique set of challenges, and this task is not for the young, timid, or novice rider.

American Standardbreds, bred for harness racing, usually are trained for either the trot or pace. Some trotters can learn to canter and jump quite well, but pacers are not mechanically inclined to do well in those tasks.

At least one gaited breed, the Icelandic Horse, is prized for its jumping ability, but the best jumpers in that breed tend to be from specific families that—not surprisingly—possess the strongest, most rhythmic trot and canter.

Appendix Quarter Horses, Paints, and Appaloosas can be wonderful jumpers if there's enough thoroughbred or warm-blood ancestry to create the right conformation and movement, but the classic-style Quarter Horses (with low withers, straight shoulders, bulky muscles, and upright pasterns) are just not built for the task of jumping. Sporthorse-bred American Saddlebreds, Morgans, and Arabs—especially the larger ones—can be very talented jumpers but, again, the conformation must be right. Many of the smaller, classic-type Arabs, for example, exhibit a very flat croup that makes it difficult for them to coil the loins and create a good bascule over a jump.

Consider crosses: Many breeders are now selecting for performance and temperament, deliberately combining the athletic attributes of thoroughbreds with the calmer temperament of draft and part-draft crosses. Horses that are three-quarters thoroughbred and one-quarter light draft can be excellent athletes with very calm attitudes. (Be sure you know what you're getting size-wise, however. Many draft breeds continue growing well past the age of 5, and sometimes the delightful 16-hand 4-year-old turns into an equally delightful but gigantic 17.3-hand, 1,600-pound 6-year-old. Big can be good, but there's such a thing as too big!)

PARENTAGE: WHO'S YOUR DADDY?

If you want to buy or breed a good jumper, it makes sense to look at the sires and dams that seem to enjoy and excel at jumping. Parentage does matter, and recent studies have confirmed what breeders have known for centuries: Jumping ability can be inherited.

In a study of 5,347 Hanoverian mares conducted from 1987 to 1993, Dr. Ludwig Christmann, assistant breeding manager of the Hanoverian Verband in Germany, evaluated mares and their offspring using standard mare inspections and performance tests. *Standard mare inspections* judge each horse's conformation (frame, neck, head, saddle position, fore and hind legs) and *performance tests* evaluate the correctness of the gaits, free jumping abilities, and rideability (responsiveness, cooperation, willingness to work with energy and suppleness).

The highest measure of inheritability (40 percent) was shown in free jumping—leading to the conclusion that you can indeed breed for jumping ability. And a strong correlation was shown between the quality of the canter and the ability to jump. However, the study also revealed that perfectly correct conformation does not guarantee jumping ability.

If you don't know your prospect's actual parentage, don't let that become a problem. If jumping ability is inherited in 40 percent of offspring, there's the remaining 60 percent of foals born who do *not* inherit a parent's jumping ability. So don't buy a jumping prospect just on bloodlines alone! When you buy a horse, you're buying that horse based on his unique characteristics—you're not buying the whole family.

TEMPERAMENT

Temperament and attitude are certainly just as important as conformation and parentage. Inherited characteristics include basic temperament as well as physical conformation. Temperament is different from attitude. *Temperament* is what he's born with (nature), and *attitude* is what's developed by his relationship with humans (nurture). Your jumper needs a good temperament *and* a good attitude, but it's impossible to develop the attitude without the good basic temperament.

A horse's temperament can be described by evaluating four *personality scales:* friendly to standoffish; energetic to apathetic, curious to fearful; and dominant to submissive. Understanding his position on each of these scales can help you understand whether he'll be easy to train, whether he'll be suited to the tasks you ask of him, and whether he'll suit *your* personality.

Friendly or Standoffish? A gregarious horse understands the dynamics of the herd, understands how to follow a herd leader, and can relax in a group because he isn't overly intimidated by the other horses. A friendly horse is often a curious horse, interested in new tasks and willing to investigate his surroundings.

The standoffish horse may become worried when he's asked to work in close proximity to others. An aloof horse is often cautious in new situations, and may be reluctant to trust or accept a human as his leader. Training may be a little more difficult with the standoff, because rewards such as praise and treats are less meaningful to him.

Energetic and Sensitive, or Lazy and Dull? Energy level is often a breed characteristic, and jumping requires more energy than more relaxed equestrian activities. A high-energy horse will put extra effort into everything he does, and he usually has an excellent work ethic. An energetic horse is often easy to teach but may be a challenge to keep focused on the task at hand because he may tend to be sensitive and restless. The most competitive jumpers usually display a high degree of sensitivity, responsiveness, and natural energy.

The overly relaxed or apathetic horse has to be urged into giving adequate effort. He may be a wonderfully safe and predictable jumper for young and inexperienced riders, or he may be so lazy that he becomes clumsy in his jumping. In either case, he's probably not a candidate for the Grand Prix jumping circuit.

Curious and Bold, or Fearful and Cautious? Humans can encourage curiosity in horses, and we can certainly create fearfulness, but all horses are born with a varying measure of both curiosity and fear. Some horses are born with great boldness and curiosity, while others seem to retain a very high measure of fear and mistrust, despite our best efforts in careful handling and training.

Curiosity, confidence, and boldness are the opposite of fear. The bold horse is willing to be the leader and make confident decisions. A confident horse can take care of a timid rider. On the other hand, a little caution can be a good thing: A cautious horse will make the extra effort to clear the rails, and won't make foolish mistakes based on overconfidence.

A horse with lots of fear is a dangerous horse, and will not make a good jumper no matter what his physical talents. His fears will overwhelm him and create panic; he cannot fully trust his partner.

For the Coach and Rider: Assessing Temperament

You assess a horse's personality largely by observation.

Define the Task and Purpose for the Horse

When developing your own checklist to assess a horse's temperament, you should first define the task and purpose for the horse. For example, a reliable lesson horse for young or novice riders should score high for friendliness and curiosity, and low-to-moderate for energy and dominance.

An open jumper or eventing prospect, on the other hand, should demonstrate a lot of energy, boldness, and dominance. Friendliness in this case is less important, and good jumpers and eventers are often a little aloof. They don't compete in a group, and they must be confident when setting out on a stadium or cross-country course with no other horses to follow.

A hunter or equitation horse *must* have good manners, so your hunter prospect must remain friendly, calm, and comfortable with groups of strange horses in the hunt field or in a flat class. Boldness needs to be balanced with caution, so the horse will want to jump clean and clear. A dominant horse may challenge his rider and spoil the smoothness of a good hunter round.

Write Down Your Checklist

If you're shopping for a new horse, a temperament assessment checklist will help. If possible, observe each prospect in the paddock, in the stall or aisle, when he's being led, ridden, longed, free-longed, or worked in a round pen. If you're looking at a young horse, ask about the temperament of the horse's parents, also. Bold, dominant mares, for example, tend to produce bold, curious foals.

Make written comments about each horse. Then assign a score of 5 (energetic, friendly, curious, dominant) to 1 (lazy, standoffish, cautious, submissive), based on the following questions.

1. Energetic or Lazy?

✓ Does he stand quietly, or is he restless during grooming, saddling, or mounting?

✓ Does he need to release energy at the beginning of a ride by bucking, shying, or going too fast, or does he settle into his work quietly?

✓ When he's asked for more energy, does he overreact, respond appropriately, or have to be prodded with spurs or a stick?

Try to test the horse in different situations to be sure that what you're observing is a true measure of his usual energy level. Workload, weather, or an exciting new environment can all create temporary changes in a horse's natural energy level.

2. Friendly or Standoffish?

✓ How easy is it for humans to approach the horse in the stall or paddock? Does he show interest, or does he ignore or avoid people?

✓ If possible, watch when he's turned out. How friendly does he seem with other horses? Is he friendly with his neighbor in the next stall? Does he display bad manners (ears back, threatening to bite or kick)? How does he respond if another horse threatens him?

✓ Can you ride him in close proximity with other well-behaved horses? Can you ride him away from the group, or is he herd-bound? Does he seem to relax more in a group, or is he more comfortable when he's the only horse in the arena?

3. Curious or Cautious?

✓ Drape a jacket over a fencepost or drop a towel on the ground, and see how he approaches it. Is he curious or suspicious?

✓ Does he shy or spook at any time when he's being handled or ridden? Does he overreact to a gesture with a longe line, whip, or rope?

✓ Does he show tension in his eyes, ears, neck, or body when he's asked to perform work that he's familiar with?

✓ With a very green or very young horse, place a rail on the ground, lead the horse over it, then move it to a new position. How willing is he to approach, investigate, and step over the rail? How careful is he about trying to step over, rather than just stumble through?

✓ With more experienced horses, ask the seller to move rails and jump standards out of their accustomed places. Is the horse overly anxious about the jumps being moved from one position to another, or does he seem comfortable figuring out what to do with the new configuration?

4. Dominant or Submissive?

✓ When you handle him from the ground, is he pushy or respectful? If you correct, does he respond with respect, ignore you, or overreact?

✓ If he's in a pasture herd, can you tell where he is in the pecking order? Does he appear to be a leader, or just one of the herd?

✓ When ridden or led in a group, will he willingly go first, last or in the middle? Does he *prefer* to be in the lead, or is he content to follow?

Assessing Your Checklist

It's the *individual* scores for each category and the way they combine that are important. Decide what's important to you, based on an honest evaluation of your riding level, your own personality, and your goals. The ideal show-ring hunter for a timid novice rider, for instance, might score a 3 for energy, a 5 for friendliness, a 4 for curiosity, and a 2 for dominance. The best open jumper prospect for a talented, experienced and highly competitive rider might score 5 for energy, 1 for friendliness, 4 or 5 for curiosity, and a 4 for dominance. And you'll want your backyard lesson horse to pull a 2 for energy, 5 for friendliness, 5 for curiosity, and 3 for dominance.

Dominant or Submissive? The highly confident, dominant horse may be highly competitive, but he's also going to challenge his rider frequently during training. In jumping, the horse and rider must work as a team, so control and decision-making pass back and forth between them as the situation requires. An overly dominant horse will fight his rider for control.

The very submissive horse, on the other hand, relies on the rider for all the direction, and can't be trusted to make good decisions on his own. He often lacks confidence and may be slow to learn, because he needs constant direction and reinforcement from his rider. A very meek horse may also be a fearful horse.

Physical Development

All the potential in the world won't produce a great horse if there are gaps in nutrition and health care, skills development, or strength training. These key factors are even more important in jumping than in most other equestrian sports, because of the additional demands placed on the equine athlete—and the potential for damage when good management is lacking.

NUTRITION AND HEALTH

Good nutrition, grooming, regular deworming and vaccinations, appropriate trimming and shoeing—it goes without saying that all these factors should be carefully managed to support the horse's needs. It's a good idea to keep the following key points in mind, however, when you're purchasing a prospect for jumping or considering management changes for the horse you already have.

1. *Body condition of a mature horse.* How fat should your athlete be? It depends, again, on the task at hand. A show-ring hunter should carry more weight than an eventer or show jumper, but the hunter should look sleek, not pudgy. On the Henneke Body Condition Scoring System, a hunter should be a 5 (moderate) or a 6 (moderately fleshy), but never more than a 7 (fleshy). An eventer needs to be lean and muscular, not fat, with a body condition of 4 (moderately thin) or 5. (Don Henneke, PhD, developed the Henneke Body Condition Scoring System during the 1980s to describe a horse's condition. It is a 9-point scale based on visual appraisal plus palpable fat covering 6 major points of the horse that respond most readily to changes in body fat. A 1 is "poor"; a 9 is "extremely fat." [Don Henneke, et al., "A condition score relationship to body fat content of mares during gestation and lactation." *Equine Veterinary Journal* 15 (1983): 371–372.])

2. *Body condition and growth rate of a young horse.* Nutrition and condition are extremely important with still-growing horses. Weanlings and

yearlings are especially susceptible to developmental problems if they've been fed a high-carbohydrate diet in an effort to help them grow fast and put on weight. This can contribute to *osteochondritis dissecans (OCD),* a condition that occurs when cartilage in the legs of a rapidly growing young horse does not convert properly to bone. OCD can cause inflammation and lameness, which may show up when the horse is still young, or may not be noticed until the horse is older and started in training. Be sure to have your veterinarian X-ray the legs of a young prospect for signs of OCD, and don't be impressed by breeding farms that produce fat babies!

3. *Shoeing.* Foot balance and traction are critical to help a horse take off and land safely and comfortably, and to help maintain soundness. All horses need regular, careful trimming, and almost all will need shoes when jumping, because of the added stress on feet and the increased demand for reliable traction. Many ponies can go barefoot on grass or sand, even when jumping, because they carry less weight and are generally sturdier than large horses. A barefoot pony may have all the traction he needs to safely negotiate a pony hunter course, but he'll probably need shoes for cross-country jumping on hard ground or mud.

   Many jumpers wear shoes that have been drilled and tapped for removable studs. There are many types of studs, designed for different footing: slick grass, deep mud, mud and ice. All studs are designed to reduce slip and increase traction. They all alter the balance of a horse's feet, and they always create additional stress on tendons and joints. Studs should *never* be left in the shoes longer than absolutely necessary. (For example, they should be removed *immediately* after a cross-country ride.) Some farriers recommend that studs be used only on the hind shoes, to minimize front-leg stress. When evaluating a jumper prospect, ask lots of questions about shoeing, especially if he's wearing corrective shoes (for example, bar shoes or wedge pads) or shoes tapped for studs.

4. *Care of the older horse.* Every horse needs proper conditioning and nutrition to do his job, but this is especially true with jumpers. Extra stress on leg joints—especially hocks, stifles, shoulders, and fetlocks—requires extra care. Any horse over the age of 10 should be on oral joint supplements (usually a combination of glucosamine, chondroitin sulfate, MSM, and antioxidants). Many trainers feed joint supplements to all their horses, regardless of age.

Many horses go through a period of *temporary hind-leg lameness,* beginning usually around age 8 to 12 (sometimes earlier), during which the *lower tarsals,* the small bones of the hock, exhibit signs of mild arthritis and then fuse. Once the fusion has occurred, generally after a couple of months, this should not affect the horse's abilities long-term. Some veterinarians recommend injections of hyaluronic acid or steroids to help this process along; others recommend pasture rest or light exercise with an occasional dose of bute as you wait for nature to take its course.

It's important to have a good pre-purchase veterinary exam, with X-rays of the hocks and front feet, whenever you're considering the purchase of a new horse. Hock X-rays can reveal where the horse might be in the hock-fusion process, and will show if other problems are present. X-rays of the front feet and fetlocks can help you identify any issues with the navicular, sesamoid, and small bones of the pastern, which is where problems most commonly appear as a result of the stresses from jumping.

SKILLS TRAINING

It's logical to assume that before a horse can become responsive, safe, and reliable over fences, he must be responsive, safe, and reliable on the flat. But it's a sad fact that many riders don't devote enough time to developing a horse's flatwork basics before starting him over jumps.

If the horse's basic training on the flat is lacking, he shouldn't be asked to carry a rider over jumps. Even in the most intense round of competition, a horse and rider spend no more than 5 percent of their time actually airborne. The rest of the time is spent on the flat, managing the speed and rhythm, balancing through turns and along straight lines, and lengthening and shortening strides.

RICHARD VALCOURT

Before learning to jump, a horse must be thoroughly responsive on the flat, shortening and lengthening stride, bending through turns, and moving forward off the rider's leg.

What's a good test to determine if a horse's flatwork is solid enough to begin jumping with a rider on board? Many successful trainers use the requirements of a First-Level dressage test as a standard. First Level requires balance and bending on 15-meter circles at the trot and 20-meter circles at the canter, leg-yielding, and lengthening stride at trot and canter. Rhythm, relaxation, obedience to the aids, smooth transitions between gaits, straightness, and willingness to go forward are all basic requirements. A horse ready to show in the hunter or equitation ring should also demonstrate flying changes of lead.

So if you're considering a jumper prospect that's "doing three-six courses" but you find he can't balance on a corner or lengthen stride, or if he rushes or balks or won't pick up his right lead or won't move forward off the leg, then you know you'll have to take him back to kindergarten basics before you can make any progress in his jumping career.

STRENGTH, STAMINA, AND AGILITY TRAINING

Carmakers know how to set performance standards for the products they manufacture. They can determine, for example, exactly how many times a car door can be opened and closed before the hinges break and the door falls off. It's easy to determine this: Simply open and close the door on the test vehicle as many times as it takes until that final time when the hinges fail.

Horses also have a mechanical breaking point. Every jumper has an optimal number of jumps in him: an unknown number of times he can jump an obstacle at a certain height and width, before the stress of jumping and landing will cause him to go lame and end his jumping career.

We cannot know what that number is until his career has been suddenly ended by that last jump. But horses are *not* cars, and your goal should not be to "find out how many jumps he has in him." In fact, the goal should be exactly the opposite: Keep the horse sound and healthy for a long, productive life, so you will *never have to learn* what that number is.

Like any athlete, a horse must be in excellent physical shape to perform at his best. Many soundness problems, especially in older horses, could be prevented if riders always made sure that their horses were properly conditioned (through training) for strength, stamina, and agility. A well-trained, experienced horse does not need to jump very often to keep his skills sharp, but he *does* need regular work to build muscle strength and stamina. Distance work, hills, and occasional agility exercises with cavalletti and small grids are far more beneficial (and less stressful) than repeated drilling over high jumps. Many people are surprised to learn that advanced-level event horses and Grand Prix jumpers who participate in the most demanding jumping sports, usually spend only 1 hour a week in actual jumping. The bulk of their training regimen consists of conditioning work on the flat that includes lots of exercises to increase suppleness and strength.

When you're evaluating a prospect to purchase or lease, learn the horse's level of fitness. Try to find out if he's been correctly conditioned, and ask how much and how often he's used for jumping. A hard-working lesson horse might be jumping 30 or 40 small fences nearly every day, but if he's fit and sound, he can be successful at his job. Be especially careful, however, not to demand too much, too soon, of the experienced jumper that's been out to pasture for a month or more. Just because the horse *can* jump a course of 4' fences, doesn't mean he *should.*

Partnership Development

Jumping requires a higher level of partnership, communication, and cooperation than any other riding sport. In jumping, the horse and rider must both make rapid decisions. Control passes back and forth between rider and horse as the rider organizes the approach and then must trust the horse to figure out how to clear the obstacle and land safely. If the pilot (rider) and copilot (horse) can't trust each other to make the appropriate decisions, the partnership will fail. The partnership requires mutual trust, responsiveness, and good judgment.

TRUST AND CONFIDENCE

Good training is built on logic, sequence, and repetition. Each step in the learning process needs to be based on a solid foundation of basic skills, so the horse knows what to expect from the trainer and vice versa.

Be sure that an experienced trainer with a proven record has taught your jumper prospect. The experienced trainer knows how to nurture and maintain trust in the horse-human partnership. This is done by giving the horse appropriate work in a step-by-step training program that leads to learning and greater confidence.

Trust can be quickly destroyed if the horse is frightened or hurt. This can happen in many ways, because a horse's balance is especially fragile when he's jumping. Trust-busters include:

- Poorly fitted equipment that pinches, hurts, or restricts the horse's ability to move freely and keep his balance
- A rider who gets left behind, jabs the horse in the mouth, or unbalances the horse with jumps that are set at impossibly short or long distances
- Frequent bad approaches (too fast, too slow, crooked, unbalanced) that require the horse to jump awkwardly, stop, or crash
- Over-facing the horse by making the jumps too difficult
- Punishing the horse for an honest mistake or for being afraid
- Overworking the horse when he's lame, sick, or exhausted

If your horse has lost trust in his rider, you'll need to give him time to recuperate from physical ailments and then go back a few steps in the training program. If you notice signs of these problems in a horse you're thinking of buying, ask for a second opinion and consider what may be involved in the retraining process. Even a very talented jumper can learn to hate his job as a result of bad riding, rushed training, or simple overwork.

RESPONSIVENESS

Jumping demands good two-way communication and prompt responses. The horse needs to pay attention to his rider, respond to requests promptly, and put an honest effort into his work.

To pay attention, the horse must always attend to both the rider and the job at hand. You can tell if your horse is paying attention if he is using both *soft eyes* (peripheral vision) and *hard eyes* (narrowed, focused vision) as he negotiates a course of obstacles. (Just like his rider, the horse also uses similar shifts in visual focus.) The position of the horse's ears will tell you where the horse is looking, because the eyes and ears work together. As the horse works on the flat, most of his attention should be on his rider and his general surroundings. He may have one ear forward and one back, signifying that his attention is split between where he's going and what his rider is communicating. Many horses travel with ears slightly floppy and at "half-mast," signifying relaxation and soft eyes as they take in their surroundings. On the approach to a jump, ears and eyes should be focused forward to assess the obstacle. On landing, the horse's attention shifts back to the rider.

A horse should have prompt responses to his rider, which means that the horse *begins* to respond correctly *as soon as* the rider issues a request. It doesn't mean drastic, hypersensitive behavior! When asked to halt, for example, the horse shouldn't perform a dramatic sliding stop. Instead, he should immediately begin shifting his weight back to his hindquarters in a smooth, balanced manner. It may take him twenty strides to complete the halt if he's traveling, say, at a forward gallop, but the important point is that he's begun to respond promptly, without any hesitation or argument.

A horse that enjoys his work will put a good effort into it. Many horses seem to genuinely enjoy jumping, perhaps because the exercise and sense of freedom makes them feel good. For a confident, energetic horse, it's an acceptable way for him to release energy and earn the praise of his rider.

Don't confuse "good energy" with speed and anxiety. The horse that grabs the bit, flings his head up, and charges at the jumps does not love to jump, no matter what his owner says. This horse is rushing to get the job over with, and is worried and anxious about the process. A horse with *good energy* puts the necessary effort into his job, but always stays attentive and responsive to his rider.

EXPERIENCE AND JUDGMENT

It's often said that good judgment comes from experience, and experience comes from bad judgment. So horses and riders both need to make many small mistakes in order to learn. The trick is to make sure the mistakes are small, and to allow them to happen in a safe, low-risk environment. Mistakes should generate learning, not fear.

Jumping demands partnership. Rider and horse are pilot and copilot, and there are no passengers. Both must play an active role in the partnership and make good decisions. A rider who tries to micromanage every step the horse takes isn't creating a safe jumper, she's creating a robot-horse that can't think for himself when he gets into a sticky situation. Good training encourages the horse to take care of himself and his rider, to use his own judgment, and sometimes to ignore a rider's bad signals.

A horse should *never* be punished for knocking down a jump or miscalculating the takeoff. It's *never* the horse's fault when a rider gets left behind, loses a stirrup, or ends up on the horse's neck after landing. *Never* punish an honest effort, an honest mistake, or confusion. And never punish fear!

Skill-building and good judgment take both time and a variety of experiences. Horses develop confidence not by jumping over the same big jump a thousand times, but by being asked to jump a thousand different little jumps.

A horse with a good range of experience will be able to tackle new, unfamiliar jumps with confidence, because he recognizes the similarities between the new jumps and all the others that he's jumped before. So when you evaluate a horse that's advertised as an "experienced jumper," find out what his experience has been: how many places has he gone, how many different types of jumps and courses has he tackled? Colored rails, flower boxes, coops, panels, oxers, natural brush, water, ditches, banks? Every new experience that is successfully mastered builds confidence, experience, and judgment.

Evaluating Talent: Yearlings and Two-Year-Olds

A "natural" jumper shows his abilities early, often as a weanling cantering by his dam's side. He seems to have an intuitive understanding of where all four legs are, and how to negotiate obstacles. Just as a cutting horse trainer looks for those young horses that show a lot of "cow" at any early age, so a trainer of jumpers looks for the young horses that seem to be born with "jump."

One of the best ways to evaluate a young prospect is to watch him free-jump, or loose-jump. Free-jumping has long been used in Europe to determine a young horse's ability before he's grown enough to begin work under saddle. The warmblood sales catalogs contain spectacular photos of young horses (from 4-year-olds right down to weanlings!) sailing over obstacles in marvelous style. The ones that can fold their knees up by their ears always command the highest prices.

In *free-jumping*, one or more jumps with wide wings are set up next to the wall, and the horse is guided around the perimeter by the trainers, who use various barriers, voice commands, and longe whips to control the horse's speed and direction. The horse should be trained well enough in longeing techniques so he is responsive to voice and whip cues—in other words, he should be free-longed, not just chased wildly around the arena. (See chapter 8 for a discussion of free-jumping and training on the longe.)

In the past, free-jumping wasn't used much in North America, as either a training technique or a selling tool, but it has rapidly gained favor at larger training stables and elite breeding farms. It helps you assess the horse's natural talents and watch how he approaches and handles a jump. It's also valuable in the early stages of training and as a loosening-up exercise, for jumpers and non-jumpers alike. Most training stables in Germany, including the dressage barns, use free-jumping once a week as part of the regular training program.

Free-jumping requires a suitable training area, usually an indoor or covered arena with 6' or higher surrounding walls and a straightaway length of *at least* 100'. (A round pen is *not* suitable for anything larger than a very small crossrail. Galloping and jumping while constantly turning in a 65'-diameter enclosure puts excessive stresses on developing leg joints.)

A variation of free-jumping in the arena uses a *jumping lane,* a straight outdoor track 10-12' wide, with high barrier fencing along the sides and jumps set up at intervals across the track. A jumping lane has the advantage over free-jumping in the arena because the horse can't duck out. If you're trying to evaluate a sales prospect, however, it's sometimes hard to see exactly what's happening in the jumping lane.

If you have a chance to watch your prospect free-jumping, then what should you look for? A good jumper will:

1. First, *notice* the obstacle and focus on the problem it presents. He should approach a jump with all neurons firing, figuring out how to go over instead of around it.

2. Jump smoothly and steadily, without rushing, and find a comfortable take-off spot that doesn't cause him to "prop and pop" from an awkward, too-close spot or take off so far back in such a wild "space shot" that he has to make a desperate effort to clear the rail. Ideally, takeoff and landing spots should be approximately the same distance away from the jump, so the arc of flight is centered over the obstacle.

3. On take-off, plant both hind feet nearly simultaneously for the thrust. In mid-air, fold both front legs "tight, square, and even," so he can lead on either lead.

4. Demonstrate both suppleness and scope. *Suppleness* means all the body parts move and work easily together, without stiffness. The horse appears to "sit down" on takeoff, the legs fold and unfold easily over the jump, and the loin coils strongly so the horse's back rounds up into a bascule while in the air. *Scope* means he can easily adjust the length of his stride and the arc of his jump, shortening his frame to jump a tight vertical without losing *impulsion* (momentum), and lengthening his body to extend the flight time over a spread fence.

5. Stay safe and balanced in the air. This means he doesn't trip over the jump, fall, dangle a leg, twist his legs or body sideways, or land off-balance. The joints of the front and hind legs should fold snugly. Ideally, he should be *square* in front, meaning both knees should come up to the same height, with forearms raised to or above the horizontal, and the knees and fetlocks folded to 90 degrees or tighter. (Hocks should tuck neatly under the belly, and not trail behind the horse or twist to the side. If he takes off from a long spot and has to reach to clear a wide jump, he should be clever and flexible enough to "hang his knees over his ears."

6. Judge the height of a fence so he jumps high enough to clear it but without a lot of unnecessary effort. Green horses often over-jump in an effort to avoid touching the fence, and this desire to go clean is certainly a plus. But landing from a consistently too-high effort can be difficult to ride or it may indicate that the horse is overanxious about jumping, and ultimately it will shorten the horse's useful jumping career because it puts undue stress on his legs.

7. Manage the landing well, raising his head and neck as he touches down so he can come back into balance and continue going forward smoothly without tripping or losing balance. He should be able to take off and land on either lead.

A green horse won't exhibit perfect consistency in his jumping, of course, but he should show attention, balance, suppleness, and scope. He should also appear to learn from any small mistakes, and not become terrified if he rubs a rail or occasionally takes off from a bad spot.

And remember that if the horse has jumped out of a trot, rather than a canter, it's nearly impossible for him to snap both front legs up evenly on takeoff. The sequence of steps (alternating diagonal pairs) in the trotting stride makes it hard for him to fold both front legs together. The *hind* legs should always plant and push together, regardless of whether the horse is trotting or cantering the approach, but to properly evaluate the ability of the front legs to fold evenly, you should see the horse jump from a canter.

Now that you're able to spot talent in a horse, how can you develop confidence in the rider? I cover this topic in all of the following chapters, beginning with chapter 3, "Getting Started: Readiness and Equipment."

Chapter 3

Getting Started:
Readiness and Equipment

L earning to jump should help you improve your balance and coordination in all your riding, while also helping you to develop more confidence, trust, and better communication with your horse. Of course, you've got to be sure your balance is secure before you begin jumping . . . so it should be an enjoyable, positive, upward spiral of success.

Jumping *should* be just plain fun. But if you don't have solid skills on the flat, good communication with your horse and the right equipment, you'll just be frustrated.

Rider Readiness

Unfortunately, many riders try to start jumping before they've acquired the necessary skills and balance, so they get scared and hurt. Or they inadvertently destroy the horse's confidence, so he's no longer a safe, willing jumper. Or they're determined to overcome fears and memories of past accidents and injuries, but those anxieties create tension and imbalance, which just leads them into a *downward* spiral of fear and tension. But you can avoid that downward spiral by making sure the basics are solid.

Skills, Partnership, and Responsiveness

These basics include physical skills, an understanding of the partnership involved, and an ability to create prompt, appropriate responses. And I'm not talking just about the horse—it's the *rider's* physical skills, partnership abilities, and responsiveness that must come first.

Physical Skills. Learning new physical skills is a step-by-step process. You can only focus on one new skill at a time, and you can't learn new ones if the foundation is shaky. So before any jumping occurs—before anyone even *suggests* that jumping might happen—you have to be sure the basics are solid on the flat.

Partnership. Part of the challenge of jumping is that it requires a level of partnership between horse and rider that generally isn't required in riding on the flat. In jumping, the rider and horse must share the pilot's chair and help each other make decisions. The rider is the "senior partner," but ultimately, it's the horse who decides where to place his feet, how high to jump, and how to recover on landing.

Are You Ready to Jump?

Before you start jumping, you need to have the right horse to learn on. He should be quiet, steady, predictable, very experienced, and willing to forgive your small mistakes. He should seem to enjoy jumping without rushing, pulling, or getting anxious.

And you need correct basic skills. You should be able to perform all of the skills in this checklist:

✓ Ride at a walk, sitting trot, rising (*posting*) trot, and canter on both leads, with or *without* stirrups, with the horse on light contact. *Light contact* means your legs *and* hands can work independently, in steady, quiet contact.

✓ Not have to grab the saddle or mane, or lose a stirrup at any gait, unless your horse spooks or stumbles.

✓ Know your diagonals and leads without having to look down, and be able to fix a wrong diagonal or lead quickly and smoothly.

✓ Understand and use your aids correctly to control your horse's speed and direction. This includes rein aids (direct, indirect, and opening or leading rein), legs (positioned on the girth or behind the girth), and seat/weight (active to encourage, following to maintain, quiet to slow down).

✓ Bend and balance your horse through turns by using your inside-leg-to-outside-hand connection.

✓ Shorten or lengthen strides at trot and canter, using your aids in simple half-halts.

✓ Move your horse forward *promptly* with a squeeze from your calves (or a squeeze plus a cluck or a tap from a stick), and move your horse laterally off either leg, in a turn on the forehand or leg-yielding at walk and trot.

Responsiveness. There's also a "rapid response" factor in jumping that can be disconcerting if you're accustomed to having plenty of time to create a steady rhythm and fix mistakes in your riding. You and your horse both need to make decisions, sometimes very quickly, about where to go and what to do.

You need to give your horse immediate feedback when he's responded promptly and correctly. In the excitement of jumping, many riders forget to reward, praise, and thank their horses. Good riding is its own reward, for horse and rider, but it also helps to have an excellent rapport with your horse, so he knows—and you never forget to tell him—when he's done well, or even when he's just *tried* to do the right thing.

This book assumes that you've been riding long enough, and well enough, to acquire solid skills on the flat, both in the arena and out on the trails. You may be taking regular lessons, you may be returning to riding after a few years away from the sport, or perhaps you're making the change from another riding discipline. But you should be able to pass all the tests in the "Are You Ready to Jump?" list before you move into jumping.

YOUR SUPPORT TEAM

To get started in jumping, you'll also need to assemble your support team. It's possible to work through all the lessons and exercises in this book by yourself, but you'll be much happier and safer if you work with a coach, a buddy, or a knowledgeable friend (or several friends!). Your riding buddy can give you feedback, help solve problems, act as your "eyes on the ground," and—most important—replace jump rails, move *cavalletti* (ground poles), and pull out the tape measure to check distances and heights.

Equipment

Hunt seat equitation, the foundation for jumping, evolved from the *forward seat* developed by an Italian cavalry officer, Federico Caprilli, at the beginning of the twentieth century. Through close observation, Caprilli determined that a horse can jump best when his rider shortens his stirrups, keeps his center of gravity over the horse's center of gravity, stays off the horse's back, and interferes as little as possible with the jumping motion. It was a simple concept, but a revolutionary one, and all modern jumpers use a variation of Caprilli's forward seat.

To support his revolutionary concept in rider position, Caprilli also developed a new forward-seat saddle. A wide variety of jumping saddles is available, but all are based on some variation of the Caprilli saddle. And the rest of the equipment used in jumping is designed with the same principles in mind: stay in balance, stay safe, and interfere as little as possible with the horse's jumping efforts.

HORSE EQUIPMENT

Saddle

A good saddle should help both you and your horse find balance. It should fit the horse—meaning it sits level and even when viewed from front, back, or either side; it shouldn't pinch or press on his spine; and it should allow his shoulders to move freely. The saddle should also fit and support you, with moderately forward flaps and a medium-shallow seat so you don't have to struggle to keep your balance forward enough, or get your seat out of the saddle enough, to move with your horse over a jump.

Padded flaps and knee rolls are a matter of preference as long as they support your leg in the correct position and don't "trap" you in the saddle. Some saddles also come with *thigh blocks,* which are designed to keep the legs from slipping back. A very deep seat, big knee rolls, and thigh blocks can give you a trapped feeling and make it hard to get your seat clear of the pommel in jumping. Save these models for serious cross-country galloping and foxhunting, where you'll want that extra measure of security.

Flap position is another variable. The higher the fences and the faster you travel, the shorter your stirrups will be, and the more forward the flap on the saddle should be. Don't buy a saddle with an extremely forward flap when you're just starting to jump though.

The different jumping disciplines all have their favorite saddles and these change somewhat according to fashion and fad. See what saddles are currently recommended for your discipline, and then see what fits your budget. Ride in as many saddles as possible, and ask a trusted instructor or saddle-shop salesperson to help you with fit for you and your horse.

If you're just beginning to jump, a general-purpose hunt or close-contact saddle will do just fine. Many older models of close-contact saddles have a plain flap with a very small, "pencil" knee roll (or none!), but you'll probably be more comfortable and feel more secure with at least some padding at the front of the flap to help you keep your leg from slipping forward.

If you're interested in eventing, with its three disciplines of dressage, cross-country, and stadium jumping, but you don't have the money to purchase two (or even three!) specialized saddles, start with a general-purpose saddle that supports you well for the dressage phase. It's much easier to jump small jumps in a medium-deep dressage saddle than it is to ride dressage correctly in a forward jumping saddle. The jumping-specific saddle can be acquired later.

Bridle

Start with the mildest bit that you and your horse are comfortable with. Resist the temptation to over-bit your horse just because you're going to jump. Don't follow fads! If your horse goes well in a snaffle on the flat, stick with that as you begin jumping. If your horse goes well in a *bitless bridle, sidepull,* or jumping *hackamore,* that's even better. It's harder (though not impossible) to interfere with a horse's balance with a bitless bridle than with a bit, so horses will often go with more confidence.

Do *not* use any kind of *curb* (shank) bit. If you normally use a kimber-wicke or pelham, and you're just beginning to learn jumping, remove or greatly loosen the curb chain so you won't punish your horse as sharply if you catch him in the mouth over a jump. Using bit converters on a pelham also softens its effect.

My favorite bit is a French or double-jointed snaffle, with a medium-weight, curved mouthpiece. If a more experienced horse begins to get a little exuberant or I need a little more control, I often go to a pelham, which allows me to adjust the actions of the curb and snaffle reins independently. Many riders are not comfortable, however, with handling two reins.

The rings of a snaffle bit can be eggbutt, D-ring, full-cheek, or loose-ring. A loose-ring snaffle is a good bit for flatwork (and a favorite of dressage riders) because it transmits small vibrations from the fingers to the horse's mouth, to more effectively ask for a soft poll and jaw. Most hunter riders prefer an eggbutt or D-ring because the feel through the reins is steadier and less wiggly. A full-cheek snaffle can help with the horse that's a little stiff in turns, because the sides of the bit exert pressure on a larger area of his face. For safety reasons, however, don't *ever* use a running martingale with a full-cheek bit. (See the sidebar "Check Your Equipment!" for more information about safety issues.)

The cavesson can be plain, dropped, flash, or crossed, depending on what your horse is accustomed to and what is allowed if you're aiming to show. Make sure you know the equipment rules for the type of competition you're interested in!

Be sure your reins provide good grip. Laced or braided reins are traditional for hunters and hunt-seat equitation. Jumpers and event riders often prefer rubber reins or some combination of rubber and sewn-in hand grips.

Martingales and Breastplates

In the United States, hunters, hunt-seat equitation riders, and open jumpers below a certain level can use standing martingales, which steady a horse by applying downward pressure to the noseband of the bridle when he raises his head to escape the action of the bit. Running martingales, which apply downward pressure to the bit when the horse raises his head and the rider applies pressure to the reins, are allowed at all levels, in all competitions over fences, though they are seldom seen on hunters and equitation horses except in schooling shows or jumper-type equitation classes. This is because hunters are expected to jump quietly on a light or loose rein, so a running martingale would have no effect. Equitation riders are expected to keep their hands tactful and quiet so a running martingale isn't needed.

A martingale can help remind a horse not to fling his head upward if he gets a little excited, but it *must* be adjusted appropriately so the horse has complete freedom to use his head and neck in jumping. The strap to the girth should be snug under the horse's chest, not dangling, and the strap to the noseband on a standing martingale should be as long as the underside of his

Find the Saddle That Fits!

Your most important piece of equipment, and your most expensive purchase (after your horse), is a good saddle. Take the time to find a saddle
that fits both you and your horse.

Used Saddles

Many wonderful saddles can be purchased over the Internet through eBay
and similar online auctions. But unless you're familiar with the exact
model and size of saddle that you're purchasing, and you trust the seller,
you're running a big risk of buying a badly designed, poorly constructed,
and downright dangerous piece of equipment. Be especially wary of any
new saddle with no model name or maker's mark, offered at a ridiculously
low price and advertised as a "starter package."

   At best, cheap saddles will make your horse uncomfortable and cause
you to struggle with your balance. At worst, they'll cause an accident
through equipment failure.

   Here are some of the signs of a poorly made saddle:

- The saddle tips back so the deepest point of the seat is far to the rear
  and the flaps stick forward over your horse's shoulders.

- The leather feels like cardboard, stiff and dry and slippery. Many
  poorly made saddles are finished with a slick, painted-on surface
  dye; well-tanned leather is conditioned with oils that penetrate and
  preserve the leather. It should be supple even when new.

- The nailheads and d-rings are rusting. Rust weakens the leather.

- The stirrup bars are set too far forward or back, so stirrups don't hang
  straight below the deepest part of the saddle.

- Stitches are large and loose. Billet straps are thin and flimsy. Holes
  in the billets are unevenly punched.

- Saddle is not symmetrical or it sits crooked.

- Panel padding on the underside of the saddle is uneven or lumpy.

   If you're on a tight budget, don't purchase a new, cheap saddle. Instead,
look for a used name-brand saddle that's been well cared for. Good leather
saddles are expensive when new, but they can last for decades.

Synthetic Saddles

I never appreciated synthetic saddles until I moved to a tropical climate,
where mold and mildew blossom overnight. You won't see synthetic saddles used on the "A" show circuit, but in training and at the lower levels
of competition, a well-made synthetic saddle can be a sensible choice for

anyone on a budget. Again, be sure to buy quality by sticking with known brands. And remember that the synthetic saddles aren't indestructible.

Well-cared-for leather generally lasts longer and is easier to repair than synthetic material. Also, some synthetic saddles have a nearly slip-free saddle surface, which gives a false sense of security. If you become accustomed to the extra *grippiness* provided by a synthetic, and then find yourself in a friend's leather saddle, you may discover your legs aren't nearly as secure as you thought they were!

Saddle size

The seat size of a saddle is measured in inches, from the center of the cantle to the nailhead on either side of the pommel. This measurement roughly corresponds to the length of the rider's thigh, as measured from hip to knee. A standard saddle for someone 5' tall and of average build is 16". Most adults of average build will do well in a 17" or 17½" jumping saddle, though this will vary depending on the rider's conformation. A saddle's fits also depends on the depth of the seat, the length and position of the flaps, and whether it has a cut-back pommel, which lessens the available space for your seat.

Testing for Fit

You should have a knowledgeable coach or saddle fitter confirm that your saddle fits you and your horse, but you can do a preliminary check.

Put the saddle on your horse, girth it up, and check to be sure the deepest part of the saddle sits over the lowest part of your horse's back, just behind the withers. Sit in the middle of the seat. You should have a 3"–4" clearance between the back of your buttocks and the cantle of the saddle. Pick up the stirrups at jumping length and rise into jumping position (stand in the stirrups, lift your seat up so it just clears the saddle, and fold forward at the hips). Be sure you can rise easily without bumping your crotch on the pommel. Your knee should tuck into the knee roll behind the farthest-forward part of the flap. The flap should be long enough so it doesn't catch on the top of your tall boots or half-chaps, but short enough so you can feel your horse's barrel from mid-calf downward.

The stirrups should hang straight down so it's easy for you to keep your feet underneath your body without having your legs slide back off the flap or pop forward over the knee roll. The saddle should feel as if it's supporting you, not pushing you forward or back so you struggle for balance.

Be sure you can see all the way through the gullet from front to back, so the saddle isn't pressing on your horse's spine. While you're in the saddle, check to be sure nothing's pinching his withers or restricting his shoulders. Then have an observant friend stand behind you and ensure that your spine, the center of the saddle, and the center of the horse all line up vertically.

neck plus the underside of his jaw. The rings of a running martingale should reach to the level of his withers when contact is taken on the reins, so the martingale doesn't interfere with the straight line from the rider's hands to the horse's mouth. Anything shorter will interfere with his ability to balance during takeoff and landing, when the head and neck must be able to lift.

A breastplate is a good idea, especially for cross-country jumping. It helps to hold the saddle in place and may also provide a strap for you to hold on to. Be sure a polo-style breastplate is adjusted correctly so it doesn't ride up into the horse's windpipe—it should sit just above the points of the shoulder, with horizontal attachments securely fastened to the billets above the girth buckles. A hunting breastplate, to which a running or standing martingale strap can be attached, should be adjusted so the centerpiece is in the center of the horse's chest. The neck strap on a hunting breastplate will probably sit too close to the withers to provide you with a properly placed handhold for jumping, but it can still be useful as an emergency grab strap.

Elastic inserts in the breastplate or martingale may give the horse more freedom to use his shoulders. These are often seen on jumpers and event horses, but are frowned upon in the more traditional-minded hunter shows.

Jumping Strap

The *jumping strap* is a specific piece of equipment that will provide you with a handhold while practicing two-point position and jumping. The jumping strap is placed around the horse's neck, about one-third to one-half of the way between the saddle and the horse's poll, in the proper place for you to take hold of with one or both hands. It should be made of something that is comfortable to hold, provides a measure of security, yet can also be moved a little forward as your hands move forward in a crest release. And it needs to be wide enough so it doesn't cut into the horse's windpipe.

The neck strap of a polo-style breastplate can be used as a jumping strap, if it's in the right position. (Most sit too close to the saddle, but a small rider on a long-necked horse may be able to use a breastplate strap.) You can also wrap a stretchy track bandage twice around your horse's neck, if you can secure it so it doesn't pull loose.

A spare stirrup leather makes an excellent jumping strap. Be sure to double the *bight* (loose end) of the strap back through the buckle, and use a rubber band for a keeper if the bight is longer than a couple of inches. Use a shoelace or a foot-long piece of twine to secure it to the front of your saddle so if your horse puts his head down, the strap won't slip down to his ears where he can catch a front foot in it.

Yes, the horse's mane is always there to grab if you need to, and it's always better to grab mane than yank your horse in the mouth if you get left behind, but the mane doesn't grow in the right place—it's attached to the top of the neck, not 2" down on the side of the neck, where your hands should be. In a good crest release, your hands should be on either side of the crest, not floating above or on top of it. (See "Using Your Hands: The Release," in chapter 4.)

After your balance is really secure, you won't need the jumping strap.

This photo shows a horse who is ready for schooling over fences: protective boots, a spare stirrup leather to be used as a jumping strap, polo-style breastplate, and snaffle bridle with rubber reins.

Horse Boots

When you're schooling, always use *splint boots* (also called galloping, brushing, or tendon boots) on your horse's front legs. They should cover the leg from just below the knee to the bottom of the fetlock. Their purpose is to prevent cuts and bruises on the skin and tendons from contact with jump rails or the horse's other feet. The hind legs aren't as likely to suffer serious injury, but if your horse is prone to interference with his hind feet, add rear splint boots or ankle boots as well. *Bell boots* (overreach boots) are also useful for the front feet if your horse is likely to clip a front heel with a hind shoe. This is a frequent danger when jumping in mud or on uneven ground.

Open-front boots are popular with show-ring jumpers, because they want their horses to "feel the sting" if the horse hits a rail, but all boots should cover and protect the tendons at the back of the front legs. For general schooling, closed boots are best because they protect the front of the cannons as well as the tendons.

Boots don't have to be fancy or expensive, but they do need to fit securely without being over-tightened. Suitable protective boots may be made from vinyl, leather, rubber, or neoprene, with an extra layer of padding down the inside of the leg to cover the fetlock. They fasten with Velcro straps or buckles, and are shaped to protect and fit the inside of the leg. If you ride often in wet, muddy conditions, avoid fleece padding and polo wraps, which may become heavy when waterlogged and cause the boots to slide down the legs.

Check Your Equipment!

Using your equipment correctly is just as important as having the right equipment. Review this list to improve your chances for safety and success.

1. *Never* tie the stirrups to the girth or any other part of the saddle. This creates a major safety hazard if you fall. If you're not able to keep your legs steady without tying the stirrups, stop jumping and go back to the basics to gain the proper control.

2. Safety stirrups (peacock or spring-loaded) are a good idea, especially for very young riders. However, be sure *peacock-style stirrups* (open side secured with elastic band) are strong enough to bear the rider's weight and won't stretch out of shape.

3. *Never* use a full-cheeked snaffle with a running martingale, because there's always a chance that the martingale rings might catch on the top half of the bit's cheek. And *always* use rein stops when you use a running martingale, so the rings won't slide forward and catch on the rein buckles.

4. Keep your tack clean and well-conditioned. Jumping places more demands on equipment, as well as on horse and rider, than riding on the flat. And tack is expensive! Buy good-quality tack, take good care of it, and it should last a long time.

5. Inspect all tack frequently for loose stitching, cracks, splits, and worn spots. Jumping a cross-country course is challenging enough with two stirrups; think how much more difficult it would be if one broke! (This very thing happened in 1995 to New Zealand Olympic gold medalist Mark Todd, the eventing world's most successful and celebrated three-day rider. A stirrup leather broke one-third of the way into his round on the grueling cross-country course at Badminton CCI****—a four-star Cours Complete Internationale is the highest level of eventing competition—and he rode the rest of the course quite successfully with only one stirrup. For most riders, that would spell certain disaster!)

6. Don't use track bandages to protect your horse's legs unless you're an expert at wrapping them *and* your horse will be working only on dry ground. Inexpertly applied track or polo bandages can become a major hazard when they become saturated with mud or water, because they will slip, become unwound, tangle, and trip your horse.

7. Ultimately, you are responsible for your own safety. Check the condition of your equipment every time you ride, especially if someone else has saddled your horse or you're riding with someone else's tack.

For showing, you'll need to learn the rules for each type of competition. Boots on the horse aren't allowed, for example, in most hunter classes.

Horseshoes

For lower-level jumping on secure arena footing, you shouldn't have to change your horse's shoeing. Simply be sure his feet are well-trimmed and balanced, wearing his usual shoes. Smaller horses and ponies may do well without shoes, but you may find that your normally barefoot pony will get better traction on hard or slippery footing if he's wearing shoes all around.

If you become serious about competing at higher levels, or if you're going to be doing a lot of cross-country jumping in muddy terrain, talk to your farrier about shoeing your horse with small caulks or removeable studs.

RIDER EQUIPMENT

I hope you're already riding with a safety helmet, comfortable breeches and supportive boots. But here's a review of how these essential elements should function to help keep you safe and effective in your riding.

Helmet

Buy a helmet that's comfortable, secure, and well-ventilated. Then wear it. Wear it *every* time you ride.

And be sure it's ASTM-SEI certified, so it meets American safety standards. Not all of the helmets sold in Europe or Australia meet American standards. Check the tag: If it says "ASTM/SEI certified," you're set. But if the tag says "for apparel use only," the helmet is *not* certified for use as protective headgear by the American Society for Testing and Materials (ASTM), the organization that sets standards for many types of safety equipment. (The Safety Equipment Institute, or SEI, is the laboratory that does the testing to ensure that equipment meets the ASTM standards.)

Boots, Breeches, and Chaps

Wear paddock boots or tall boots that have a solid sole and a 1" heel. They should give your ankles good support but still allow you to flex at the ankle and get your heels down. Leather is best. Synthetic leather is acceptable, but remember that the leather-like synthetics wear out much more quickly than real leather. Synthetic paddock boots are a good choice for youngsters who are growing and will need a larger pair of boots every couple of months. Don't wear boots with heavily ridged soles. A little security in the stirrups is nice, but you may need to get your feet out of the stirrups quickly, in case of a fall.

Rubber boots may seem like a money-saving choice, but they're hot in the summer, cold in the winter, and—more important—they have no "material memory," so the boots resist being reshaped into a heels-down position. It's very hard to get your heels down and keep them there in rubber boots.

"Riding sneakers" are not suitable for jumping, because the soles aren't rigid enough to support the foot securely. Putting weight in your heels can make the sneakers curl around the stirrups.

If you wear paddock boots for schooling, half-chaps are also a good idea. They help support your legs and provide a little more friction than plain breeches against the saddle and the horse's barrel. Some riders love the snug feel of full chaps for schooling, but remember that a pair of suede chaps can give you a false sense of security. When you swap the chaps for breeches and boots on show day, you'll feel as if your legs are sliding every which way!

For schooling, any kind of snug-fitting pant with no inner-leg seams will do. Breeches, jodhpurs, riding tights, or riding jeans are all fine. Full-seat breeches are preferred by jumpers and eventers, while hunter and equitation riders favor traditional breeches with suede knee patches.

Protective Vest

A body protector that covers the rider's torso, shoulders, and tailbone is required for jumping in Pony Club activities and the cross-country phase of horse trials. It's also highly recommended for all other types of jumping. Good vests are lightweight, comfortable, and easily adjustable. You may be able to borrow or share a vest for schooling. You'll be expected to provide your own for competitions that require them.

Gloves

Gloves should fit comfortably, prevent blisters, and give you a good grip on reins and crop. There are many kinds of leather, synthetic, or cloth gloves to choose from and the priciest are not always the best. Smooth leather gloves look nice but can be slippery when the reins get wet or sweaty.

Spurs and Crop

Take the spurs off if you're just learning (or relearning) to jump. If your horse needs spurs on the flat, try to get him moving forward more promptly from your leg and a crop so you won't need spurs, at least to begin with, over fences. Later, *if* you can ride reliably off the inside of your leg and control the position of your foot so you don't jab him unintentionally, put the spurs back on if he's sluggish. But be sure they are the correct type and are placed correctly on your boot. Use Prince of Wales (POW) or hammerhead spurs with straps, not western-style slip-ons, so you can place them behind your ankle, not low on the heel of your boot. Ride with your foot parallel to the horse when you don't need them; when you want to apply the spurs, simply turn the toe of your foot out a little (not the whole leg!) so the spur contacts the horse's barrel. You should not have to raise your heel, swing your legs, or otherwise disturb your position to use them.

It's a good idea to get in the habit of carrying a crop or jumping bat, and practice switching hands with it so you're comfortable using it on either side of your horse. The stick is a useful aid to remind your horse to listen to your leg when you ask him to go forward or move over. To use a stick correctly, put both reins in one hand in a single bridge (see the illustrations on page 71) and tap the stick just behind your leg or further back on your horse's hindquarters. Never try to apply the stick while holding a rein in the same hand, unless you are merely tapping the horse on the shoulder to help him through a turn.

You can school on the flat with a dressage whip, but don't jump with it. For jumping, your crop or jumping bat should be no more than 18" long. Anything longer is awkward to carry and swap from hand to hand, the moving tip can distract your horse, and it may catch on the jump standard.

Practice handling reins and crop on the flat, so you can switch hands smoothly and you never have to look behind you to see where you're applying the crop. (See "Lesson #1: Managing Reins, Crop, and Jumping Strap" in chapter 4.)

Other Items

Whenever you ride, please tie back long hair, remove dangly or noisy jewelry that might distract you or your horse, and don't wear any expensive items that you can't afford to lose!

If you're riding on the trails or away from the barn, it's a good idea to carry a cell phone with you for safety reasons, but if you're riding in a lesson or clinic, please leave the cell phone in the tack room. It's disrespectful to your fellow riders and coach, as well as distracting and potentially dangerous, for you to make or receive phone calls while riding.

Please, no chewing gum while riding! And no one should *ever* smoke on or around horses or stables—the fire hazard is just too great.

Dressing for Success in Shows and Clinics

When you're ready to compete in a show or ride in a more formal event such as a foxhunt, you'll want to acquire "show-worthy" clothing. Check with your coach or watch other riders at the local shows to see what you'll need to borrow or purchase. By adding a well-fitted coat in navy or black, a white shirt and choker, tall boots, a hairnet and black gloves to your regular clothing, you should be able to hunt or compete with confidence.

If you're invited to ride in a clinic with a nationally known instructor, please take the time to be sure your horse, tack and clothing are super clean. A tailored polo shirt, gloves, your best breeches (no rips or stains!) and well-shined boots are appropriate.

Chapter 4

BALANCE BASICS:
CENTER OF GRAVITY

our horse has a natural balance. He knows how to move without stumbling or falling down. If he's been trained correctly, then he also knows how to carry the added weight of a rider without losing his balance. And if he's a horse with plenty of experience carrying novice riders, he also knows how to stay steady even when his rider is a little unbalanced. He may even know what to do if his rider loses her balance completely: slow down or stop.

That's the kind of horse you want to learn on! For obvious reasons, you should not try to learn to jump on a horse who doesn't already have loads of experience teaching novice or unsteady riders.

The Rider's Center of Gravity

You, too, have developed a natural balance when you're on your own two feet. But learning to balance on a moving horse is much harder, because you have to respond to his shifting center of gravity. Your goal is to always keep your center of gravity over the horse's center of gravity—or sometimes, behind it. (And once in a very great while, ahead of it. But more about that later.)

Being in balance with your horse means keeping your center over his center, no matter what shifts occur in the horse's center of gravity. If you can do this, you will never fall off.

So where is your center of gravity? It's the point in your body where the vertical force of gravity is perfectly balanced between left and right, top and bottom, and front and back. If you were sliced into symmetrical halves, top to bottom, left to right, or front to back, each half would weigh the same as the other. Your center of gravity is in your middle, approximately behind your belly button.

You learned to stay in balance on the ground as a toddler. As you walk, sit, stand, or run, your muscles and ligaments make thousands of tiny automatic adjustments to keep your whole body aligned with your center of gravity.

When you're balanced, movement is easy and relatively effortless. But when you're in danger of tipping forward, back, or to the left or right, you struggle to avoid losing your balance and falling.

If you have long legs and a short torso, you'll find it easier to balance than a rider with a long torso and short legs, because your center of gravity is a little lower and closer to the horse's. (That's why a very tall man finds it tougher to balance on a horse than a shorter woman. His long torso puts his center of gravity up higher. The ideal physique for riding combines long legs with a relatively short, slim, and light upper body. Only a few of us are so lucky!)

When the balance is right, everything lines up vertically: the rider's center of gravity (the star) is over the horse's center of gravity (the circle) with her foot (the square) firmly underneath both, in a vertical line.

RICHARD VALCOURT

But when the rider can't respond quickly enough to fold at the hip and stay in balance, the centers of gravity become misaligned. Here, Lisa's too-long stirrup has caused her to push herself upward to stay with her horse. Her hip and knee angles are too open and her lower leg has slipped back, creating insecurity—yet she's managed to keep her hands forward and not interfere with her horse's effort.

The Horse's Center of Gravity

When he's at rest, your horse's center of gravity lies perhaps 8" to 10" behind the point of his shoulder, in the middle of his body, a little behind where your knees rest when you're sitting in the saddle. And that's good, because a well-balanced saddle puts *your* center of gravity right above *his* center of gravity.

But as soon as your horse moves, his center of gravity begins to shift, as he moves the various parts of his body. The faster he goes, the more rapidly his center of gravity shifts. When he's galloping and jumping, some shifts are quite large and abrupt: toward the back as he "sits" to push off, forward and up on takeoff and flight, forward and down on landing, and back into the middle during recovery.

The Combined Center of Gravity

Not only do you have to follow the horse's shifts in balance, but the horse also has to adjust to *your* shifting center of gravity. The *combined* center of gravity for both of you is *higher* than for just the horse alone. Your horse is larger than you, and your weight can't influence him as much as his weight can influence you, but you probably weigh at least 10 percent of his body weight and yes, you *can* pull him off balance.

But since we humans came up with this idea of riding horses over jumps, it's up to us to solve the problems of balance.

First, you need to find a seat position that's both secure and flexible.

BALANCE BASICS: POSITION

To stay in balance while jumping, you need to ride in the forward, or jumping, seat. The forward seat is not just a classical dressage seat with the stirrups shortened. Riders who move into hunt seat from dressage, stock seat, or saddle seat often find it hard to adjust to the jumping seat. Because the goal of hunt seat is to *stay in balance while galloping and jumping*, you need to understand these differences:

- *The stirrups are shorter.* In fact, your stirrups should be two or three holes shorter than a dressage or western stirrup. The higher the jumps or the faster your speed (as on a cross-country course or in the hunt field), the shorter the stirrups must be. How short should your stirrups be? To find a good starting length, drop your stirrups and stretch your legs straight down. The bottom of the iron should hang at your ankle bone, or just above it. For jumping small fences (up to 4'), the angle at the back of your knee should be about 100–110 degrees.

- *Your legs and weight play a larger role than your seat to communicate with your horse.* When you're riding in a full-seat position, as in dressage or western, your *seat* is an effective aid because both seat bones are in contact with the saddle. But in jumping, your seat bones are often out of the saddle, so you must rely more on your legs and weight to communicate with your horse.

- *The positioning of your knee, lower leg, foot, and the stirrup are vitally important in jumping.* In other riding disciplines, your seat is your foundation for balance. For example, if your lower leg is a little out of position while riding a counter-canter or cueing a lope, you may not get the results you want but you're probably not going to fall. In jumping, your *leg and foot* are the absolute foundation for your security. A lower leg that's out of position can mean disaster.

- *Because your stirrups are shorter, you have "less leg" against the horse's sides.* Your horse must be willing to *go forward* and put effort into his movement without constant micromanagement from you. If your horse stalls or drops into idle without constant reminders to keep going, you'll need to do some re-schooling to make him more self-propelled. If, on the other hand, your horse is hot, overly sensitive to the leg, or accustomed to being *ridden off-contact*—without steady leg contact—you'll also need to retrain him so he'll accept the calm presence of your legs without rushing or becoming anxious.

- *The jumping position places specific demands on the human body, especially the "body-balancing" and weight-carrying parts of your lower back, thighs, and calves.* You'll need to strengthen muscles and stretch ligaments so your balance will be secure without exhausting or straining yourself.

- *Jumping requires you to learn a new way of using your eyes.* You and your horse will need to make prompt decisions about direction, speed, stride, and balance, so you'll need to shift smoothly between using *soft eyes* (peripheral vision) and *hard eyes* (narrow focus).

These points are discussed in more detail in the following sections. Five lessons in chapter 5 give you a chance to practice these skills.

Four Basic Positions for Jumping

There are four basic positions used in jumping. Which position you use is determined by the situation you are in. You change positions by opening or closing the angles of the hips, knees, shoulders, and elbows.

Opening or closing these angles creates changes in your center of gravity so you can align your balance with your horse's center of gravity.

The four different positions used in jumping are:

1. A three-point (light, or slightly forward) seat
2. A moderate two-point (forward or half) seat
3. A closed (very forward) two-point seat
4. A very open safety position

You'll still use a *full seat* (vertical back, with weight in your seat) when riding on the flat.

Three-Point (Light or Slightly Forward) Seat

The *three-point seat* is when you have three points of contact with the saddle: two legs and a light seat. The three-point seat is closest to the full seat you've been using for dressage or basic balanced-seat flatwork. A three-point position is used for traveling between jumps. In three-point, you lean forward a little and close the hip angle slightly, so your weight is in your stirrups but there's no daylight visible between your seat and the saddle. You can't really use your seat bones to influence your horse from this position because all your weight is in your heels, but it's easy to shift back into a full seat if you do need to re-balance your horse when he gets quick or on the forehand.

These photos show a good stirrup length for work on the flat and over cavalletti: stirrups are short enough to provide flexion in the hip, knee, and ankle . . .

. . . so the rider can rise into three-point, or light, seat to work over cavalletti. These stirrups are too long for jumping, however, when the rider needs to rise into . . .

CAROLE GEBALLE

CAROLE GEBALLE

RICHARD VALCOURT

. . . a secure two-point seat for takeoff.

RICHARD VALCOURT

Equally important, but often neglected, is the safety position. You're not really leaning back; instead, you slip the reins and ensure that your back and stirrup leathers remain at a "true vertical" to keep you balanced behind the horse's center of gravity for security. Your weight is still in your heels. Use this position for galloping downhill or jumping down a bank or drop jump.

Two-Point (Forward or Half) Seat

Your two-point seat is what you'll use for actual jumping. In *two-point,* you lift your seat clear of the saddle, but not by standing straight up. Instead, you lean forward and lift your seat a couple of inches clear of the saddle as you close your hip angle.

As your balance and timing improve, you'll learn to move from three-point to two-point *as the horse jumps,* allowing the horse's jumping motion to close the hip angle on the way up and open it again on the way down.

When you're first learning to jump, however, you should shift into two-point position two strides (about 15–20' at a trot, about 25–30' at a canter) *before* the jump, and hold it for at least two strides *after.* This will help you stay with the horse's motion without having to try to time a change in position.

As you lean forward and the angle of your hip changes, obviously the position of your upper body, arms, and hands must also change. The farther

RICHARD VALCOURT

What happens when my stirrups are too long? Although my hip angle has closed nicely, the thrust of take-off has caused me to misplace my leg: I'm standing in my stirrups, my knee has opened too wide, and I've lost my deep, secure heel.

forward your shoulders and arms go, the shorter your reins must be to keep light contact with your horse's mouth.

As you shift from three-point to two-point on the approach to a jump, ideally you'd shorten the reins even further. But when learning to jump, it's much too easy to lose your balance, grab the reins, and catch your horse in the mouth if you're trying to ride with rein contact. So in the beginning, you should simply move your hands forward and hold the jumping strap (or the mane) along with your reins, to be sure your hands will not interfere with your horse's mouth.

See Lesson #3 in chapter 5 for exercises that can help you practice changing from two-point to three-point positions.

As in all riding, your eyes should be looking straight forward, over your horse's ears; your back should be flat, not roached (rounded or convex) or stiffly arched (concave); your shoulders should be square; and you should maintain a straight line from your elbow to your horse's mouth. See the "Position Check" sidebar, later in this chapter, for a list of points to review.

Closed Two-Point Seat

The *closed two-point seat* isn't really a different seat, just a more extreme version of the two-point. To fold into a closed seat over a 5' or taller jump, you'd also need to ride with shorter stirrups.

Over a high jump, leaping up a steep bank, or when an athletic horse makes a big effort, you'll need to fold quickly into a more forward or *closed two-point seat*. When you jump very high, your hips and knees must close even more on takeoff than in the two-point seat, you shift your weight (balance) forward even more, and your arms and hands must reach farther to follow your horse's head and neck.

Safety Position

The safety position is very useful when you're galloping or jumping downhill, when you'll need to help your horse balance by staying a little behind the motion.

Position Check

Whether you're in two-point, three-point or safety position, the same principles apply. Be sure to:

1. Look up and straight ahead, between your horse's ears.

2. Keep your shoulders square; don't let them drop, round, hunch, or twist. Keep your back flat, neither arched (concave) nor roached (convex or rounded).

3. Keep your lower legs firmly underneath you, with the stirrups on the balls of the feet and the heels lower than the toes. The stirrup irons should be straight across your feet, with your little toes resting against the outside branches of the irons.

4. Your stirrups should hang vertically next to the girth, not swing forward or back.

5. Allow your weight to push your heels down through flexible ankles. Keep the feet turned out at a natural angle—about 30 degrees. Don't brace against the stirrups or shove the feet forward in an effort to get the heels down.

6. Ride off the insides of your thighs and calves, not the backs of your legs. The flat insides of your legs put more surface area against the saddle and horse, and this allows the knees to stay close without pinching.

7. As you bring your seat out of the saddle from a full seat into three-point or two-point, think of folding your hips closed.

8. Don't *grip* with the legs—especially not the thighs—but *do* maintain an even *friction pressure* along the length of your lower thighs, inside of the knees, and upper calves. A strong grip will exhaust you in minutes; an even, steady friction pressure can be comfortable for an hour or more.

9. As your hips close in two-point or three-point, your upper body angles forward, so you must carry your hands and arms forward the same distance that your shoulders have moved forward—perhaps 2" for three-point position, 4"–5" for two-point position.

10. Maintain a straight line from your elbows through your forearms, wrists, and hands to the bit. This means your hands must be slightly below the crest of the horse's neck and evenly spaced on either side of it. Don't let your hands float above the mane. Support your *hands and arms* on the horse's neck, but support your *torso* with your back and legs.

Unless you're an experienced jumper and confident in your ability to keep your hands quiet and independent, when you jump keep the reins a little loose. Take hold of the jumping strap on both sides of the horse's neck, and don't try to maintain contact with his mouth.

In the *safety position,* you open the angles of your hips and knees, pushing your heels down to keep your weight anchored low. You keep your seat upright but still light in the saddle, and let the reins slip (see "Slipping the Reins" in "Using Your Hands: The Release," on page 65) to allow the horse full freedom of his head and neck.

Although it looks like you just lean back and shove your feet forward in safety position, you actually keep your back and stirrup leathers vertical. In other words, you're just staying upright and balanced over your knees and feet. It's the ground and the horse that are dropping down beneath you.

For many riders, this is a scary position to think about, but after you've practiced it you'll see it's the most secure method you can use to tackle downhill terrain and drop jumps, where the landing is lower than the ground on the take-off side. In fact, it's so important that you know how to do this that Lesson #1 teaches you the safety position *before* you begin to actually jump.

Strengthen Your Position on the Ground

Riders must be athletic. You don't have to be a marathon runner or a weightlifter, but you must be fit enough so you are able to move with your horse and not increase his burden. An unfit, uncoordinated rider makes it much harder for the horse to do his job, because he must constantly adjust his own balance to compensate for the rider's unsteadiness and unpredictability. In other words, you need to be in control of all your body parts.

What can you do to improve your balance and position quickly, especially if you're riding only one or twice a week? Consider trying any sport or activity that requires you to crouch, balance with bent knees, open and close hip angles, use your inner thigh muscles (*adductors*), strengthen your abdominal core, or stretch your hamstrings. Any of the following activities will help increase the strength of these key riding muscles and help you maintain balance over your feet:

- Bicycling (especially climbing hills)
- Skiing, surfing, and snowboarding
- Tennis and fencing
- Yoga, Pilates, tai chi, gardening, and any dancing that doesn't require high heels
- In the gym, use the thigh machines and do heel lifts, abdominal crunches, lunges, and squats

Riding requires you to lower your heels and ride off the insides of your legs, so there are some activities that *don't* help your riding. These activities include:

- Ballet, which requires your legs to turn outward, as in a plié
- Wearing high heels, which shortens the tendons at the back of your lower legs

See Lesson #2 in chapter 5 for a few exercises you can do to strengthen your legs and make your balance more secure.

THE ANCHORED LEG

How can you use your legs both to support your position *and* cue your horse when you're jumping?

It's important to understand that a rider has two *anchor points,* which are specific parts of the leg that provide stability and help you hold your balance while jumping.

The first "anchor" is in the *heel.* By keeping your weight in your heels, and your feet under your center of gravity, you can stay secure. But your feet need to move into different positions to cue the horse. You may be riding without stirrups or you may need to move one or both legs back to bend through a turn or move your horse into a more forward stride. Then the "anchored heel" becomes less secure. You can't simply rely on "heels down" to stay secure over a jump. It's necessary, but not sufficient.

The other important anchor is at the *inside of the knee.* That's the point that provides steady, secure contact with the saddle, and also serves as the pivot point for the parts of your body that are above the knee (the upper leg and torso) and below it (the calf and foot).

With a solidly anchored knee, you can pivot your upper leg and torso *forward* from that point to follow a forward thrust over the jump. You can also bring the lower leg *back* slightly to apply leg or spur, without upsetting your balance. And you can open the hip and knee angles for a sharp downward descent. But the position of the well-anchored knee *does not change.* It's the point around which everything else rotates.

And if you, your horse, and your saddle are a good fit in both size and shape, then that *anchored knee* is also the part of you that's closest to the horse's center of gravity, so it's easier for you to stay in balance

Look at the pictures in this chapter and the next, to see if you can identify which riders are demonstrating an anchored leg: heels down, stirrup leathers vertical, and the inside of the knees flat against the saddle.

USING YOUR EYES: SOFT EYES AND HARD EYES

When you ride on the flat, you're usually using your peripheral vision to stay straight and balanced as you concentrate on feeling the horse beneath you, while still remaining aware of your surroundings. That wide-angled approach to vision is called *soft eyes.* Soft eyes promotes a holistic approach to riding by encouraging you to feel what your horse is doing, instead of relying purely on vision to tell you what's happening beneath you. Soft eyes helps you relax, let go of tension, breathe, and become more aware of your surroundings.

The opposite form of riding vision is called *hard eyes,* which means using your eyes to narrowly focus on one particular object as a goal. If your riding requires precision in a pattern—a dressage test or a trail class, for example—in which you must pay attention to a specific marker or obstacle in the arena, then you are probably shifting briefly from soft eyes to hard eyes to establish a brief, pinpoint focus so you can ride with accuracy to that precise spot.

Your horse already uses soft and hard eyes. When he's relaxed, rhythmic, and moving steadily in a familiar arena with no obstacles to negotiate, the ears of an attentive horse are often at *half-mast,* neither forward nor back; or one ear may be forward and the other back, showing that he's watching and listening simultaneously to his rider and his surroundings. In this situation he's using soft eyes. But when presented with an obstacle—a bridge, a ditch, a jump—his attention sharpens and his focus narrows as he "locks on target" with hard eyes and decides how to deal with it.

So jumping requires quick shifts back and forth between hard eyes, which you use on the approach and over the jump itself to maintain a very focused direction; and soft eyes, which you use to maintain your rhythm, speed, and direction when you're not approaching a fence.

A good horse and rider team often synchronize their use of hard eyes and soft eyes as they ride a course. They enter quietly, taking note of the whole arena in a soft-eyes view during their opening circle. The rider scans the arena and notes the placement of the judge, the jumps, and any other obstacles, while her horse travels quietly with ears and eyes flicking back and forth a bit, attentive and alert but waiting for direction. Then they both focus on the first jump in the first line, using hard eyes to establish a straight, steady approach. They revert briefly to soft eyes as they ride their large, flowing turns and seek the next line or jump on the course.

Through the rider's use of her eyes and other subtle shifts in balance, the horse *knows* which jump to look at—and he also knows which ones to ignore. He knows when to simply maintain rhythm and when it's time for both of them to lock on target.

Eyes Always Up and Ahead

No matter what type of focus you're using—soft or hard eyes—your eyes must always be up, ahead, and preparing well in advance for any change in direction. Soft eyes does *not* include looking down to see what lead you're on, tilting your head, or gazing around at your buddies as they ride by. Using soft eyes *increases* your awareness of your surroundings; it should not make you careless or oblivious.

And using hard eyes should not make you tense or stiff. It simply narrows your focus, so your attention is focused on one simple goal: landing on the other side of the next obstacle. (Yes, *landing*, not just taking off. Instead of thinking only of how to get *to* the jump, you should also think of what happens *after* the jump—the smooth recovery and the balanced turn.)

You will go where your eyes lead you. As legendary rider, trainer, and judge Victor Hugo-Vidal used to say, "Ride *with* a point, ride *to* a point." Look forward and you'll go forward. Look down and, well, that's where you'll end up.

USING YOUR HANDS: THE RELEASE

When a horse jumps he needs the freedom of his head and neck to help him maintain balance, so the rider needs to *release* his head and neck, enabling him to do that vital work.

There are three types of releases you can use when jumping. When you begin jumping, you'll start with a *long crest release* and hold on to the jumping strap. Then you'll move to a *short crest release* and eventually an *automatic release*.

At times, you'll also need to let the reins slip through your hands in a very long release. *Slipping the reins* can help you stay safe when jumping downhill or if your horse stumbles.

Long Crest Release

In a *long crest release,* you jump on a loose rein, maintaining contact on the approach but then pushing your hands far enough forward (about a third but no more than half of the way up his neck) to ensure that the horse will not be

caught in the mouth if you lose your balance. After landing, you retrieve the contact gently to guide the horse around the course. Using a long crest release with a jumping strap pretty much ensures that you won't catch your horse in the mouth by accident.

Obviously, your horse must be steady and honest enough to jump on a loose rein. You can't develop confidence and skills on a horse who tries to duck out or stop just before a fence.

RICHARD VALCOURT

This photo shows a good example of a short crest release. Lisa keeps her eyes up and her hands forward throughout the jump. She uses Nani's neck to keep her hands steady, but her body is supported by her legs and the weight in her heels, so she doesn't collapse on Nani's neck or interfere with the horse's balance.

Short Crest Release

After you've gained enough experience and feel that your balance is secure, you won't need the jumping strap and you'll be able to move to a short crest release. In a *short crest release,* you maintain light contact with your horse's mouth on the approach, and then push your hands forward a shorter distance on the crest of the neck at takeoff to follow the jumping motion. See Lesson #4 in chapter 5 for several exercises on developing crest-release skills.

Automatic Release

Accomplished riders can follow the action of the horse's head with a light, steady contact—never interfering, but always communicating through the reins. This technique is called an *automatic release,* meaning the rider's hands maintain a straight line from elbow to bit.

However, it may take *years* of practice to develop a sensitive automatic release. You must have total control over your own balance and be able to use each of your aids—legs, hands, and weight—independently.

When your balance is so secure that you can stay with the motion while jumping through grids without reins or stirrups, *and* you've developed a good eye for distances and can accurately gauge the moment of takeoff (see chapter 6, "Understanding Strides, Distances, and Grids"), then you're ready to try an automatic release.

In an automatic release*,* your goal is to maintain contact with the bit throughout the jumping stride. This means that your hands and arms must smoothly follow the entire jumping motion, from lift-off and in-flight bascule to descent and landing. The biggest difference between an automatic release and a short crest release is that your hands need to move *below* the crest of the neck, especially over a big jump on an athletic, bascule-producing horse, to maintain the elbow-to-bit line. And you must always be prepared to let the reins slip a little, especially on the descent, if your horse has put in a really big effort.

Slipping the Reins

An especially important skill in jumping is knowing *how* and *when* to let the reins slip safely. *Slipping the reins* means letting them go longer—smoothly, and without dropping them.

Essentially, you'll need to let your reins slip whenever you discover your arms are too short to follow the motion of the horse's head and neck. To produce a steady hunter or equitation round, you shouldn't need to let the reins slip at all, unless your horse puts in an awkward jump. But on varied cross-country terrain, or if you're riding a horse who doesn't always meet his distances perfectly, you'll probably have to let your reins slip to avoid catching him in the mouth when you need to sit back or you find you've gotten left behind.

Whenever a sudden motion of the horse's head threatens to pull you forward and down, you must relax your fingers and let the reins slide longer on both sides simultaneously. Keep your heels down and don't let your feet go back, because this will tip you forward.

There will be times when you know you'll need to let the reins slip—on a drop jump, for example, or the descent from a large jump—and lots of other times when you're not expecting it, but you must react quickly to avoid being pulled over the horse's neck if he trips, bucks, or shies suddenly. Slipped reins are also very useful if you're riding one of those notorious ponies who dive into the grass for a snack at every opportunity.

Remembering to Reward:
It's Not All about the Rider

Sometimes you can focus so hard on technique that you forget to think about how you're communicating and building a partnership with your horse. Yes, the focus here is on developing *your* riding skills, but every time you ride, you're also affecting your horse's training. You're always teaching him new things, confirming what he already knows, or teaching him to forget what he's learned before.

Make every time count as a positive experience for your horse!

Whenever you and he have done something well together—maintained your rhythm over a ground rail, executed a smooth turn, performed a balanced transition—think of the reward your horse needs.

Everyone has used negative reinforcement—that's when we initiate an action by rein, leg, or weight pressure, and then remove that pressure when the horse performs correctly. But you should also think of using positive reinforcement, such as giving a reward when the horse has done a good job. Positive reinforcement can be small, like a little scratch at the withers or a quiet "Good boy," or big, such as a rest break or the end of work.

Each time you ride, and especially as you concentrate on each of these lessons, be sure to keep your horse's needs in mind. He's willing to work for you as long as he gets the positive rewards he needs: rest, comfort, approval, and your gratitude. (Treats are optional!)

I use three kinds of positive reward for my horses, and I use them frequently, especially with young horses, whether I'm working specifically on their skills or mine. These rewards are:

1. **The reward voice.** This is a quiet "Good boy!" or "Good girl!" always said with the same tone and inflection. I use it frequently on the ground, while grooming, leading, and handling, so my horses also understand and appreciate the reward voice when I'm riding.

2. **The reward rub.** A withers scratch or mid-neck rub can go a long way to helping a horse relax and bring his attention back to you, while also letting him know of your approval. This is often delivered in combination with the reward voice. (Some riders seem to think a hearty thump or vigorous smack on the neck, combined with a loud voice, lets the horse know the rider is pleased with him. Please don't do this—horses don't like it.)

3. **Rest.** When we've both done well, my horse gets a *big* reward: voice plus neck rub plus an immediate rest. We walk, I drop the reins, and tell him he's wonderful.

Not only does this reward system help you build a great partnership with your horse, it will also help *you* relax and enjoy the moment!

Riders who can maintain a firm but relaxed feel of the reins, with supple elbows, wrists, and fingers, often have an instinctive feel for when they need to let the reins slip. On the other hand, those who ride with tension in their arms and hands often have trouble letting the reins slip when they need to.

The last photo in the sequence on page 58 shows the rider in safety position, slipping the reins on a downhill slope. See "Lesson #1 in chapter 5 for an exercise that teaches you how to slip the reins.

There's a lot of material to absorb here, but it's important to understand the reasons *why* you need to have independent aids (especially the hands), a good foundation of support (legs), and the ability to stay in balance with your horse as he moves.

The lessons in chapter 5 will help you develop these vital skills.

Chapter 5

PREPARING FOR THE JUMP

There are several skills you need to master before actually beginning to jump. This work may seem a little boring, but it will greatly improve your balance—and your confidence—when you begin riding over actual jumps. It's okay to move quickly through these skills, but don't skip anything!

Each "lesson" is broken down into a series of exercises, Depending on your experience, your level of skill and the cooperation of your horse, you may be able to complete all the exercises in a lesson within one hour-long riding session. But if this material is new for you, or your basic riding skills are a little shaky, you'll probably need to devote several practice sessions to a single lesson.

Lesson #1: Manage the Reins, Crop, and Jumping Strap

Your reins must fit your hands well, so you can comfortably close your fingers around them. To keep the reins from slipping when you don't want them to, always hold them in a double grip: the reins should pass between your pinky and ring finger as well as between your index finger and thumb. Close all the joints of your fingers so the tips of the fingers touch the palms. Your thumb should rest on top of the index finger, closed but not clamped.

Carry your hands so you have a straight line from your elbow, down your forearm, through your wrist and hand, and along the rein to the bit. This will ensure that the bit will work correctly in the corners of the horse's mouth. (If you hold double reins, as with a pelham bit, the straight line should be along the snaffle rein. The curb should have less tension than the snaffle.)

Carry your crop along with the rein in whichever hand you feel you need it. If your horse drifts left on his turns, for example, you'll want to carry it in your left hand so you can brush it against his shoulder. If you're carrying a crop because he's lazy going forward off the leg, probably either hand will do.

Carry the crop with the end down, never up in front of your face. And don't put your wrist through the wrist loop, if it has one. (I cut wrist loops off so there's no temptation.) If you need to drop the crop in a hurry—in case you fall, or you discover that the crop has become a distraction to the horse— you'll want to simply open your fingers and let it go, without having to pull your hand out of a wrist strap.

It takes practice to handle the reins, crop, and jumping strap. Practice the exercises below until you can smoothly shorten, bridge, and slip your reins; change hands with your crop; and take hold of and let go of the jumping strap, all without dropping anything or interfering with your horse's mouth.

If you don't need to carry a crop with your own horse, great! But these are good skills to have, regardless, because they help you develop independent hands. If your balance is secure, your hands will be able to function independently of your seat and legs—and that's an absolute requirement for jumping.

EXERCISE #1: BRIDGE YOUR REINS

Bridging your reins—holding both reins in one hand, or holding both reins with both hands— is an important skill to learn, so you can quickly shorten the reins or free up one hand for another task. Here's an exercise to help you develop this technique.

1. Walk your horse, holding your reins evenly and in light contact with both hands. Now take both reins into your left hand in a single bridge, as shown in the first photograph on page 71, by using the thumb and three fingers of the left hand to take up the right rein as well as the left. Do this without disturbing your horse's rhythm or changing the contact. Your right hand should now be free.

   The grip on your left rein should not change, but now you're also holding your right rein in the same hand, so it enters between thumb and index finger and exits between pinky and ring finger. Contact should feel the same on both reins.

2. Return to two-handed contact, then bridge your reins in your right hand.

3. Now look straight ahead, not down at your hands. Change back to two-handed contact, then practice bridging the reins first in the left hand and then in the right.

4 Finally, repeat this exercise at the sitting trot, rising trot, and canter. Don't look down; do it all by feel.

EXERCISE #2: CHANGE HANDS WITH YOUR CROP

Many horses that go well enough on the flat without a stick need a little more encouragement to go forward over jumps. Or perhaps you're accustomed to riding with spurs on the flat, but your instructor says "no spurs over jumps" until your leg is really secure, so you need to carry a crop to encourage your slightly-too-quiet lesson horse.

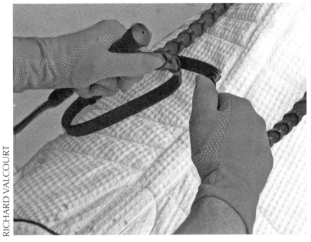

These photos show how to bridge the reins and change hands with your crop. First, take both reins and the crop in your left hand.

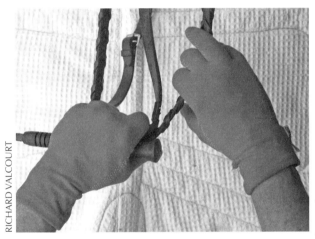

Let go of the right rein with your right hand, so you can . . .

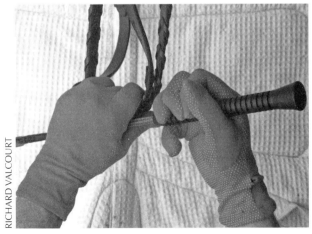

. . . pull the crop through from left hand to right hand.

71

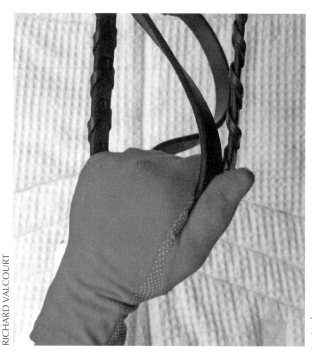

Now your left hand holds both reins in a bridge while your right hand is free to use the crop. Then pick up the right rein in your right hand again.

To use a crop behind the saddle, you'll need to have your reins in one hand and the crop in the other.

1. Start at a walk, with two hands on the reins and a short crop in your left hand, as shown in the first photograph on page 71.

2. Bridge the reins in your left hand, so both the reins and your crop are in your left hand and your right hand is free.

3. Use your right hand to pull the crop up out of your left hand, being sure to keep the reins steady.

4. Settle the crop in your right hand. Now, with your crop in your right hand and your reins in your left, you can reach back to tap the horse with the crop behind the saddle. Practice moving the crop back to the correct spot (behind your leg on the horse's barrel or haunches, to reinforce your leg aid). You don't have to tap him if he doesn't need it, just reach back quietly and find the right spot without quite touching him.

5. Now bring the crop forward again and take up the reins in two hands. Practice switching hands and using the crop on both sides, without fumbling or jerking your horse in the mouth and *without looking down or behind you.*

6. Repeat this same exercise at sitting trot, posting trot, and canter.

7. Finally, repeat this exercise at trot and canter while holding your two-point position.

Why is this a necessary skill to have? Aside from being able to use your crop quickly, smoothly, and correctly when you need it, you're also learning to develop independent hands. It's impossible to bridge the reins or change hands with the crop if you're clinging to the mane or the saddle for balance!

EXERCISE #3: SLIP THE REINS

One of the best ways to learn to slip the reins is to have a friend stand in front of your horse, take hold of the reins, and try to pull you forward and down. (Use an extra pair of long reins so no one pulls on the horse's mouth!)

Try it with your eyes closed, so you learn to respond quickly by feel. As the "horse's head" comes back up, take your reins up smoothly.

1. Start in full-seat position at a halt, holding your reins with normal contact. Close your eyes. As your friend pulls down on the reins, *before* you get tipped forward out of the saddle, open your fingers and let the reins slip longer, but *don't* drop them. Sit up, keep your heels down and your elbows slightly bent so you have a little "give" in reserve. Then ask your friend to let up on the pull so you can shorten your reins smoothly back to regular contact.

RICHARD VALCOURT

Here's a good example of when you will need to slip the reins. Sit up, keep your legs under you with a deep heel, and allow your fingers to open so you can let the reins slide longer without dropping them. In this photo, I've let my elbows open almost to the limit and I'm looking down. Instead, I should look up and keep a little more bend in my elbows.

2. Now begin riding at walk, trot, and canter. At each gait, practice letting the reins slip long, then take them up again quickly but gently. Maintain your leg position and balance so you can help your horse stay straight.

3. Find opportunities out on the trails where you might need to slip the reins—for example, heading down a steep hill or bank, or letting your horse stop for a drink in a stream. Practice keeping your eyes up and your weight in your heels.

Most situations that call for rein-slipping happen because the horse needs to use his head and neck to balance himself. You can slip the reins safely because you can trust your horse to do the right thing and keep you both balanced. But if he puts his head down in disobedience, you'll need to deal with it differently.

Some otherwise reliable horses (and many ponies) are known for screeching to a halt and diving into a patch of grass. If this happens, you need to regain control quickly. You may have to let the reins slip initially so you can stay in the saddle, but then you must quickly bring your shoulders back, brace against your stirrups, and pull up sharply with one hand, to bring your horse's head to the side. Immediately urge him forward with legs, voice, and stick. Keep him moving!

RICHARD VALCOURT

Take hold of the jumping strap at a specific point as you trot or canter around the arena. Don't look down; instead, find it by feel. Take hold, then let go again a few strides later, without disturbing your balance or your horse's rhythm.

EXERCISE #4: ADD THE JUMPING STRAP

After you're comfortable with all the other rein-handling exercises, practice hooking two fingers of each hand through the jumping strap at predetermined points in the arena. Each time you pass a tree or a marker cone, for example, take hold of the strap. Then let go of it four strides later. Keep your rhythm steady and don't look down—feel for the strap! Your reins should go a little loose as you reach for the strap.

1. At a rising trot, reach forward with both hands, hook your index finger through the strap, and hold it for four strides. Each trot stride has two beats, so you can take hold, say to yourself, "One-two, two-two, three-two, four-two," and then release the strap and return your hands to your regular riding position. Look up and keep posting in a steady rhythm. Make the changes in rein contact smooth and quiet so you don't disturb your horse as you move from light contact to no contact, when your hands move forward, and then back to light contact again.

2. At a canter, count four strides as "one-two-three, two-two-three, three-two-three, four-two-three." Be sure to keep your horse moving forward as you release the strap and bring your hands back into contact.

Lesson #2: On Your Feet—Gain Balance and Strong Legs

A rider must be an athlete. There are many things you can do before and after you ride to help improve your balance, strength, and coordination on horseback. Exercise programs designed specifically for riders can be very helpful when you have only limited time in the saddle.

Three exercises I've found particularly useful are discussed below. They combine elements of Pilates and yoga, they can be done pretty much anywhere, and they require no special equipment.

EXERCISE #1: HEEL LIFTS AND HAMSTRING STRETCHES

Stand on a step or a block with the balls of your feet near the edge, feet about shoulder-width apart, and your heels hanging off the edge. Bend your knees and hips to approximate the angles that you use when riding in a full-seat or three-point position. Place one hand on a wall or counter for stability, if you like, and then gently and slowly raise yourself so your heels are up, then gently let your weight down into your heels to stretch the hamstrings. Don't bounce or jar yourself. You should feel a stretch in the tops of your thighs as well as along the ankles and the backs of your calves.

Start with perhaps five or six lifts and drops, then take a break, and do a few more if you're comfortable. Between sets, sit down and rotate your ankles to keep them from becoming stiff.

These photos show the heel lift and hamstring stretch. Keep the knees bent, and hold onto a railing or wall for balance.

Next is the half-squat exercise. Bend, close angles, and breathe!

EXERCISE #2: HALF-SQUATS

Stand straight and relaxed, with equal weight on the balls of both feet, and feet about shoulder-width apart. Breathe in and place your hands on your hips or knees (or hold them in riding position). Keep your back straight and look straight ahead as you slowly fold into a half-squat position. Try to keep your feet flat on the floor and your back straight.

From the half-squat, fold down into the egg exercise. Hold and breathe.

Tighten your abdominal muscles to hold this position and feel your center of gravity, just behind your navel. Breathe out.

Try to hold the half-squat for at least 3 seconds and keep breathing. Then straighten up smoothly. Repeat for a total set of six half-squats.

EXERCISE #3: THE EGG POSITION

Next, instead of straightening up from the half-squat, fold all the way down to the floor as shown in the last photo on this page. Tuck your head down, stretch your back, and breathe deeply. Hold for a count of three, then slowly roll back up into standing position. This position is also wonderful for stretching sore back muscles in between rides at the barn or in a show.

Lesson #3: Two-Point and Three-Point Positions

These exercises will help develop your balance and ability to change positions smoothly at a trot and canter. Take a look at the photos on pages 57–58 to review the positions, then work on the following exercises.

Be sure your stirrups are the right length. With your feet out of the stirrups and hanging relaxed, the stirrup iron should touch your ankle or just above. Pick up your stirrups and go into rising trot in a large circle or along the rail of your arena.

EXERCISE #1: RISING TROT TO THREE-POINT POSITION

Change from rising trot to three-point position, without changing your horse's rhythm. To do this, think of three-point position as a pause in your posting motion. Simply stop posting in the "up" position, and be sure your seat is still lightly grazing the saddle. You should be angled forward at the hip just enough to bring your shoulder over your knee. And your knee should be over your stirrup. Shift all weight from your seat into your stirrups, so you feel your ankles flex and your heels go down. Feel the security of your *anchored knee*, the spot on the inside of your knee that will keep your leg secure through friction pressure.

Your hands should be about 3" forward of where you carry them when you're riding in a full seat. Try to maintain a straight line from your horse's mouth to the bit, and press your knuckles firmly into the crest of your horse's neck. Don't let them float or wander *above* the neck.

Hold the jumping strap if you need it to get or recover your balance, but then try to hold your three-point position without it.

Stay in three-point position at the trot for one circuit of the arena, or one large circle, and then shift back smoothly to posting, being sure to rise on the correct diagonal. Check your rein length and adjust if necessary to maintain light, steady contact.

EXERCISE #2: RING FIGURES IN THREE-POINT POSITION . . .

After you've given your horse a break, go back to three-point position, be sure your balance is secure, and then begin riding ring figures: circles, serpentines, and changes of direction. Use your aids correctly to ask your horse to bend through turns: Keep contact on the outside rein to support your horse as you direct the turn with the inside rein, while the inside leg presses at the girth to maintain impulsion and the outside leg rests slightly behind the girth to hold the hindquarters steady.

Tips for Maintaining Your Position

- Keep your horse moving forward. He should feel as if he's a little in front of your legs, ready to move forward or shorten whenever you ask.

- Whenever you lose your balance or feel that your horse isn't out in front of your legs, shift back into a full seat, reorganize, and then move forward again.

- Use both hard eyes and soft eyes to find your path and stay on track: Look ahead with peripheral vision (soft eyes) to see your entire work area, then locate the next set of cones with sharp focus (hard eyes). At least five strides before you reach the next cones, shift back to soft eyes to find the next pair, and so forth.

- Remember to keep your head and shoulders even—don't lean or duck down into your turns!

- Keep your shoulders parallel to the horse's shoulders and your hips parallel to the horse's hips.

Try riding these exercises, in three-point position:

- *Spiraling circles.* Set four cones as quarter-circle markers on a 65' (20-meter) diameter circle. Then place another four cones outside the first set, with 6' between each pair of cones to form your track. Establish a medium trot or canter rhythm on a large circle (approximately 98' [30 meters] in diameter) just outside the outermost cones. Keeping the same rhythm and speed, spiral in so you're traveling between each pair of cones on a 79' (24-meter) circle. And on your third circle, spiral in even more so you're traveling just inside the innermost cones, on a 65' (20-meter) circle. Use your outside leg to bring your horse in on the smaller track, and your inside leg to push him back out.

- *Large figure eights with simple lead changes.* Add a second circle to make a figure eight. Keep your circles big, round, and even. Ask for a simple change of lead by shifting into trot for a few steps as you straighten and then change to the bend in the middle. If you can stay in three-point for the lead change, great; if you're losing your balance and getting disorganized, then post or sit the trot, reorganize, and then pick up the new lead and shift back into three-point.

- *Next, add trot-canter transitions.* You may be tempted to sink back into the saddle for the upward transition, but try instead to maintain your three-point position and cue your horse mostly from your leg, not your seat. Use diagonal aids to ask for the canter, taking a slight feel of the inside rein as your outside leg moves back for the cue.

- *To get the correct lead, try to time your request when the horse's outside hind leg strikes the ground—he takes the first step of canter with that outside hind leg.* (How do you know when the outside hind foot is about to strike the ground? Use your feel and your soft eyes—peripheral vision—to know when the *inside shoulder* is farthest forward. That's the moment in trot when both the inside front foot and outside hind foot touch down.)

After your balance is secure in three-point, drop and cross your stirrups and repeat the above exercises!

EXERCISE #3: . . . AND NOW IN TWO-POINT POSITION

Now do all of the preceding exercises in two-point position. Close your hip angles and lean forward until your seat clears the saddle by 2"–3", and shorten the reins to correspond to your farthest-forward hand position. Be sure to look up and keep your back flat, not arched stiffly or roached in a slump.

Traveling in two-point position on her trot circles, Lisa works to get Nani more out in front of her legs without resorting to sitting or posting.

In the upward phase of the canter, Lisa stays balanced over her feet and allows her hip and knee angles to close in response to the push upward and forward . . .

. . . and then, in the downward phase of the stride, lets her hip angle open and her hands stay forward to follow Nani's head and neck as they stretch out and down. It's essential that your hands be able to follow the canter motion before you try to follow the jumping motion!

Even though you may feel as if you're riding a little "high in the tack," you must remain balanced over your stirrups with weight in your heels. Your horse should not speed up unless you ask him to. If your horse gets quick or feels like he's falling on his forehand, ease back into three-point (you may need to sit down) to take your weight off his front end. Use half-halts, transitions, and circles to lighten him and keep his hindquarters active. Then go back to two-point.

Try to maintain a consistent rhythm, bend, and speed, no matter what seat you're in.

EXERCISE #4: THE TEST

Can you ride a simple dressage test while in two-point or three-point position? When you can do a reasonable job of riding the first two Training Level dressage tests in two-point position, you'll know you've mastered the art of relying on legs and weight, instead of seat, for transitions and balance.

Lesson #4: Focal Points and Crest Releases

Jumping requires mental focus, visual focus, and the ability to move all your body parts independently without losing your focus. Knowing *where* to look and *how* to look will help you keep your balance, because it will help you keep your head straight and above your shoulders.

This lesson will help you use your eyes correctly while you smoothly release and then take up the reins again. Why is it important to develop both skills simultaneously? Because you can't guide your horse if you're not looking where you're going, and you can't look where you're going if you're focused on your hands instead of what's in front of you.

To set up for this lesson, place two pairs of jump standards on the track of your arena, one in the middle of each long side. Use just the standards, no rails, and be sure each "jump" is set on a straightaway, at least 60' from a turn or corner. These "phantom jumps" will indicate places where you'll execute a crest release while cantering in two-point and three-point position. (You can also use pairs of cones to mark the location of your "phantom jumps," but standards are better because they'll simulate actual jumps.)

Set a cone or other marker approximately two quiet canter strides (25–30') before each "phantom jump." This is the point where you'll move from three-point into two-point position.

If you're new to jumping, you should begin each exercise below with the long crest release and a jumping strap. If you're somewhat more experienced, use a short crest release. *Before you start the exercise, however, be sure you know how to execute a proper crest release.* Specific instructions for using both releases are included below, too.

> **Long Crest Release.** To perform a long crest release, you'll maintain light rein contact and press your knuckles on the crest of your horse's neck. One stride (10'–12') before the "jump," push your hands 2"–3" forward along the horse's crest. Plant your hands and *keep* them there. Press your knuckles into the crest of the neck and keep them steady over the jump and through the landing. Keep your hands and arms forward as the horse's jumping motion comes up underneath you.
>
> If you have a problem with keeping your hands steady and forward in a long crest release, take hold of the mane or jumping strap with your thumb and index finger. If you still can't keep them secure, go back to exercises on the flat, because your balance and security aren't ready yet for jumping.
>
> Don't lie on the horse's neck or throw yourself forward. Instead, try to feel the motion as the horse lifts his shoulders in a regular canter stride, and allow the motion to close your hip angle. Keep your hands out in front of your face and *keep your heels down.* The steadiness of your hands is directly related to the steadiness of your legs!
>
> As your horse passes the standards, straighten up a little but *keep your hands out in front of you for at least one stride after the "jump."* Don't snatch the reins back! Practice releasing and reestablishing contact in a quiet, smooth fashion.
>
> **Short Crest Release.** This is the same as the long release, except your hands don't move as far forward and you strive to maintain light contact with your horse's mouth even while your knuckles are pressing into the crest. As your horse passes the standards, keep your hands forward but straighten your arms a little so your upper body can come back up and open your hip angle while your hands stay forward. Then gently take back your regular rein contact two strides after the "jump."

Lisa pushes her hands forward in a short crest release as she passes the markers. A few strides later, after a phantom "jump," she'll smoothly take back the contact.

EXERCISE #1: FOCUS AND RELEASE

Remember that good balance and control require you to look up and forward, even while you're releasing and following the motion of the horse. This exercise asks you to identify a focus point for your eyes, while your hands release to follow with the horse's motion.

1. On your horse, begin by walking through one of your "phantom jumps." Walk straight along the path you'll follow when you're cantering, and look ahead to identify a focal point for your eyes to lock onto as you approach the "jump." This focal point can be a tree, a fence post, or anything else that's stationary and at least 40' beyond the jump.

   Then walk your horse through the second "jump" and identify a focal point for that one as well.

2. Pick up a steady canter, and begin traveling in three-point position toward your first "jump." Find and look at your focal point. Use peripheral vision to see your marker cones, set two strides before the "phantom jump." As you pass the cones, shift into two-point position. One stride before the "jump," close your hip angle a little more and push

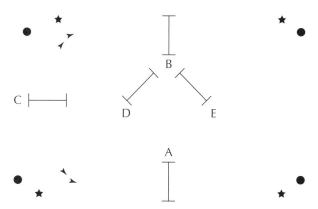

This figure shows the recommended layout for the "focus and release" and "simple rails" exercises. Begin with the jump standards at A and B, then add a rail on the ground at A and B. Next, place single rails at C, D, and E. (You can use just rails or, for more precision, include jump standards at C, D, and E, as well.) The dots indicate straight-line focal points—where your eyes should be looking—for the approaches to A and B. The curving arrows indicate the "moving focal points" for rail C, and the stars show the focal points for the diagonal-line approaches to D and E.

your hands into a steady, quiet crest release. And two strides after, shift back into three-point and gently take back the rein contact. *Do not look down or move your eyes from your focal point* until you have shifted back into three-point. The jump standards will remain in your peripheral vision as you pass them.

3. When your horse has cleared the "jump" and you're back in light contact, prepare for your corner by shifting into soft focus, turning your head and letting your eyes follow a traveling point around the turn. When you've located the next "jump," find your new focal point, change back to hard focus, and ride with laser-like precision down your straight track to your next "jump."

EXERCISE #2: SIMPLE RAILS

Now add a single ground rail between each pair of standards and repeat the preceding exercise, first trotting and then cantering over each rail.

At the trot, you may feel your horse make a quick, extra-long or extra-short step to avoid tripping or stepping on the rail. More experienced horses know how to measure and adjust the last few steps of the approach so they don't have to make an abrupt, last-minute correction. Whatever your horse does, your job is still the same: Stay straight, stay secure, and stay out of his way.

At the canter, an experienced horse will place himself correctly as if he were actually jumping: His hind feet push off on the take-off side, and then his front feet land on the far side. Some less-experienced horses will split up the canter stride, plopping a single forefoot on the landing side. And some cautious horses may actually give a little hop over the rail, so you'll be jumping before you really expect to.

Again, no matter what your horse does over the rail, don't look down, don't try to "place" your horse, and don't try to anticipate when he will step over the rail. Simply keep a steady rhythm, shift quietly into two-point position at two strides out, move your hands forward into crest release one stride out, and let your horse do what's necessary to carry you over the rail.

The only time you need to make a correction is if your horse gets a little quick and enthusiastic about this work. If he's merely a little quick, he should settle down as the work becomes a bit tedious.

But if your horse shows signs of real anxiety by rushing, spooking, leaping high in the air, or trying to avoid stepping over the rail altogether, stop your work. This horse has too many training issues for you to deal with and he's not a good partner for you to learn on.

Whether cantering or trotting over your single rails, your goals should be the same: Keep your eyes on your focal point, stay balanced over your stirrups with weight in your heels, give a crest release, and remain in two-point until two strides after the rail.

Concentrate on these key points during this exercise:

- Use your eyes correctly. Find your focal point when you're on a straight line and look around your turns. Don't shift your eyes rapidly from place to place; just move from a simple hard-eyes focus on the approach to a soft-eyes focus for turns.

- Keep your heels down and your feet under you as you land.

- Hold your two-point for at least two strides after the jump, then move smoothly back into three-point position.

If you have room in your arena, place additional ground rails (C, D, and E) as shown in the diagram on page 83. Don't try to create any combinations (in-and-outs) yet. Place your rails as unrelated distances, so they are never closer than 60' along the path you will travel.

Trot and canter over these for both directions, changing position and practicing your crest release. Pay particular attention to finding your focal point and holding a straight line as you travel over the rails placed across the diagonals, and focus your eyes on a "moving focal point" as you find the approach to any rail placed on the short side of the arena. (For example, rail C.) Unless your arena is very wide, this rail will have to be ridden as if it were placed on a curved path—hence the "moving focal point."

Now you can create a small course with rails in this order: A, C, D, E, C, B.

- Begin with a large, clockwise circle at a trot on the end of the arena opposite rail C. Midway through your circle, pick up a right-lead canter and look for rail A.

- As you canter over A in two-point, look for rail C and establish a moving focal point to take you around the turn.

- As you canter over C, turn your eyes to find D on the diagonal. Turn and lock onto a straight-line focal point for D.

- After D, continue deep into the corner ahead of you, and transition to trot for a simple change of lead and a left turn. Turn your eyes left, continue around the end of the arena into a left turn, and find your focal point for the approach to E.

- As you canter over E, you'll look for the moving focal point that will take you through the right-hand turn to C and onto the straight line for B.

- After B, transition smoothly back to a rising trot and finish with a smooth circle. Then give your horse a reward with a long rein, a pat, and a rest. You've just finished your first course.

Tips for Riding the "Simple Rails" Exercise

Note that the approach to rail D must always be from a right-hand turn, and the approach to rail E must always be from a left-hand turn.

Get in the habit of riding long, straight lines across the diagonals. Use your corners and the full length of the arena—no cutting corners.

Be sure you are moving smoothly into two-point and executing a crest release for each ground rail. The crest release doesn't have to be huge, because the horse's jumping effort isn't huge, but it *must* be a real release.

Do *not* look down to change leads after D. If you and your horse are comfortable with a flying change of lead, great, but many riders will need to do a simple change of lead (dropping to a few steps of trot) to stay organized.

Tips for the Coach

You don't have to be a professional trainer to help a friend or riding buddy improve her balance and focus. Ask her to tell you where her eyes are looking at each point on the course. Remind her to find a focal point and "lock on."

Ask the rider if she felt she was giving a good crest release over each rail.

Did she lose her balance and need to grab the mane at any point? If so, try to learn why. A loss of balance is often caused by an unsteady lower leg: the foot swings back or forward, the heel comes up, and the rider falls ahead of or behind the horse's center of gravity.

Lesson #5: Stirrups and No Stirrups

This is another of those "basic skills" lessons that may seem like a no-brainer: *Of course* you can drop and pick up your stirrups while riding. *Of course* you can ride without stirrups. (See the "Are You Ready to Jump?" sidebar from chapter 3.)

You've done these exercises on the flat. (I hope.) But now you raise the challenge level a bit.

EXERCISE #1: RETRIEVE THE STIRRUPS

This exercise is simple. Just go back through the previous four lessons and repeat the exercises. But this time, practice dropping and picking up one or both stirrups.

As you ride in two-point, three-point, and over your single rails, have a helper call out these commands: "Drop your left stirrup," "Pick up your left stirrup," "Drop both stirrups," and so on. Your goal is to become so adept at retrieving a dropped stirrup that you won't have to slow down, fumble, lose balance, glance down, or poke your horse in the ribs.

EXERCISE #2: RIDE WITHOUT STIRRUPS

Riding without stirrups is every rider's favorite (not!). But it's the single most effective exercise you can do to strengthen your legs. For this exercise, just pull the stirrups off your saddle and repeat Lessons #1 through #4.

When you ride without stirrups, your legs should remain in the same position as when you have stirrups. Your legs may lengthen slightly, but they should *not* be pulled up higher with pinched knees or clamped thighs.

The only difference when you're riding without stirrups is that you can't really push the heels down—instead, you have to pull the toes up a little to stretch the hamstrings and make the lower leg a little snugger.

Be sure to take frequent breaks. Breathe. Relax and rotate the ankles from time to time so you don't develop cramps in your feet or calves.

ARE YOU READY TO MOVE ON?

If you find that riding without stirrups for 10 or 15 minutes at a time in posting trot, canter, and two-point is difficult, that's a sign your legs aren't ready yet to support you in jumping.

And if you can't hold a two-point position (with stirrups) for 3 or 4 minutes at a time without collapsing and rounding your back, that's a clue that your back and abdominal muscles don't yet have the stamina they need to support your upper body. But keep working and your strength and balance will improve!

Chapter 6

UNDERSTANDING STRIDES, DISTANCES, AND GRIDS

ounting strides. Finding the right distance. Long spots, short spots, deep spots, a "waiting" distance.

What does it all mean, and why do you need to understand strides and distances? Can't the horse figure all that out on his own?

Yes, the horse can figure it out on his own, *when* he's on his own. But for him to produce a smooth, steady, safe performance over fences at your request, when he's carrying *you*, you have to help him. So you've got to develop a feel for striding, and learn when and how to ask your horse to make adjustments in his stride and balance.

Depending on your horse's experience, training, and temperament, your horse relies on you for direction. When you're riding on the flat, you determine direction, speed, balance, and stride length, so he's probably going to expect some help from you when you ride over fences.

On the other hand, you shouldn't have to micromanage your horse's every movement. He should respond to your requests for direction, speed, stride length, and takeoff point, but, ultimately, he's the one doing the jumping. *Essentially, your goal should be to help your horse exercise good judgment about his jumping.* Then you can simply sit quietly and stay out of his way.

Many riders today seem to think that overriding—doing too much—is better than under-riding. In my experience, overriding gets you into far more trouble than under-riding. And I'd much rather ride a horse that will take care of me than one that has to wait for my commands before lifting a hoof.

The better you are at having a feel for stride length and seeing a distance *early,* the better you'll be at communicating the necessary adjustments to your horse.

In this chapter, we tackle the problems of strides and distances by creating jumping grids, combinations of cavalletti and small jumps set at carefully measured distances. When constructed properly, these gymnastic jumping exercises will help develop the rider's sense of rhythm, timing, and "eye for distance." The exercises also help the horse by increasing his agility and strengthening the muscles in his back and hindquarters.

Measuring Strides

Developing a feel for strides and distances is an art, but is based on math. And it's not that complicated. Essentially, you look at the canter stride as covering a certain distance: The standard for a 16-hand hunter or jumper traveling at a medium canter is 12'. He can lengthen his stride to 13' or shorten it to 11', 10', or maybe even 9' if his rider is accomplished at maintaining impulsion and collection. But if you ask for anything shorter than that, your 16-hand jumper is in danger of losing impulsion and rhythm. (An upper-level dressage horse, of course, can shorten the canter stride even more to produce a fully collected canter or pirouette. But here I'm talking about the average hunter or jumper, with the average rider.)

For many smaller horses and novice riders, a 12' canter stride can seem too big and fast. So you should begin working with an 11' distance instead. If you're riding a pony or if your small horse is a little lazy, you may even want to start with a 10' distance when you set up your jumping grids and courses.

If you want to compete in events that require a 12' stride, however, you'll need to develop that larger stride in your horse.

If you don't know how long your horse's canter stride is, don't worry. You'll find out soon enough. Measuring stride length is tackled under the next section, "Your Horse's Jumping Stride at the Canter."

Your Horse's Jumping Stride at the Canter

In chapter 1, you reviewed the mechanics of the canter and the jumping stride. Essentially, when a horse is traveling in an 11' stride at a medium canter, he's covering the ground in 11' increments. He can shorten or length that increment but he *cannot change the sequence of steps or leave out any part of the sequence* without breaking stride or putting in a dangerous jump.

In jumping, the horse splits the canter stride into two parts: half on the takeoff side (where hind feet push off), and half on the landing side (where front feet land). So he must complete the last canter stride approximately 5'–6' in front of the jump. The smaller the jump, the more leeway he has for takeoff and landing. The higher the jump, the more precise the takeoff must be.

Ideally, the horse with an 11' canter stride will complete his second-to-last stride 16.5' in front of the jump, leaving room for one more 11' stride and a smooth takeoff about 5' or 5.5' in front of the jump.

But what happens when the horse completes that second-to-last stride 20' before the jump? The next stride—the last one before takeoff—will place him 9' away from it. A takeoff from that far out is dangerous, because his 11' jumping stride will cause him to land only 2' beyond the jump, and it will be impossible for him to clear the fence.

The Eleven-Foot Canter Stride

Why does this book start with exercises set for the 11' stride, instead of the competition standard of 12'?

Because it's safer. When you're just beginning to jump, you will want your horse to offer a quiet canter over small jumps, not a forward 12' stride over big fences. It's better to be a little quiet in your canter stride until your balance is secure.

The 11' stride is also easier for small horses. Many wonderful, highly experienced lesson horses are not 17-hand thoroughbreds or even bigger warmbloods. They're more likely to be 15.2 hand quarter horses, or even 14.3 hand pony crosses. They're very good at packing a novice rider around a 2'6" course based on 11' strides, but they'll find it a challenge to do the same thing with 12' distances.

Well-designed low-level competition courses, especially those at schooling shows and beginner-level horse trials in which horses and ponies compete together, often use 11' distances. Novice-level stadium-jumping, with jumps at a maximum height of 2'11", often feature a one-stride in-and-out set at a distance of 22' or even 21'.

When should you work with a 12' (or larger) canter stride? When:

1. You have a big-enough horse. If you *are* riding that 17-hand warmblood, his natural canter stride probably is 12' or even a bit longer.

2. You're ready to jump a course of fences higher than 3'. Your horse will need the added impulsion, which translates into more scope and stride length.

3. You know you *must* deal with 12' or even 13' multiples in the show ring. A 12' multiple is the standard for most equitation, hunter, and jumper courses on the open circuit.

Unfortunately, the 12' distance is also the recommended standard for the American Quarter Horse Association's hunter hack classes, in which horses are asked to jump two low fences (often as low as 2') set at 24' apart. That 24' distance should be ridden as a one-stride in-and-out, but how often do we see the hunter hack horses chip in a second (or even a third!!) stride in that combination? Unless the jumps are 3' or higher, this combination should be built on a 21' or 22' distance to give the quarter horses (who are often a little smaller and shorter-strided than open-circuit hunters) a chance at making it through in the correct single stride.

RICHARD VALCOURT

The accuracy of the take-off spot is less important on small jumps than large ones, but it still matters. When the final canter stride ends too far away from the jump, the horse must make a bigger effort and reach to get over the jump. This mare is reaching: struggling to make the distance from a too-long take-off spot.

When a horse ends a canter stride at such an impossible distance, he has four choices:

1. Go for that dangerously long takeoff spot, putting in a huge effort to lengthen his jumping stride so he can land safely.

2. Add another tiny stride, perhaps only 7' long, rocking way back on his haunches, taking off only 2' in front of the fence, and shooting almost straight up in the air to avoid hitting it.

3. Stop.

4. Break stride by lifting off with the front feet 9' out and "hopping" an extra step with one or both back feet to bring them closer to a reasonable take-off spot.

A very clever horse can get by with option 4, but it's a survival move that tends to make spectators and judges gasp. Open jumpers may be prized for their nimbleness when they "put a fifth leg down," but it's penalized as unsafe jumping in an equitation or hunter round.

And what happens to the rider in each of these scenarios?

1. She gets left behind because the horse takes off earlier than expected. She catches him in the mouth because she hasn't learned how to grab the mane, slip the reins, and help him by sitting still. And maybe she falls off on landing.

2. She falls forward because the horse has almost stopped in order to create that last tiny stride. The straight-up-in-the-air jump then dislodges her seat, so she thumps down on his back and catches him in the mouth, thus punishing the horse for his honest effort. And maybe she falls off on landing, too.

3. She falls forward and probably off.

4. She feels as if the horse has become suddenly disorganized and double-jointed, and may be left behind the motion.

So what's the solution in this scenario?

When the takeoff is too close to the fence, even when it's a very small fence, disaster can result. My green horse isn't experienced enough to understand she must shorten the last few strides before takeoff, so she's "buried" herself too deep to this log. She has barely enough room to get her knees up out of the way, and we're in danger of falling. (We landed safely, though a bit shaken.)

Horse and rider need to adjust the stride length much earlier in the approach—not just in the *last* stride, but in each of the *previous* four or five strides. If the rider can see early on that her horse's canter strides will put her too close or too far back from a jump, she can make small adjustments before they get into trouble. In the preceding scenario, if the rider lengthened the last three strides by just 1'—going for a forward 12' stride instead of a steady 11' stride—the horse would complete the last stride 6' in front of the jump, a reasonable take-off spot, instead of that dangerous 9' spot.

An experienced and careful horse knows how to make these early-on adjustments, even without direction from the rider, but ultimately it's the rider's job to manage the approach and help the horse get to that comfortable take-off spot. The following lessons should help both you and your horse discover an eye for distances so you can produce a smooth, safe, rhythmic jump with as little effort as possible.

To accomplish this, you need to learn how to:

- Measure distances with your *own steps*, on the ground.
- Judge the *length* of your horse's stride.
- Measure the approach with your *eyes*, when riding.
- Decide *when and how much to adjust* the length of your horse's stride.

Approach at the Trot, Land at the Canter

When you start jumping, you begin with an approach to the jump at a trot.

Why trot, if the horse finds it easier to jump from a canter? Because the trot is slower, so you'll have more control and more time to respond and make decisions. And, although it's more effort for the horse to jump from a trot than a canter, neither of you will have to worry about striding at a trot.

Because the trot is a symmetrical, two-beat gait in which the horse takes evenly spaced steps, it's easy for him to shorten or lengthen just one of those steps and take off at any reasonable spot in front of the fence. The horse doesn't have to complete an entire sequence of footfalls at the trot as he does at the canter. Instead, he can just plant the hind feet together and push off from any point in the trot stride.

Gymnastic Grids

One of the best ways to build your horse's agility and confidence is by riding through *gymnastic grids*, in which the placement of ground rails, cavalletti, and small jumps will help you and your horse develop rhythm and balance. It's crucial, however, that the grids are constructed correctly, so that the distances between elements will make it easy for you and your horse to find a comfortable rhythm and develop your eye for distances. Distances in grids are set fairly tight to encourage the horse to rock back on his hindquarters and not seek a "long" spot for takeoff.

Some grids require an approach at the trot, others at the canter. This will also affect the distances you'll use between elements, because the first canter stride after a trot fence will be a little shorter than your horse's regular canter stride.

Correct distances are especially important when jumping grids, where you'll use related jump elements to help you and your horse find comfortable take-off spots and develop a feel for pace and distance.

Setting up a grid with incorrect distances, on the other hand, is dangerous and can destroy confidence. Even 6" too long or too short can create difficulties with novice riders or green horses. When you're ready to begin riding through grids, use the "Distances for Elements in Gymnastic Grids," chart on page 104 for reference.

Before you set up grids to ride through, however, you'll need to get off your horse and learn how to use your own steps to pace out distances. (This is covered in the following lesson.) It's important to know how to measure distances on foot, so you can set your jumps at a safe, comfortable distance for your horse. And as you develop your eye for distances, you'll be able to relate what you're measuring on the ground to what you're feeling when you ride.

LESSON #6: CALIBRATE *YOUR* STRIDE

To develop your feeling for measuring a distance on foot, you'll need a tape measure (25' is adequate, 50' is better, 100' is best) and four ground rails. This lesson is set up based on 11' distances, but if you already know your horse canters in a 12' or a 10' stride, go ahead and adjust the distances accordingly. See the "Distances for Elements in Gymnastic Grids" chart on page 104.

Exercise #1: Create a Measuring Step

First, you'll start with three of the basic distances used to construct a grid for a horse with an 11' stride.

Using the tape measure for accuracy, place two ground rails 4'6" apart. Then place a third rail 22' beyond the second, and the fourth rail 33' beyond the third one.

The first two poles represent the distance between trotting poles, the 22' distance creates a one-stride combination (approached at a canter), and the 33' distance creates a two-stride combination.

The 22' distance is called a one-stride because the horse lands 5.5' beyond the first rail, puts in one 11' canter stride, and then takes off 5.5' in front of the second rail, for a total of 22'. The 33' spacing creates a two-stride distance because there will be two complete non-jumping strides between. (When counting canter strides, *don't* count the landing steps or the take-off steps, just the non-jumping strides.)

Leave the tape measure stretched out on the ground between the second and third rails so you can see it clearly. Stand with your heels against the middle of the second rail, facing the third. Now walk straight toward the third rail,

22' away. Take *big* steps, every one the same size, and count the steps to the second rail. If you're 5'4" or taller, you should be able to stretch your steps to a full 36"—that's a handy measurement. Try to walk the distance in seven large, equal steps, with a one-third-size step (12") left over.

If you're shorter than 5'4", you may not be able to make a 36" step. Instead, aim for a 24" step, and walk the distance between the two rails in exactly eleven steps. (And if you're still growing, you may have to recalibrate yourself every few months.)

This is your measuring step. Practice it several times with the 22' distance until you can maintain accuracy without looking down at the tape measure. Then come back to the 4'6" distance between the trotting poles, and see if you can accurately pace out that smaller distance with one and a half 36" steps, or two and a quarter 24" steps. Finally, practice with the 33" distance and see how close you can come to fitting a perfect eleven 36" steps (or sixteen-and-a-half 24" steps) into that distance.

Exercise #2: Walk a Multiple-Stride Line

On one long side of your arena, set two ground rails 55' apart. On the other long side, set two rails 66' apart. You can set just the rails, or include jump standards to help guide your eyes when you ride this set-up in the next lesson.

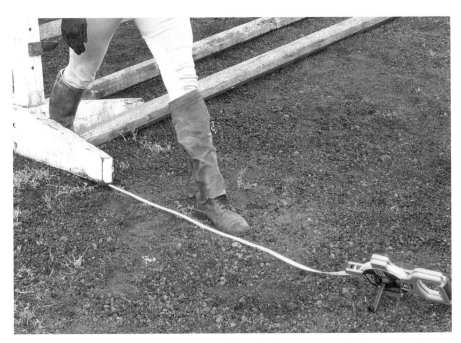

Learn how to develop a "measuring step" by placing your heel back against the bottom of the first rail and then striding forward in 3' or 2' steps. Be consistent, and measure from heel to heel.

66 Feet: Five non-jumping strides

55 Feet: Four non-jumping strides

Use this set-up to practice measuring the distance with your own stride. Then ride the lines at a canter, counting strides. Keep your eyes up and find the focal points (indicated by dots) for each line.

Each pair of rails represents a jumping line with two ground rails placed at a "related" distance: They have an expected number of complete strides between them. The 66' distance is a five-stride line, and the 55' distance is a four-stride line.

After you've used the tape measure to ensure accuracy for these distances, practice pacing off the two lines until you can determine, within 6", the distance between ground rails for both lines. This will prove invaluable when you're walking a course before a class.

LESSON #7: FIND YOUR HORSE'S BASELINE STRIDE

Now get on and ride, preferably while you're still fresh from having walked the distances.

Exercise #1: Feel the Rhythm

After you've warmed up simply canter quietly, in three-point position with light contact, around your track and over the rails placed in the 66' and 55' lines. Pay attention to how you're using your eyes: Find your focal points and think about how much you can notice with peripheral vision (soft eyes) while still remaining focused on the point for each line. If you meet each rail in a steady, rhythmic canter, your horse should make the small adjustments he needs to step over the rail with his front feet so the rail fits "under" the canter stride.

Change direction and canter two or three times each direction, then give your horse and yourself a break.

Exercise #2: Count the Strides

Now you need to determine the length of your horse's *baseline stride,* which is the length of stride that he's most comfortable with. First, be sure you're able to count each separate stride.

Repeat the same work as above, but this time count the number of strides between each pair of rails. Don't look down at the rails—stay focused and use peripheral vision so you know when your horse has "landed" over a rail.

Begin counting with the first full canter stride *after* the rail. If your horse has met it correctly, his front feet will land and pick up, and then his back feet will touch down. *That's* the beginning of the first canter stride. Don't count the last beat before the rail, when the front feet push off in the beginning of the next "jumping" stride.

So look up, feel for the rhythm, listen to the beats, and say: "*Land*, one, two, three, four, *off*." "Land" is the touchdown of the front feet after the first rail, and "off" is the hind feet pushing off for the second rail in the line.

Lisa rides the four-stride and five-stride lines from Lesson #7 in a medium canter, making sure Nani stays in front of her leg. Nani has just completed the last non-jumping stride; the next beat with her hind feet will be "off" (for the takeoff).

Four eleven-foot strides
The 55′ distance

5′6″   11′   11′   11′   11′   5′6″

You should ride the 55' distance in an even four strides, unless you have a larger horse or a pony. Adjust the distance between ground rails so it works well for your horse in a medium canter. The canter rhythm should be steady so it feels the same at the end of the line as at the beginning.

Why not just use a tape measure to find the distance between two prints left by the same hoof? That can help you determine stride length, certainly, but the purpose of this exercise is to feel the way the striding feels while moving, so you can "become your own tape measure."

If the 55' line doesn't ride well in four strides—if you've got a bigger-striding horse who can do the distance in three-and-a-half strides—then go ahead and change the distance to 60' for the four-stride line and 72' for the five-stride line.

If, on the other hand, you're maintaining a forward, medium canter but your small horse is struggling to make the 55' distance in four strides—if he's putting in an extra stride or two on each line—then shorten the distances to multiples of 10' (50' for a four-stride distance, 60' for a five-stride distance).

This is where a knowledgeable assistant can be a big help, to confirm that what you're feeling is what is actually happening.

Remember, the goal right now is not to make adjustments to his stride, but to find the *baseline* that you can both be comfortable with. Adjustments happen later, after you're very secure over very dependable distances.

Whenever you ride from now on, you should be able to count strides and maintain the same rhythm along a line or around the arena. Practice counting strides *everywhere,* even when you don't have rails to canter over. Use markers along the arena perimeter, or between two trees when you're in a nice open space on the trails. See if you can guess how many strides it will take you to canter all the way around the arena, then count and see how close your estimate was.

If you practice in a dressage arena, how many strides does it take you to canter across the diagonal from the markers H to F, or along the long side from K to H?

Find Your Breathing Rhythm

A good way to help you increase your awareness of rhythm and find your center of balance and relaxation is to breathe in rhythm with your horse's canter stride.

Your horse naturally breathes with his own motion. The movement of his body makes it easy for him to inhale on the upward phase of the canter and exhale on the downward phase as his body swings forward and pushes air from his lungs. But riders often get out of breath because their breathing doesn't match the rhythm of the horse's canter.

Have you ever seen a rider finish a 1-minute round over fences gasping for air and short of breath? Have you ever felt like that? (How would you ever survive galloping a 7-minute cross-country course?)

Getting short of breath while riding is not just about exertion and lack of stamina. Often, it's more a matter of jittery nerves, body tension, and poor breathing skills. When your breathing is quick, shallow, and erratic, what happens? You get tense, awkward, and fatigued. And when you're tense, your breathing becomes quick and shallow. It's harder for you to stay in balance, and harder for your horse to carry you.

Try this exercise to help you find a relaxed breathing rhythm as you canter:

1. You'll need a large arena or field, where you can canter steadily with no sharp turns. Establish a medium canter in a light seat, with your body angled just slightly ahead of the vertical and your weight securely in your stirrups.

2. Use soft eyes to guide your horse along your path and think about your breathing. Make each breath very regular and a little deeper than normal: in through your nose, out through a slightly open mouth.

Riding through Gymnastic Grids

Now that you're comfortable with counting strides and you've found your horse's baseline stride length, it's time to set up a grid and begin to jump.

Lesson #8: The Basic Grid

The basic grid begins with a cavalletti and then you'll add actual jumps in a logical, step-by-step fashion. This lesson also introduces the idea of channel poles to help you and your horse stay straight.

3. Where does your breath go? Make each breath go deep into your abdomen, not just your upper chest. Breathe from your center of gravity—it will help you stay centered on your horse.

4. Now count. How many strides does your horse cover in the time it takes you to complete one full, comfortable breath?

5. Try to match your breathing to your horse's strides. If you're on a large, big-striding horse with a relaxed canter, you may find yourself breathing in on one stride and out on the next. A smaller horse may complete two strides as you inhale and two more as you exhale. Try to inhale as the horse lifts up at the beginning of a canter stride, and exhale during the downward phase of a stride. And try to make each breath last at least two strides.

When jumping, often both riders and horses take in a big breath on takeoff, hold their breath while in flight, and exhale on landing. That's fine. It helps with focus and the jumping effort. But if you're not breathing in a steady, regular, relaxed manner in between the jumps, then you'll quickly run short of breath.

So, practice rhythmic breathing in a rhythmic canter. Your goal is to develop a relaxed, ground-covering canter with rhythmic breathing that you can maintain for at least 2 minutes. (If you want to ride in three-phase events or go foxhunting, you'll need considerably more than 2 minutes of rhythmic canter—but this is a good beginning.)

Then, see if you can do the same exercise in two-point position. Breathe in, breathe out. Look ahead, use soft eyes. Relax into the rhythm. Breathe from the center of your body.

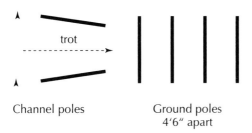

trot

Channel poles

Ground poles
4'6" apart

To build a grid, start with ground poles or cavalletti, and channel poles to help guide a straight approach. Use cones to mark the spot where you should put your hands forward in a crest release.

Terms: Types of Jumps

- **Ascending (ramped) oxer:** The rail on the back element is higher than the front. This is one of the easiest fences to judge for distance, jumping effort, and take-off because the ascending spread creates visual perspective and invites a rising arc.

- **Cavalletti:** Italian for "little horses." A series of raised poles or planks that can be placed in series for trotting or cantering over. Cavalletti are often built so they can be raised to varying heights, from 6"–18". Also called ground poles when they are not raised off the ground.

- **Combination:** A jumping line that includes at least two fences set at related distances of 39' or less. A combination may include a bounce (no strides between fences), a one-stride in-and-out (usually set at 22' to 26'), or a two-stride combination (33' to 39'). In competitions, a *disobedience* (refusal) at the second or third obstacle in a combination usually requires the rider to re-jump the first element because there isn't enough room between the elements for an approach to the second or third jumps. Jumps in a combination are labeled 8A, 8B, and 8C to indicate that they are all elements of the same obstacle.

- **Coop:** Triangle-shaped wall that simulates the look of a chicken coop, with a wide base, angled sides, and a narrow top.

- **Crossrail:** A simple jump made with two rails. One end of each rail rests in a jump cup; the other end rests on the ground. The lowest point is always the middle.

- **False ground line:** A jump with its lowest horizontal line (bottom rail) *not* at ground level is said to have a false ground line. A false ground line makes it difficult to judge the true height of the jump.

- **Filler:** Any material used to "fill in" the face of a jump so it appears more substantial. Flowers, brush, panels, and gates can all be used as filler.

- **Ground line:** A rail placed on the ground underneath or 2'–3' feet in front of a fence to help the horse and rider judge height and takeoff. All jumps set for beginner riders and green horses should have a ground line.

- **Ground poles:** 10' or 12' poles or rails placed on the ground in a measured series for trotting or cantering over. May also be referred to as *cavalletti.*

- **Jumping line:** Any track that the rider follows, which includes at least one jump. A "line" may have only one jump, or it may have several set at related distances (multiples of canter strides). Most riders think of a jumping line as straight, but it can also be a "bending" line, around a turn or with the jumps slightly offset.

- **Oxer:** Any fence with a spread. Usually constructed with two pairs of jump standards set close together so both elements are jumped at one time. The back rail of the oxer should never be set lower than the front, because the horse cannot see it on his approach. There are several types of oxers discussed in this list

- **Roll-top:** An oxer with a half-rounded wall, often covered with artificial turf, which simulates a small bank (to be jumped over, not onto).

- **"Skinny" or narrow jump:** Most show-ring jumps are 12' wide across the face, but many course designers are now including 9' or 8' jumps as a test of accurate riding on equitation, hunter, and event courses.

- **Square or parallel oxer:** Both elements are set at the same height. This jump is more difficult to judge than an ascending oxer.

- **Swedish oxer:** Rails on the front element are higher on one side and rails on the back element are higher on the other side, so they create a modified crossrail with a spread.

- **Triple bar:** An oxer with three pairs of standards and three elements to be jumped. The front rail is lowest and the back rail is highest. Requires accuracy and scope to clear both height and width.

- **Vertical:** Any jump without a spread. The most difficult verticals are *airy* (without ground lines or filler material), because it is hard for horse and rider to judge size and distance. Verticals with fillers or many rails are easier to gauge.

- **Wall:** A rectangular box, solid and substantial looking, that simulates a brick or stone wall. May be used as a filler under a rail, or may have movable blocks at the top that can be knocked off.

Exercise #1: Build a Simple Grid

Begin with four ground poles (trotting poles) spaced 4'6" along your track. In front of the first ground pole, place a pair of "channel poles" on the ground as shown in the diagram on page 101. About 10' in front of the first ground pole, near the ends of the channel poles, place a pair of cones.

The cones will remind you to put your hands forward in a crest release, and the channel poles will keep your horse focused and straight on the approach. You can also add a pair of jump standards on either end of the first ground pole to help guide you into the trotting poles.

Approach at a steady but slightly forward rising trot. Find your focal point to hold a straight line. Shift into two-point two steps (one trotting stride) before the cones and give a medium crest release when you pass between the cones. Hook a finger through your jumping strap if you're using one.

Hold the position as the horse steps over the rails, and feel how his slightly higher trot steps lift his body up. Instead of letting him throw you up,

Distances for Elements in Gymnastic Grids

Element	12' stride	11' stride	10' stride
Trotting poles	4'9"–5' apart	4'6" apart	4' apart
Canter poles ("bounce" cavalletti)	10'–12' apart	9'–10' apart	8' apart
Trotting poles to 18" X-rail	10'–12'	9'–10'	8'–9'
X-rail to 2' vertical (trot approach)	18'	16'	14'
2' vertical to 2'–2'6" oxer (canter approach)	21'–22'	19'–20'	17'–19'
2' vertical to 2'6" oxer, 2 strides (canter approach)	33'–34'	30'–32'	26'–29'
X-rail to 2' vertical, bounce (canter approach)	12'	10'–11'	9'–10'

Note: Grid distances should be set slightly tighter than related distances for a course. So if your horse's normal canter stride is 11' you'd set up a classic grid with four trotting poles spaced 4'6" apart, and then place a crossrail 10'–12' beyond the last trotting pole, with a 2' vertical 16' beyond that, and an oxer 20'–21' beyond the vertical. You trot over the trotting poles, jump the crossrail and land in canter, take one canter stride to the vertical and a slightly larger canter stride to the oxer, and land in a canter.

think of closing your hip angle and folding forward to bring your torso down just a little: The horse comes up to meet you with each step.

Think to yourself, "Look up, heels down, anchor the base."

The steps over the rails should be slightly elevated and more energetic, but they shouldn't create a drastic change in rhythm.

Hold the position until you're at least four trot steps past the last rail, then smoothly ease back into posting trot and take up the rein contact.

If you felt as if the horse met the ground poles in a normal trot stride (or just slightly more energetic than normal), and gave you that slight lifting feeling without struggling or tossing you around, great. But if you felt he was struggling and reaching to make the 4'6" distance between ground poles, try it again with a little more impulsion on the approach. If he's still struggling to reach the distance, get off and shorten up the spacing a little.

If, on the other hand, your horse had to drastically shorten his steps to make it through the 4'6" spacing, he probably needs the spacing widened to accommodate his bigger stride.

After you've been through the trotting poles several times and you're comfortable with the rhythm, cross your stirrups and go through a few times without stirrups, posting and then holding your two-point.

Exercise #2: Cavalletti with Crossrail

And now it's time for an actual jump! (Yes, you can pick up your stirrups.) Nine to ten feet beyond your last trotting pole, add a crossrail that is eighteen to twenty inches high. Beyond the crossrail, add another pair of channel poles to help you stay straight on the landing. Be sure the narrow ends of the channel poles are at least eight feet apart. You want the channel to encourage your horse to stay straight, not trip him if he does waver off-center. See the diagram on page 106.

Ride this almost the same way that you rode the ground poles, keeping your two-point position and executing a crest release at the cones. But instead of just letting the horse keep the same trot rhythm all the way through, you're going to ask him to land in a canter after the crossrail. So two steps before the crossrail, ask for a canter with a slight squeeze of your calves. And be sure to specify which lead you want: right leg on the girth, left leg back a little for a right lead or left leg on the girth and right leg back an inch for the left lead. (You may not *get* the correct lead, but it's important to *ask* and to *expect* the canter after the jump.)

Why ask for a canter transition at this crucial moment? Because if you don't ask your horse to put a little energy into his jump and land in a canter, he may land in a disorganized heap.

But remember, all you're asking for here is a small canter transition. It's important for you to know how sensitive your horse is. You don't want him to rush forward, put just a little effort into his work so he hops over the crossrail

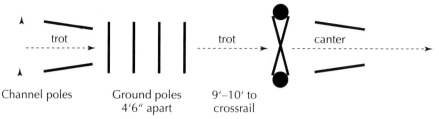

Add a crossrail after the trotting poles and another pair of channel poles to help create a straight landing.

and doesn't just try to trot a big step over it. (There's no harm if he does spring over and land in a trot, but it's uncomfortable for the rider and awkward for the horse. It's better for both of you if he lands in a quiet canter.)

On take-off, don't throw yourself forward—just fold at the hip, and let the horse "rise up to meet you" so your hip angle closes.

On the descent, keep your hands firmly planted on his neck for security. His neck, mane, and jumping strap are all there to help keep your hands and upper body secure.

What happens on landing? You look up, sit up, keep your hands forward on his neck, and keep those heels down and feet under you as your horse recovers into a steady canter.

Do not allow your hands to fly loose or snatch his mouth. Do not tip forward or look down.

Think about what should happen after the jump: a few strides of canter and a smooth transition back to rising trot.

So here are the steps:

1. Approach at rising trot.

2. Two strides before the first ground pole, move into two-point.

3. At the cones, give a crest release (a long crest release if you're a novice, a short crest release if you've done this before but are reviewing the basics).

4. One step before the crossrail, signal "go forward into canter."

5. Jump the crossrail and land in canter. Stay in two-point throughout.

6. After the channel poles, take up light rein contact and transition from canter back to rising trot.

Ride this basic grid at least fifty times (but not all in one training session!). When you feel confident that you can establish a straight approach and a steady rhythm, hold a steady two-point position, perform a secure crest release, and have your horse land cantering quietly *every time,* then you're ready to move on.

Constructing Grids

Make sure you have enough room (at least 50') before the first element and after the last element so riders can turn smoothly onto a straight approach and stay straight after the last obstacle, with time to recover their balance without having to deal with a sharp turn.

Be sure the distances between elements are accurate. Pace the distance for practice, but then get out the tape measure.

Build the grid progressively, as discussed in this book. Start with the simplest element and add one piece at a time. (Example: Single ground rail—cavalletti—crossrail—vertical—oxer.) When you run into trouble—if your horse swerves or refuses or rushes—analyze the problem, recheck the distances between elements, and go back a step or two in the construction of your grid.

If your practice ground has a slope to it, build your grid so it will be jumped uphill, because it's much easier to maintain your balance uphill than downhill.

Use *channel poles* (a pair of ground poles placed parallel to the line of travel or in a funnel position) on the approach and landing to help horse and rider stay straight through the grid.

Always use a pole as a ground line on the take-off side of each jump. The ground pole should be rolled out a distance equal to the height of the fence. Ground poles on the landing side are also helpful to remind a horse not to cut down on his arc over the jump. Ground poles make it easier for the horse and rider to judge both the height and take-off spot for a jump.

Lesson #9: The Grid—Add a Vertical and an Oxer

The easiest way to move on to a slightly larger jump is to add a second, and then a third jump, to your basic cavalletti-to-crossrail grid. You'll use your knowledge of your horse's baseline stride length to create a carefully measured distance: one stride between the crossrail and a small vertical jump.

Each element of the gymnastic grid should prepare you and your horse for the elements that follow: the trotting poles (cavalletti) establish the rhythm and path for jumping the crossrail, the distance from the crossrail to the vertical determines the correct take-off spot for the vertical, and so on.

Riding through a well-built gymnastic grid should be much easier that trying to jump a single lonely fence set in the middle of the arena. It's the relationship between the elements in a grid that will guide you into mastering your basic jumping skills.

RICHARD VALCOURT

As her horse lands, Lisa keeps her seat lightly out of the saddle and balances over her feet. Her hands are firmly pressed into the crest of her horse's neck in an excellent short crest release.

Exercise #1: Crossrail to a Vertical

Now you'll construct a combination by adding a small (18–24") vertical jump 16–18' beyond the crossrail. (See the "Distances for Elements in Gymnastic Grids" chart on page 104 for adjusting the distance based on your horse's baseline stride.) Add another pair of channel poles to help keep your horse straight, and ride this combination with the same approach and the same rhythm as in the previous lesson. The only difference is that your horse will canter one stride after the crossrail and then jump again, making a slightly larger effort over the vertical.

Treat this grid as all one obstacle, and stay in two-point all the way through. The only change in your position should be in the angle of the hip, which closes as the horse lifts off and opens as the horse descends.

Remember:

- Keep your eyes fixed on your focal point.

- Maintain quiet, steady contact with your legs. Don't grab or swing or grip with the lower legs.

- Keep your hands planted firmly on the crest of the horse's neck, and don't try to steer or make any corrections after you've released the reins.
- Use channel poles to help keep your horse straight.

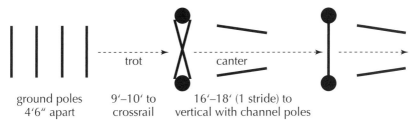

ground poles 4'6" apart | trot 9'–10' to crossrail | canter 16'–18' (1 stride) to vertical with channel poles

Add a small vertical jump 18–20' (one short canter stride) beyond the crossrail. Use additional channel poles to keep your horse straight.

RICHARD VALCOURT

Lisa's leg has slipped back a little; she'd be more secure if her stirrups were a notch shorter. But she's not interfering with Nani's jump, and her hands are following the motion in a quiet automatic release. If you're new at this, be sure to use a long crest release to give your horse plenty of rein.

What Happens after the Last Fence in the Line?

As you jump the last fence in a grid or a line, you must have a plan. Where do you go and what happens next?

Many riders pay such close attention to the jumps that they don't have a clue about what they should do after the last one. So they collapse in a disorganized heap, flop back into the saddle, let their horses drift, and cruise to a walk, looking around to see who was watching. Or they let their horses stop and wander onto the track of the arena. I've seen young riders land over the last jump, drop their reins and let their ponies grab a mouthful of grass, right in the path of the rider coming behind them!

This kind of sloppy riding creates confusion and can cause accidents in the schooling ring.

Here's how to finish your line: Look up, right straight ahead, transition back into full seat or three-point, and organize your turn at the end of the arena. If you've finished your "go," find room to make a large circle and transition back to trot and then walk, just as if you were riding your final circle at the end of a hunter round. Keep your horse balanced and on the aids, and pay attention to other riders. Neither you nor your horse should go off-duty just because you managed to get over a few jumps. Keep riding!

Exercise #2: Remember to Breathe

After you've become comfortable with the rhythm of your horse's striding through the grid, and you feel fairly balanced and secure, pay a little extra attention to your breathing as you ride through. Try to breathe in rhythm with the trot, then inhale as your horse lifts over the crossrail and exhale as he lands. Inhale on lift-off over the vertical, and exhale on landing. Keep your eyes on your focal point, don't force yourself into a rigid breathing pattern, but *think* about your breathing.

Feel the rhythm of the grid: step, step, step, step, gather, jump, land, canter stride, gather, jump, land, recover the canter.

Exercise #3: Build Security without Stirrups

Ride Exercise #1 without stirrups. Can you keep the same rhythm?

Exercise #4: Vertical to an Oxer

Next, add a small oxer 19'–20' beyond the vertical, as shown on page 111. Measure the distance from the center of the vertical to the *center* of the oxer. Make the front rail of the oxer 3" *lower* than your vertical, and place the back rail at the same height as the vertical. Keep the *spread* (the distance from front rail to back rail) no wider than the height of the highest rail. So if you're

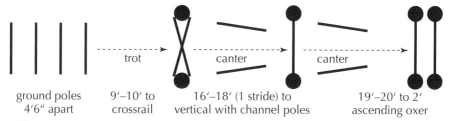

| ground poles 4'6" apart | 9'–10' to crossrail | 16'–18' (1 stride) to vertical with channel poles | 19'–20' to 2' ascending oxer |

Add an oxer to your grid, being sure to construct it properly so the back rail is higher than the front. Ascending (ramped) oxers are much easier than square oxers for a horse to see, judge and jump.

building an oxer that's 21" high at the front rail and 24" at the back rail, make the spread 24" wide.

Ride through the grid as before, approaching the cavalletti in a trot and landing over the crossrail in a canter. Hold your two-point and crest release all the way through, and feel how the horse closes your hip angle a little more with the bigger effort of the oxer. Be sure to keep your weight in your heels, and don't get tipped forward or thrown back on the descent from the last jump.

The oxer will *feel* like a bigger jump because your horse must jump a few inches higher to clear a spread than to clear a vertical of the same height.

LESSON #10: THE GRID— CANTER BOUNCES

A *bounce combination* is also called a *no-stride*, because the horse lands from one jump and immediately lifts off for the next, with no canter strides in between. Like other grid elements,

After you feel comfortable and secure in this basic gridwork, give yourself a stronger leg by riding the same exercises without stirrups. Keep your leg in the same position as when you had stirrups, and move smoothly from full seat to three-point and two-point.

bounces build strength and agility in the horse, and help the rider develop a better sense of rhythm. When it's properly constructed and ridden, a bounce combination requires the horse to shorten stride and coil his loin as he pushes off from the hindquarters. It's a particularly useful exercise for horses that tend to rush or flatten over their fences.

Constructing Safe Jumps

Rails can be made of wood or thick PVC. If you're using PVC rails, be sure they're designed for equestrian use and are **heavy**—at least 20 pounds for a 12' rail. Lighter plastic will bounce and spring when hit, tangling in a horse's legs. Even worse, light plastic may shatter on impact.

The standard length for rails and jump elements in most show rings is 12', but many classes will include narrower jumps. Many people school at home with 10' or even 8' rails, so when they go to a show, it's easy to find the center of a 12'-wide jump.

Jump standards can be made of PVC or wood. PVC is durable and lightweight, but may blow over in a strong wind. It's a good idea to purchase the kind that can have the base filled with sand or water to weigh them down. Five-foot-tall standards are plenty tall enough for schooling. PVC schooling standards such as Stackers and Blocs are excellent for home use.

Important: Be sure to use Stackers or Blocs safely. Don't place the rails so that they can fall back toward the horse's hind legs (and possibly trip him) if he dislodges a rail with his front legs.

Jump cups can be made of metal or plastic. Plastic won't rust and it's less damaging if a horse or rider bumps into one, but most plastic cups are less durable than metal. *Slide-and-lock cups*, which slip onto vertical channel strips attached to the uprights, are a good idea. They have no pins to lose and are very easy to remove when not needed.

Use flat or shallow cups for a heavy element such as a gate or panel, so it can be dislodged if a horse hits it.

Important: Remove all unused jump cups from your jump standards. An empty jump cup can create a nasty injury if a horse or rider falls against or bumps into it.

Use filler material. Substantial, solid-looking jumps are easier to see and jump than a single thin rail. Fill in open spaces under the top rail with filler material: brush boxes, flowers, a small wall, or a panel.

Exercise #1: Ground Poles in a Bounce Pattern

At its simplest, a series of bounce jumps is a set of ground rails, precisely spaced. Begin with a single ground rail on one long side of your arena. Canter over this in two-point position from both directions.

Then add a second rail, a little less than one canter stride's length beyond. If your horse's baseline canter stride is 11', place the second rail 9'–10' beyond the first, so he'll be required to shorten stride for the second rail. After you're comfortable cantering over the two rails, add a third and then a fourth, using

Don't leave unsafe gaps between adjacent jumps or a jump and the arena wall. When you place a jump next to the wall or two jumps next to each other, leave either *no* gap, or leave at least 8' between standards or a standard and the wall. If a horse ducks out at a jump, he must be able to do it safely and not try to squeeze into a very narrow space.

Use correctly placed ground lines. The ground pole on the take-off side should be rolled out a distance equal to the height of the fence. Ground poles on the landing side are also helpful to remind a horse not to cut down on his arc over the jump, but don't jump anything that has a ground line *only* on the landing side, because this makes it very hard for the horse to judge where to take off.

Build safe oxers. The back rail of the oxer should never be set lower than the front because the horse cannot see it on his approach. Don't build a square oxer for a novice rider or green horse—ascending oxers are safer because both elements can be easily seen and they invite the horse to jump in a correct arc. Don't jump an oxer from the wrong direction.

Use safety cups on the back rail of a spread. These collapse when struck, dropping the rail so a horse doesn't get hung up if he catches the back rail.

Keep your jumps low for most schooling sessions. When you're working to improve form, control, rhythm, distances, and approaches you don't need to jump big fences. Your horse will stay sound longer by jumping a thousand 2' fences than five hundred 4' fences.

Build variety. After you've got the basics sorted out and can ride a 2' course with confidence, keep things interesting by varying the width, placement, and appearance of jumps. Add plastic flowers, plywood panels, plastic barrels, or cones. Fill in spaces with foam "pool noodles" or place a blanket over the top rail. Your solid school horse should not be fearful of a strange-looking jump, but it should catch his attention so he may give you the experience of riding a bigger effort without actually raising the height.

the same spacing. (If your horse has a larger or smaller baseline stride, you'll need to adjust the distances accordingly. Refer to the "Distances for Elements in Gymnastics Grid" chart on page 104.)

As you canter through this grid of ground poles, be sure you're approaching it in a slightly shortened canter stride, with your horse on contact. Don't let him quicken or lengthen stride. Use a short crest release and ride straight through the middle. Remember your focal point. Ask a helper to let you know if your horse is cantering so that each stride is centered over a rail.

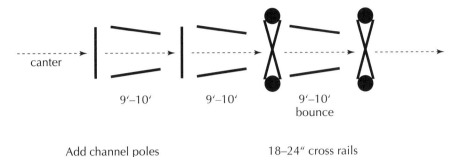

canter

9'–10'   9'–10'   9'–10'
bounce

Add channel poles
as needed

18–24" cross rails

This figures shows the bounce grid. Begin with a series of ground rails 9'–10' apart, find a good canter rhythm, then gradually replace the ground rails with raised cavalletti or crossrails.

If it feels as if your horse has to lengthen stride or speed up to get through the rails, shorten the distances a little. If he's finding the distances too tight— if he's making uneven leaps, leaving a leg behind, or breaking into a trot— then lengthen the distance a little. Going through a bounce grid should feel like being on a steady rocking horse, or riding a series of waves in the ocean: up, down, up, down.

Exercise #2: The Bounce Jump

Now replace the last two ground rails in your series with raised cavalletti or small crossrails (12"–18" high) and set at the same distances that worked well for the ground rails. Ride this from one direction only, so the ground rails are first in your series and the small jumps are last.

And finally, replace all the ground rails with crossrails or raised cavalletti, and ride the bounce grid from both directions, being sure you stay in two-point with a steady crest release all the way through.

Exercise #3: Build Bounces into Your Grid

Now create a grid that incorporates bounces, a vertical, and an oxer, as shown in the figure on page 115. You've replaced the trot poles with a canter pole to set up the striding for the first crossrail, and you've opened up the distances to accommodate a canter approach.

Ride this grid several times (in the correct direction!), with the same approach you used with the all-bounce grid—in other words, with a steady, slightly shortened stride on the approach. However, instead of feeling that your horse keeps the same steady bounce-bounce-bounce stride throughout, you should feel that he comes up higher over the vertical, then lengthens stride a little and makes a definitely larger effort over the oxer.

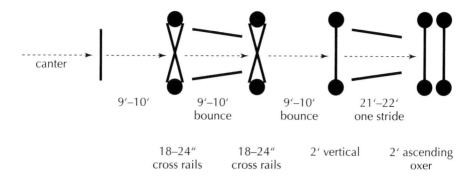

canter

| 9'–10' | 9'–10' bounce | 9'–10' bounce | 21'–22' one stride |

| 18–24" cross rails | 18–24" cross rails | 2' vertical | 2' ascending oxer |

Note: Distances are based on an 11-foot baseline canter stride

Incorporate bounces into your grid. Feel how each jump rides a little differently: tight to the first bounce, more "up" to the vertical bounce, and then forward with a bigger effort over the oxer.

So what should be happening in this exercise? You should be:

1. Trusting your horse to figure things out without your constant correction. You must manage the approach so your horse is straight and has enough impulsion, but not too much. Then you must stay centered, look up, keep weight in both heels, give a crest release, and *let your horse do his job.* Don't sit back, leap ahead, move your hands off the crest, or let your eyes waver.

2. Developing a feel for the different efforts and stride lengths that your horse must use to handle the bounces, the vertical, and the oxer. As he moves through the grid, his stride should lengthen and it should feel as if his impulsion is building. He shouldn't be rushing or flattening, just putting more energy into each successive effort.

Give your horse frequent breaks, and don't overdo these gymnastic exercises. Grids help you both develop balance and rhythm, but they can be tiring for your horse. Give him a rest before he complains.

Exercise #4: Look, No Hands!

Lessons #11 and #12 will require you to begin thinking about and then adjusting your horse's stride as you jump a line of fences, and you'll need to ride with a short crest release so you can give better direction to your horse. Your balance should now be secure enough, and your use of the aids independent enough, so you can use a shorter crest release without catching your horse in the mouth or upsetting his balance in the air.

How can you tell if you're ready to employ a short crest release? It's simple: See if you can ride the grid used in this lesson, but without reins or stirrups.

1. Start with stirrups but without reins. Knot your reins so your horse won't step through them. Approach your grid as above, move into two-point position, and drop the reins on his neck as your horse starts over the cavalletti. Hold the mane or jumping strap with your left hand and hold your right arm out to the side. Try to hold the mane lightly and move with the motion. After the last jump, smoothly take up the reins to guide your horse.

2. Ride the grid again, switching hands so you're holding on the mane with the right hand and holding your left arm out to the side.

3. If that goes well, ride the next time through with both arms out to the side.

4. Ride the grid again, this time without reins *or* stirrups.

If you can keep your balance through this grid without using your hands, then you're ready to move to a short crest release. Review the information in Lesson #4: Focal Points and Crest Releases, in chapter 4, and practice riding your grids with a short crest release.

These first ten lessons should give you a solid foundation for gridwork that can be easily varied (with different elements, distances, and heights) so you can increase the challenges without over-facing yourself or your horse.

The next chapter will take you out of the grid and on to the challenges of single jumps and course work.

Chapter 7

BEYOND THE GRID: RIDING
SINGLE FENCES AND COURSES

rids are essential training tools that help provide the gymnastic foundation for athletic development of the horse and rider. They help a horse and rider learn striding, timing, and balance.

But grids are just the beginning. The next steps are to learn how to ride single jumps and combinations, and then how to put those elements together into a smoothly flowing course of jumps.

Lesson #11: A Single Jump

Single jumps are much harder to jump than grids. In a grid, each element is built in relation to the first, simplest element. And the first element—often a rail on the ground—sets up the striding for each successive jump, so everything should flow smoothly.

Therefore, it makes sense to set up your first "single" jump at a related distance from the previous jumping effort. A *related* distance is in multiples of your horse's baseline canter stride. Assuming you're working with an 11' baseline stride, a related distance would be 44' for three strides, 55' for four strides, or any other multiple of eleven. (Remember that you have to allow half a stride for landing and half a stride for takeoff. So a 55' distance gives you 5'–6' for landing, 5'–6' for takeoff, and four non-jumping strides between the two jumps. A 44' distance gives you three non-jumping canter strides between the jumps.)

EXERCISE #1: GRID TO A CROSSRAIL

Use the grid shown on page 109, and add a small crossrail 55' beyond the grid. Place channel poles in front of the single crossrail to help keep your horse straight, and position a cone or marker 5'6" in front of the single crossrail to indicate the ideal take-off spot.

Be sure you have plenty of room to jump the entire line and reorganize before you need to deal with a turn or transition. You should allow at least 50' after the last jump before a turn or the end of the arena. You don't want your horse slowing down in the middle of a jumping line because he has no place to go after the last jump.

Here's how to ride this jump:

1. Approach the grid in a medium trot. Find your focal point beyond the last jump in the line: the single crossrail. Hold your two-point position and crest release through the grid.

2. Then, one stride after landing in a canter over the last fence in the grid, come smoothly back to three-point position and take up light contact (legs and hands) to be sure your horse stays straight on the approach to the single fence. Keep your eyes on your focal point and *don't worry about your lead.* Just maintain the rhythm.

3. Count strides as follows: "*Land*, one, two, three, four, *off.*" Keep the canter balanced, steady, and straight. On "four" (one stride in front of the crossrail), go back into two-point position and give a short crest release.

4. Take back the contact one stride after your horse clears the rail, and rebalance to turn or create a downward transition at the end of the arena.

If you've maintained your steady canter rhythm and measured your distance accurately, then the single jump should ride smoothly. Try to analyze how it felt. Have your helper tell you whether your horse's *takeoff* (where he pushes off with the hind feet) is at the marker, in front of the marker (*long spot*), or after the marker (*short spot*). Ask yourself these questions:

• Did it feel as if your horse was *chipping in* (getting too close on his takeoff), even though you had the correct number of strides? If so, then your horse was speeding up and lengthening his stride, or the distance was too tight for him. If the rhythm felt steady but he still chipped in, you'll need to move your single fence back 2' so it's 57' beyond the grid.

• Did your horse appear to take off before you felt ready, leaving from a long spot? This may have happened because you allowed the canter to get too slow and short-strided, or because the distance is a little too long for his baseline stride. If the rhythm was too slow, remind yourself to ride more forward next time. If the rhythm seemed okay but your horse still took off "long," change the distance to 53' or even 52' so he doesn't have to reach so much in the takeoff.

If it rode well, great! Ride it a few more times to be sure you're consistently arriving at a good take-off spot for your single fence, close to the marker cone.

Don't try to adjust your horse's stride yet (unless he was obviously speeding up or slowing down). The point of this exercise is not to fiddle with your horse's baseline stride, but for you to become very familiar with an *even stride and a correct distance.* You can't learn to make adjustments until you know exactly what the *right* takeoff feels like.

Developing a Feel for Distance

A feel for distance is one of the most valuable skills a rider *and* horse can develop. Being able to locate a good take-off spot and then being able to adjust your stride to *get* to that spot in a completed canter stride can make the difference between a winning round and a so-so round at the lower levels. And it's absolutely critical over higher fences.

How can you develop this feel for strides, distances, and take-off? By doing the following:

1. **Watch other riders jumping.** Count strides between fences and see if you can predict how many strides a horse will put in on a related line. Then see if you can tell from five or six strides before a jump whether a horse will have a short spot, a long spot, or a just-right takeoff. When you get good at observing stride lengths and approaches, you can spot a smooth, flowing takeoff five or six strides before it happens!

2. **Always measure accurately.** Get off your horse and pace the distances in a line of jumps, then double-check with a measuring tape. (See Lesson #6, "Calibrate *Your* Stride," in chapter 6.) Learn what correct three-stride, four-stride, and five-stride distances look like, both on the ground and from the back of your horse.

3. **As you ride, count strides.** Count canter strides on the flat and between jumps to keep a steady rhythm, to help you center yourself through breathing, and to help you develop the feel for where you are in relation to the jumps.

4. **Jump many grids and small fences at related distances.** Jumping a single fence in the middle of a field, with no reference points for distance and stride length, won't help. Instead, use cavalletti, ground poles, and cones for markers.

5. **Keep the jumps small.** Don't raise the height above 2'6" until you really *have* developed a feel for rhythm and can begin to make small adjustments to the canter stride when necessary.

6. **Ride quietly and trust your horse.** Don't over-manage the approach. Some riders become overanxious when they can't "see" a distance, so they automatically shorten stride until the horse is practically cantering in place, or they charge forward to create momentum and "bury" the horse too close to the jump. Your horse must be able to use his good judgment—after all, he's the one doing the jumping.

EXERCISE #2: VERTICALS AND OXERS

Change the single crossrail to a 2' vertical and ride the line. If that rides well, change the vertical to a 2'-wide ramped oxer. Set the front rail 3" lower than the back rail. Remember to measure your 55' distance from the center of one fence to the center of the next, so the front element of your 2'-wide oxer should be 54' from the center of the last jump in your grid.

The distance should feel the same but your horse will need to jump a little higher over the oxer. He will probably take off a little earlier to manage this, but as long as you remember to set the rhythm, use your focal point, give the release before the jump, and sink your weight into your heels, you should do fine.

Troubleshooting

Here are some common problems you may encounter in riding the line to a single fence:

- *Your horse manages the grid fine but you're not traveling straight to the single fence.* Are you keeping your eyes glued to your focal point? If your eyes are wandering, your horse can't stay straight. Is your horse "stalling" after the grid? Send him forward with legs and stick as soon as you land over the last jump in your grid. And add channel poles.

- *Your horse lands over the grid and rushes forward to the single jump.* You may be grabbing with your legs, jumping ahead of the motion, or ducking over the jumps with an exaggerated crest release, all of which can make your horse quick. Ask someone to watch you to help identify the problem, and then concentrate on riding quietly and waiting for your horse to carry you to the last jump.

- *Your horse refuses and seems reluctant to jump.* Assuming he's sound and comfortable in his tack, likes his work, and isn't soured by hours of overwork in the arena, you've got to assume there's something you're doing wrong. Make sure you're not getting left behind, falling onto his back, or catching him in the mouth when he jumps.

Problems when jumping are usually caused by a lack of balance, a lack of confidence, or a lack of control. And these are all related: When your balance is secure you will be more confident. And when you know you can control your own body, your confidence and balance will be better. Review the "A Second Position Check" sidebar to be sure you're staying in balance with your horse.

Whenever you have a problem with a particular element of an exercise, try to figure out what's happening. Then go back to the previous lessons and review the basics. Lower the height or remove a jump, check the distances, change a crossrail to a ground pole, or go back to your flatwork exercises to reestablish balance, confidence, and control.

A Second Position Check

Review "Position Check" and the pictures in chapter 4. Using these pictures as a guide ask your coach or helper to critique your position over fences. You need to be sure you consistently remain with your horse's motion, staying balanced over his center of gravity all the way through the jumping motion.

Major problems can occur on landing when the rider isn't balanced. Some common problems include:

- **Jumping ahead of the motion.** This often happens when your stirrups aren't the right length. (See the photos on page 122.) You stand in the saddle on takeoff in an effort to stay with the horse's thrust, and your leg slips back behind you. You lose security and your horse's take-off effort is hampered by your insecure position so he can't bring his legs up evenly.

- **Ducking.** When you throw your body ahead of the motion and duck down, you're probably also looking down to one side or the other. This can cause your horse to "get quick off the ground," twist in mid-air to compensate for your off-center position, and land quickly to try to regain his balance.

- **Using an exaggerated crest release.** If you throw your hands more than a third of the way up the horse's neck, you've sacrificed control and your own balance. Use a more modified crest release so your arms can help support you.

- **Jumping behind the motion.** This can ruin a willing jumper if it's accompanied by the rider thumping onto the horse's back and catching him in the mouth. There will be times when you may need to go behind the motion in a safety position (for instance, down a drop jump or when approaching a spooky fence), but *only* after you've learned to jump reliably *with* the motion. Riders who school green horses or horses that habitually refuse often tend to ride behind the motion because that's the safe place to be if the horse stops or ducks out—but riding this way burdens the horse's back and hampers his ability to jump cleanly and with a good bascule. Check your stirrup length, keep your legs under you so your stirrups stay vertical, and review Lessons #1 through #5 to strengthen your base of support.

Ride through this line several times, counting strides. And pay attention to what you're seeing and feeling all the way through. As you land over the last grid element, tell yourself, "From four strides out, *this* is what it looks and feels like." Try to see when you're three strides or two strides before the last jump.

My stirrups are too long and I'm behind the motion on this green mare. I've reached forward and let the reins slip to avoid catching my horse in the mouth, but when I land I'll be disorganized, with too-long reins and a precarious balance. This position might provide security over a drop jump but certainly isn't needed over this small log.

Here I'm with the motion and doing much better, demonstrating good balance with a short crest release.

As the jumps get bigger, you'll need to close the angles of hip and knee even more. Standing in the stirrups and leaning on the horse's neck puts Scott in an insecure position so he must throw his weight onto the horse's front end to stay with the motion. As a result, his horse is dropping one shoulder. Scott needs to keep his heels deep, and fold the "hinges" at his knees and hips.

HAMILTON AHLO, JR.

Scott's position is better here, so his horse is jumping in better form. There's more angle in his knees and hips, and his legs are supporting him so he doesn't have to lie on the horse's neck. This position gives greater security and helps to keep his balance closer to his horse's center of gravity. Using a shorter rein with his short crest release would also give Scott a little more control during takeoff and landing.

PATRICK O'LEARY

This photo shows an exaggerated and too-long release. In an attempt to stay off her horse's mouth over this big fence, Lily has slipped the reins and shoved her hands more than halfway to her horse's ears. Her landing will be disorganized and she'll have difficulty taking up the contact smoothly during recovery. (Lily is using a correct automatic release in the photo on page 54.)

Once you've become very comfortable riding through the grid and over the single fence at a four-stride distance, then you can try varying the number of strides. Move the fence to the appropriate distance so you can ride a three-stride, a five-stride, and a six-stride distance. Remember to set each distance as a multiple of your horse's baseline stride, plus two additional half-strides for takeoff and landing.

Lesson #12: Adjust Strides on a Four-Stride Line

In the previous lesson, you should have started to develop a feel for your approach, "seeing" the takeoff from three or four strides before that last jump. Now it's time to vary the striding and make some simple adjustments so you can help your horse manage distances that don't suit his baseline stride.

To adjust stride length while jumping, you need to ride with a short crest release or an automatic release. And a short crest release requires independent hands. If you're still using a long release, review the information in chapter 5, Lesson #4, and repeat the previous two lessons, practicing with a short release.

You'll use the same aids for adjusting strides in jumping as you do on the flat, but there are a few additional considerations:

- Don't ask for a stride adjustment in the very last stride before a jump—that's too late. Ask for small changes early and with every stride. When you get to the jump, you must sit quietly and stay out of your horse's way.

- You must be clear about your request and the horse must be prompt in his response.

- Practice lengthening the canter on a jumping line only *after* you've become comfortable with shortening the canter and adding a stride. *Be sure* your horse moves forward promptly from your legs, and has enough scope to easily lengthen his baseline stride by at least a foot.

- Don't override your stride adjustments. When in doubt, let the horse figure it out. Ultimately, he's responsible for getting both of you safely over the jump. That's why you're riding a safe, experienced jumper.

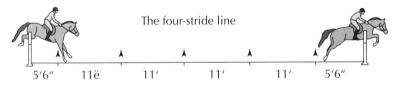

The four-stride line

5'6"   11ë   11'   11'   11'   5'6"

To practice stride adjustments, first ride a line of two fences with a comfortable four-stride distance. Then shorten the line a little: Move from 55' to 52'6" if your baseline is an 11' stride or from 60' to 57'6" if your baseline is a 12' stride. After riding the shortened four-stride line, try lengthening the distance by the same increments.

EXERCISE #1: CONFIRM THE BASELINE

Set up a line of two fences, 55' apart (a comfortable four strides), as shown in the illustration on page 124. Be sure the first fence is small, no more than a 2' crossrail or vertical.

Give yourself plenty of room for a straight approach to the first fence, because this is the first time you're being asked to canter the approach to a jump that's not part of a grid. There's no cavalletti or grid to set you up, so you must simply canter forward to the first small jump.

Remember what a good canter felt like as you came *out* of your grid in the last lesson? That's the kind of canter you want now on the approach.

1. Pick up a rhythmic canter, use a moving-point focus as you turn onto your line, then focus on a point at the end of your line, beyond your second fence. As you jump the two fences, count the strides between. You should have counted, "*Land,* one, two, three, four, *off.*"

   Don't make any adjustments to the approach on the first fence—just canter, release, jump. The second fence should have ridden smoothly, even if it felt a little short or a little long to the first fence, because landing over the first fence establishes the correct striding to the second jump.

2. If the second fence *didn't* ride smoothly, you need to fix any problems before you go on to Exercise #2. Here are some troubleshooting tips to help you ride this exercise:

   • Try to analyze your "go." Did you override the approach to the first fence? If you get a little long or a little short, that's okay, because the first fence is small. But make your adjustments *between* the two fences so your second fence rides more smoothly.

   • If your horse *chips in* (gets too close) on takeoff at the first fence, he'll lack impulsion on landing, so you must ask him to lengthen in each of the four strides to the second fence. As you land over the first fence, stay a little forward and ask him to lengthen each stride a little by squeezing with both calves. You don't want him to charge forward, just open up the canter a little for *every* stride.

   • If he leaves from a long spot at the first fence *without* putting in extra effort, he'll land close to that first fence and then have to lengthen stride to make the four-stride distance. Again, open up his stride by staying a little forward and adding leg.

   • However, if he speeds up, puts in a big effort at the first fence, and lands deep into the line, then you'll need to sink into the saddle, sit a little more upright, take a feel of the reins, and ask him to shorten slightly for each subsequent stride.

Exercise #2: Shorten the Strides on a Line

Now you'll alter the distance between the two fences and ask youself and your horse to make some stride adjustments. It's easier (and usually safer) to shorten stride than lengthen it, so you'll start with that.

1. First, shorten the overall distance in the line by 2'6". If you're working with an 11' baseline stride, move the distance from 55' to 52'6". This will require your horse to travel in 10'6" strides. Keep your ground lines close to the jumps.

   Ride the line conservatively and ask for a shorter canter stride. As you land over the first fence, sink into the saddle in a deep three-point position, keep your legs on, and take a steady feel of your horse's mouth. Think to yourself: "Steady, wait." But don't let him stall. You want a shorter stride with impulsion, not a slower pace that threatens to fall into a trot.

   Don't try to shorten him *too* much. Just balance, stay focused, breathe, and wait patiently for the next jump.

2. If that rode well, shorten the distance by a full foot from your baseline, so your original 55' distance becomes 50'.

Caution: Don't Over-Shorten the Stride

Light hands and subtlety are very important in jumping. When you're shortening your horse's stride, don't override. If you've done your job by recommending that the horse shorten his stride all along the line, the last two strides before the next fence should be smooth and flowing, not short and shorter.

Riders who have trouble seeing a distance, or those who are nervous about jumping, often feel they need to add strides to almost every line. They take their horses back into a shorter and shorter frame in an attempt to see a distance, asking their horses to "wait, wait, *wait!*" until the horse is almost cantering in place and they've driven themselves deep into an impossibly close spot.

A sensitive horse becomes nervous and tense if his rider won't let go and allow him to find a take-off spot. A more sluggish horse may "wait" until he simply stops.

For your horse to stay confident, relaxed, and willing, he's got to be free to do his job. The two of you must work together to find a comfortable stride and spot. The horse can't participate in the decision-making process when the rider is constantly taking back and waiting, waiting, waiting.

So don't overanalyze or overmanage. Breathe, soften your aids, and trust your horse.

Now you'll need to approach the *first* fence with a slightly shortened stride also, so the adjustment doesn't come as a big surprise after your horse has landed over the first fence. Ask for a shorter stride all the way through, and when you arrive at the second fence, it should ride smoothly because you've prepared well in advance.

EXERCISE #3: LENGTHEN THE STRIDES ON A LINE

Return to your baseline distance of 55' and ride through that once or twice, so the adjustment from a short to a long distance won't be too dramatic.

1. Now lengthen the distance in your four-stride line. Add half a foot to each multiple so your four-stride 55' distance becomes 57'6". (If your baseline is 12', then adjust the distance from 60" to 62'6".) To help your horse understand the bigger striding, set the ground rails 4' in front of each jump.

    Six inches sounds like a very small change in the length of a stride, but it matters. If your horse *doesn't* lengthen each stride by 6" inches, you'll arrive at the second jump having to take off from 7' out, a decidedly long spot, especially for a small horse with an eleven-foot stride at the canter!

RICHARD VALCOURT

After landing over the first fence, Lisa knows she must lengthen Nani's short stride immediately to make the distance to the next fence. She keeps her seat and hands forward and adds a strong leg aid to create more impulsion and a longer stride for a "forward" distance.

Tips for Riding a Long Distance

Open up your horse's stride *early* in the line, so you can remain quiet and balanced on takeoff. Don't make any aggressive moves that could unbalance your horse just before the jump.

If you ask for a long distance and a big effort, be prepared to go with the greater thrust and bigger jump. You may have to slip the reins if you get left behind. Give a bigger release, fold those hinges at the hips and knees, and think "Forward" all the way through and out the other end.

If you have a choice between lengthening stride and shortening to add a stride, it's safer to add a stride. But if the next jump is a wide spread, you must open up your horse's stride a little and send him forward.

If you're jumping an angled fence (see Lesson #16), be prepared for a slightly longer distance and a slightly bigger effort.

Save the lengthened-stride option for when you need it. Frequent long distances can make a horse sprawl and rush. When you need to lengthen stride, you want a smooth, scopey effort, not a ride on a freight train.

So you must ride this line with *every stride* lengthened by 6". Be sure to establish a solid, rhythmic canter. Remember to use a short release at the first fence, keep your legs on, and think, "Forward." If he lands a little short over the first fence, then you must move him forward promptly to make up ground and get to a comfortable spot for the second fence.

2. If that slightly longer line rode well, try moving the distance out another 2'6" so your horse must now lengthen each stride by a full foot from your baseline. Ride this in a definitely forward canter. With a lazy horse, you may have to pick up a stick and be a little aggressive to get the lengthened strides you need, when you need them.

Important: If the 57'6" distance did not ride well—if your horse was slow to respond or struggled to lengthen his stride, and you had an uncomfortably long takeoff; or your horse added a quick half-step or extremely short stride at the second fence—*do not* attempt the 1'-longer stride length in this exercise. Instead, you'll need to think about adding an entire stride on a longer line, which is the subject of the next lesson.

Lesson #13: Add a Stride on a Longer Line

Hunter, jumper, and equitation classes often set jumps on a five- or six-stride line, using 12' strides, so a line along the long side of an arena might consist of two jumps set 72' or 84' apart. The longer the distance between jumps, the more chances you'll have to make adjustments that suit your horse's baseline stride.

If your horse's baseline stride is 11' and you're jumping two jumps on a 72' line, you can choose to:

- Push forward into a lengthened canter all the way down the line to produce five 12' canter strides, possibly rushing and arriving in a disorganized sprawl.

- Take the safer and more conservative approach by adding a stride and riding the line in six quiet 10" strides, with 4' for landing and 4' for takeoff.

EXERCISE #1: THE ADD-A-STRIDE OPTION

To practice adding a stride, set up two jumps 72' apart: a 2' high crossrail to a 2'6" vertical, or a 2' vertical to a 2'3" oxer. Set the ground rails 2' in front of each jump.

Develop the same quiet, steady canter you used when riding the slightly shortened distance in the previous lesson, and ride the line. The canter should feel round and bouncy, not slow and ready to stall. Keep your heels deep and your body just in front of the vertical.

Count strides. You should be able to ride the line in a "quiet" six strides. If you've shortened just enough, the last stride before the second jump should give you the same feeling as every other stride in the line—no last-minute scrambling or adjustments.

EXERCISE #2: THE LENGTHEN-STRIDE OPTION

If the previous exercise rode well—if you were able to add a stride comfortably—your next goal is to ride the line in the standard five strides. For the horse with an 11' stride, this will be a "forward" five strides because you'll have to open up every stride a full foot.

Set the ground rails 4' in front of the jumps. Develop the same longer-striding canter you used in the four-stride 60' line in the previous lesson (#12). Look for your focus point and ride *forward* all the way down the line to get the five strides.

Don't rush; instead, *lengthen.* A longer stride will feel a little faster, but the rhythm should not feel quicker.

To manage the striding, your horse should land 6' beyond the first jump and take off 6' in front of the second jump. If he lands close to the first fence, you'll have to lengthen each canter stride even more to bring him to a good spot for the second fence.

This may feel like quite a stretch for you and your horse, especially if you're riding a small horse, and you may decide you're not ready to tackle these bigger distances yet. That's fine—just stay with slight variations of the 11' stride. But if you're thinking about competing, you'll need to choose your events very carefully. Many shows use those 12' strides for all the standard hunter, jumper, and equitation classes.

On a course built on 12' multiples, you'll always have options for adding a stride on a five-stride 72' line, or even on a four-stride 60' line if your horse is clever. But you *must* be able to ride a 12' stride to get safely through a 24', one-stride double—there's simply no room to add a stride safely in a one-stride combination.

Setting Your Riding Goals

Learning to jump well should proceed in a logical, step-by-step fashion, but it doesn't always happen at the same pace for everyone. Your original goal was, perhaps, to "learn to jump," but by now you've probably realized that there's far more to the process than just hanging on while your horse clears a fence.

As with all learning, it's important to set goals so you can plan the steps, measure the progress and celebrate the achievements. There are many worthy long-term jumping goals ("Someday, the Olympics!"), but all the long-term goals must be built on a foundation of short-term goals ("Jump an entire course at 2'6" and nail those lead changes.")

Goal-setting requires that the goals be specific, measurable, attainable, and challenging. And, because you never know quite what will happen when you add in the factor of a horse, goals also need to be flexible. But whatever your ultimate objective might be, realistic goals need to have certain characteristics. Goals should be:

- **Specific:** Not "Gee, I hope I find a distance to all those jumps," but "I want to ride that line in a quiet six strides, and the next in a forward five, so both lines will ride smoothly."

- **Measurable:** Instead of "I just want to do well," try "I want to qualify for the regional championship," or "We will go clean on cross-country."

- **Attainable:** "In six weeks, I'm going to win the junior jumper championship!" is going to guarantee disappointment if you haven't yet jumped more than a crossrail on your old reliable school horse. Instead, create a goal that you have a reasonable chance of reaching.

- **Challenging:** Stretch a little. If you're getting a little bored jumping through the same old grid, challenge yourself to do it without reins and stirrups. If you're comfortable on a 3' course, move the jumps up to 3'3" or 3'6".

- **Flexible:** Your horse hasn't participated in your goal-setting. If he's uncooperative or incapable or you run into unexpected problems, then make a new goal.

Exercise #3: Options for Riding a Six-Stride Line

If you have room, set the two jumps 84' apart (six 12' strides) and canter the line in both modes: the standard stride length and a shorter stride that allows you to add a stride.

Can you ride even shorter, and add two strides on this line? Smaller horses will have no trouble with this exercise. The greater the distance between jumps on a line, the easier it is to add a stride—or even two strides.

Lesson #14: Feel a Distance— Single Fence on a Circle

This series of exercises will help you develop a feel for strides and learn how you can help your horse get to the right take-off spot.

Why ride over a jump on a circle?

- Riding over small jumps on a continuous *bending line*—a circle—gives an added visual perspective that helps many riders learn to gauge the distance to a jump and find the right take-off spot.

- Riding on a circle helps keep the balance, pace, and rhythm under control—if your horse gets a little strong on a long, straight line, he'll be easier to steady on a circle.

- You're responsible for a continuous turn, so you must keep your eyes up and ahead to maintain your line. Soft eyes are especially important to help you find the jump and remain on your circle.

- If you or your horse tend to get a little quick or anxious on the approach to a jump, the steady repetition of this exercise will help you focus, relax, and breathe.

- There's a natural adjustability to the horse's stride on a circle, because one side of his body must shorten (inside) and one side must lengthen (outside) to maintain his balance on the gentle arc of the circle.

Exercise #1: Paths on a Circle

Set up a crossrail or small vertical so it can be jumped from either direction. Place a rail on the ground next to it. You'll need enough room for a large circle—at least 60' in diameter—that will take you over the jump in a continuous, steady canter. Leave enough space between your jump and any other obstacles (arena perimeter, other jumps) so you can enlarge the circle and go around the outside of the jump if you choose.

1. Start with your easier lead—for most horses and riders, this is the left. Pick up a working canter, move into three-point, and go two or three times around to establish your rhythm, traveling *outside* the jump. As

you circle, notice where on your circle you can begin to see the jump. Don't twist your body sideways in an effort to locate the jump when it's still behind you. Simply hold your position for a large left-lead circle: left shoulder back, left leg on the girth, right leg behind the girth, right (outside) rein keeping steady contact, left (inside) rein asking for the slight bend.

2. Maintain a round, accurate circle, and be sure to release with your hands as your horse jumps. You should be able to see the jump during about three-quarters of your circle. Know where it is, but don't stare at it as you approach or pass it—keep your eyes up and forward and concentrate on keeping an accurate path and steady rhythm.

3. After a few circles without jumping, quietly adjust your path so your next circle will take you directly over the center of the small jump. Give a crest release one or two strides before, and grab the mane if you need to so you don't interfere with your horse if he puts in an awkward or off-stride jump.

Each time you go over, try to make the adjustment from canter to jump as smooth as possible. Think rhythm and direction, but don't try to turn in the air. Maintain your circle with eyes, legs, and light hands. Don't lurch, duck, or use an exaggerated release. You can make small position adjustments to maintain pace and rhythm, but don't try to over-adjust your horse's stride.

Just circle, jump, re-balance. Do this for five or six circles, then come quietly back to a trot, trot one circle to the outside of your jump, walk, and take a little break.

EXERCISE #2: ADJUST THE PATH ON A CIRCLE

Now you should be starting to accurately anticipate where and when your horse will take off on your circular path. This exercise will first ask you to breathe and count strides. and then help you learn to make small adjustments to your horse's stride on a bending line.

1. Change direction and repeat the pattern: a few non-jumping circles, then five or six circles that take you over the jump.

2. Continue and concentrate on your breathing: two strides inhale, two strides exhale, or whatever feels comfortable for you.

3. How many strides does it take your horse to go all the way around the circle? Count the strides. If it's a consistent 60' diameter circle, he's probably taking fifteen to twenty canter strides to make one circuit.

   See if you can count out the last four strides before the jump. Can you see a distance from four strides out?

4. When you can feel the distance from four or five strides out, you can start to make *small* adjustments to your horse's stride. Shorten stride a little as you did in the previous exercise: Sit a little deeper with your

upper body more vertical, feel the weight in your heels, and wait. To lengthen a little, keep the hip angle a little open, the hands light, and the legs on. The adjustments must be small, subtle, and early—three or four strides out, not during the last stride of the approach.

Don't make any big moves right in front of the fence, because you must stay in good balance on landing to stay on the path of your circle.

Here are some troubleshooting tips for this circle exercise:

- If your horse lands on the wrong lead, ask for a simple change of lead through the trot and calmly canter once around *without* jumping. Then re-establish your jumping pattern, thinking a little more about how you can help him maintain his lead. Be sure to look where you're going, and keep your outside leg back to hold him on the correct lead. Carry your inside hand a little away from his neck in a leading (opening) rein, if necessary, to invite him to hold the bend *without* pulling back with your hands.

- If your horse gets quick and tries to rush, *quietly* alter your circle so you're going past the jump, instead of over it, for a few circles. Or ease back into trot, and trot over the jump a few times. Then try the canter again. Be sure not to pull him away from or toward the jump if he's in the last three strides of the approach—your decision to jump or not jump must be made *at least* four strides before it.

- If your horse puts in an awkward jump, loses the rhythm, or stops in front of the jump, review your position and balance. Ask yourself, "Where were my eyes?" Look up, find your moving point, and use soft eyes to help you hold your balance and follow your path.

Lesson #15: Leads and Turns

In previous lessons, you focused on balance, rhythm, pace, and stride length. Jumps were set at related distances on straight lines. If your horse swapped leads or landed on the wrong lead, your turns should have been large enough to accommodate a counter canter or a simple change of lead.

In Lesson #14, your goal was to stay on the path of a large circle and remain on the same lead. If your horse lost his balance and changed leads over a jump, you fixed the lead by doing a simple transition—dropping to a trot and then reestablishing a rhythmic canter on the correct lead.

In this lesson, however, you focus on balanced turns and correct leads. Your new goal will be to create smooth changes of direction with a flying change of lead over the jump.

If your horse performs reliable lead changes on the flat, he should be able to easily change leads over a jump. If he's a bit sticky about his changes on the flat, this lesson should help him find his balance and respond more reliably to your request for a particular lead.

To help your horse balance through turns and changes of direction, you'll need to clearly communicate your path and prepare him for lead changes.

Exercise #1: Hold the Lead on a Bending Line

Set up three crossrails or small verticals that can be jumped from either direction, as shown in the illustration below. Fence A can be jumped on a large (60' diameter or larger) circle. Fence B can be jumped on a diagonal from either direction, but the approach must be *from* a right-hand turn and heading *into* a left-hand turn. Fence C can also be jumped from either direction, going across the diagonal, but the approach must be *from* a left-hand turn and heading *into* a right-hand turn. Be sure you have room to make large, smooth turns at the end of each diagonal line.

You'll use fence A to help your horse create a smooth, steady, gradual turn while *holding the same lead.* You'll use fences B and C to help your horse *change direction and change leads.*

1. As you warm up with trot and canter transitions and circles, note where your focal points will be when you begin jumping on the diagonal lines (fences B and C). You'll use your eyes to lead you over a jump and into a turn that begins as soon as you land.

   You'll do this by looking straight ahead on the approach to each diagonal-line jump (B or C), and then moving your eyes into the turn on takeoff, *quietly suggesting* a change of lead while your horse is in the air.

2. Begin by cantering over fence A on a large circle, on your horse's easier lead—let's assume it's the left. Ride your left-hand circle just as you did in the previous lesson. This time, however, pay close attention to your position for the large turn so you can maintain the path of the left-hand circle: Turn your eyes a little left, turn your body slightly so your left shoulder is a little back, keep the inside leg on to support the rhythm and impulsion, and the outside leg back a little to support the lead. Think of carrying a little more weight in the left stirrup, but do *not* lean, duck, or throw your weight to one side. You want to direct a shift in balance, not destroy the balance!

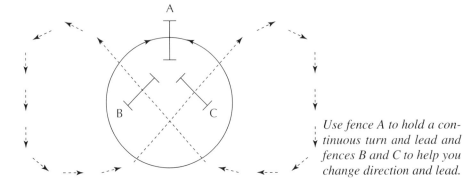

Use fence A to hold a continuous turn and lead and fences B and C to help you change direction and lead.

On the approach, takeoff, and landing, try to maintain a *very slight* inside (left) opening rein to invite your horse to look left and follow the path of the left circle. Using your short crest release, you can continue to support your upper body with your outside—right—hand, while you take a slight feel of the inside rein with your left hand.

Be sure you bring your inside hand to the left in an opening rein, not a backward-moving direct rein. You want to quietly direct your horse's path to the left, not pull back or restrict his jumping effort.

You'll know everything's working correctly when your horse jumps in a steady rhythm, maintains the path on the circle, and holds his left lead.

3. After a few circles to the left, walk, relax, reward, and then repeat the same exercise to the right.

Get Consistent Leads and Changes

Always ask for a lead in every canter transition and every jump. If you don't designate which lead your horse should be on, he'll choose his stronger lead, thus strengthening his tendency to prefer that lead.

If your horse swaps leads over the jump, don't rush him into changing to the correct lead. Simply continue cantering on your circle and maintain the inside bend and direction, no matter how awkward it may feel. Ride past the jump on the next circuit, and keep cantering.

If you know your horse can perform a flying change, then ask for the change to the correct lead, but *not during the approach to a jump*. Try to keep him from becoming anxious—you simply want him to realize that he'll feel more comfortable on the correct lead.

To reinforce your request to land on a specific lead, keep a little more weight on the inside stirrup and a little more feel on the inside opening rein.

During training, if your horse's flying changes are nonexistent or not very reliable, ask for a simple change through one or two steps of trot. Don't let him come back to a walk or relax—simply trot a step, get the correct lead, and reestablish your rhythm.

During competition in hunter and equitation classes, however, being on the wrong lead is less of an error than breaking gait for a simple change of lead. So if your horse lands on the wrong lead and won't perform a flying change, keep cantering. In eventing and jumper classes, you're not marked down for wrong leads.

If your horse frequently lands on the wrong lead while jumping, you'll need to go back to flatwork transitions to create better balance and responsiveness. An incorrect lead indicates poor balance, poor communication, or a physical weakness—all of which should be addressed on the flat first.

EXERCISE #2: CHANGE LEADS AND TURN

Now for a change of direction and a change of lead. Most horses find it easiest to change from the right to left lead, so you'll start with that. (Start with a left circle if your horse prefers the right lead.)

1. Begin with a right-hand circle over fence A, remaining on the right lead. Then widen your turn so your path takes you out to the rail and into a right-hand diagonal turn toward fence B. Ride the last three strides of the approach straight, with eyes focused straight ahead, an even feel on both reins, and your weight even in both stirrups.

    As your horse takes off, shift your eyes, weight, and position into a request for a left lead and a left turn. Make this a smooth, subtle request—no sudden moves that will disrupt his balance.

Don't shift your focus too early in a turn! Monique is demonstrating a common fault—looking for the next jump before her horse has lifted off for this one. Her balance is good, her legs are well anchored, and she's using a nice automatic release. But she's in danger of having Buddy jump crookedly, twist, or cut down in mid-air. Begin your turn and ask for the lead change in the air, not before the jump.

An instant later, Monique has to use her outside rein to keep Buddy from swerving left too soon, so he's looking right while she's asking him to turn left. He will touch down in the correct (left) lead, but they won't land in good balance for a smooth left turn.

PATRICK O'LEARY

A good smooth turn encourages the horse to land on the correct lead and in balance. Lily has turned her eyes and body slightly right, kept her left leg back, and placed slightly more weight in her right stirrup. Yes, it should be this subtle! Waiwi is responding by landing correctly on her right lead.

PATRICK O'LEARY

Look up! Don't let your concern for leads (or the height of the jump) distract your eye from your focal point. Despite dropping her eyes, Lily's balance has remained secure and centered—but when her horse lands, they'll both be uncertain about where to go next.

Upon landing, look and turn left, no matter what lead your horse lands on. *Do not look down—feel for the lead, don't look for it!* If you still need to look down to figure out what lead you're on, go back to working on the flat and keep your eyes up until you can *feel* your leads.

2. After you've made several smooth turns, with correct lead changes from right to left lead, practice a left-to-right turn: Canter over fence A on the left lead, turn to fence C, and ask for a change to the right lead over the jump.

Then continue the pattern, turning and jumping over fence B to land on the left lead. Whenever you have trouble with leads, turns, or balance, go back to the same-lead exercise on the large circle at fence A (the previous exercise). With repetition, your horse should begin to anticipate the turns and lead changes. When that happens, quit and give him a break. Anticipation can be good, such as when your horse prepares himself for what you will want him to do, and does it at the slightest suggestion—or bad, when he starts making changes *before* you ask for them, without waiting for your direction.

The first kind of anticipation deserves praise and a reward, because it increases responsiveness. The second kind needs to be altered. If you feel your horse is starting to make decisions about when to turn and when to change leads, you'll need to change the exercise so he has to pay closer attention to his rider's requests.

Now it's time to put a whole course together.

Lesson #16: Angles and Bends

The previous lessons required you to jump on a large circle path, with a very slight bend to your path, and to jump with a straight approach while preparing for a turn after the jump. Now you should be able to adjust the approach so you can either jump with an angled approach or jump while turning.

EXERCISE #1: JUMP AT AN ANGLE

1. Set up three jumps as shown in the diagram on page 139, so the distance from the center of fence A to fence B, and fence A to fence C, is 77'. The jumps can be at whatever height you're comfortable schooling over, minus 3–6", so you won't be concerned about height. Angling a takeoff makes the jump wider, so your horse may stand back a bit and put in a bigger effort over an angled jump. Be prepared for this and roll the ground poles out about 6" more than you normally would to help your horse find a comfortable take-off spot. You don't want to "bury" him in a too-close spot.

   The diagram shows a direct route (dotted line) from fence A to B. To follow this route, you'll jump both fences at a slight angle. Notice the angle of the approach.

2. Pick up a canter to the left, establish an approach to the center of fence A and immediately find your focal point beyond the center of fence B. Accuracy in your approach is very important: You are angling the jumps but your line (and your horse) must be straight.

   Don't try to ride this line with a straight approach to fence A and then a shallow S-curve to fence B. The distance will ride well in six strides if you remain straight on your path and jump each fence at an angle. As you take off for fence B, look into your left turn and ask for (or maintain) your left lead.

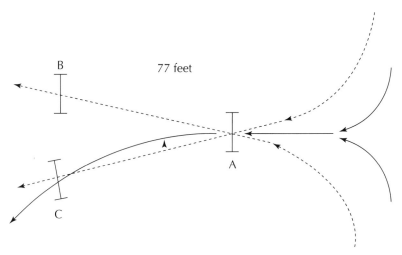

Use this set-up to practice jumping at an angle and choosing a path for a bending turn. Place a cone two strides after the landing for fence A, as shown, and be sure the distances between fences A to B and A to C are set for six strides. The dotted line shows the direct path; the solid line indicates a bending path that allows you to add a stride between fences A and C.

EXERCISE #2: JUMP AT AN ANGLE, OR BEND THE LINE?

In this exercise, you'll try two different options between jumps: an angled approach on a straight line for six strides, or a bending line that gives you room to add a seventh stride.

1. Now look at fences A and C, and place a cone 20' beyond the center of fence A, as shown in the diagram above.

   Because of the different angles of the jumps, you have two options:

   a. You can follow a direct path (dotted line) to angle the first fence and ride straight to the second, going to the left of the cone and jumping in a steady six strides.

   b. You can jump the first fence on a straight path, stay to the right of the cone, and then ride a bending line to a slightly angled approach at fence C. The bending-line option will add a stride so this should ride in a quiet seven strides.

   Note the different lines of approach for the two options: the dotted line for the six-stride direct path and the solid line for the bending path. Notice also that the direct route takes you across the diagonal and into a right-hand turn, while the bending line prepares you for a left-hand turn.

2. Ride this exercise first by taking the direct, six-stride path and angling the first fence as you did in Exercise #1. Approach the center of fence A at an angle, off a slightly shallow right-hand turn, locate fence C to establish your focal point, and ride straight toward it. Stay left of the cone and count your six steady strides. As you jump fence C, look into a right-hand turn and ask your horse to land on his right lead.

Choose Your Path: Direct or Bending?

In equitation and jumper classes (and the stadium phase of eventing), course designers often create an offset line similar to the ones used in Lesson #16.

When you're walking the course before competing (see the "Walking a Course in the Arena" sidebar in chapter 10), you'll need to decide which path to follow. Your choice should depend on several factors:

- **Can you see a distance to the first fence?** If you're having trouble seeing a distance to the first fence in a line, give yourself space and a little more time in the turn to your approach. Jump the fence straight instead of at an angle. Riding a bending line and then jumping the fence straight on will give you a better chance to find a distance, and your horse can jump more easily from a deep spot if necessary. Angling a fence requires your horse to leave the ground from a slightly longer distance.

- **What happens next on the course?** Choose the option that creates a logical flow into the next turn. In the diagram on page 139, you'd want to jump fence C on a left-angled bending line if you need to prepare for a left turn, and on a direct path if you need to prepare for a right turn.

- **How adjustable is your horse's stride?** If you're riding a small or slightly sluggish horse on a course set with 12' distances, look for the option that allows you to add a stride. Choose the bending line over the direct path (as long as you can still make a smooth turn at the end of the line).

- **How trustworthy and agile is your horse?** If you jump at an angle, is he likely to duck out? If so, choose the line that gives you the straightest approach to each fence. Does he balance well on turns, or is he awkward, green, or slow to turn? Then your best option might be to keep your horse straight but angle your approach.

- **Does speed matter?** If so, go for the direct option that requires the least number of strides.

3. Now plan a straight approach to fence A with a bending line and angled approach to fence C. Ride deeper into your turn on the approach to fence A. Look toward fence C and ask your horse to land on the left lead, but don't turn toward C until you pass the cone, two strides after landing. Allow a smooth turn toward C, keep looking left, count seven strides, and jump C at an angle, holding the left lead and finishing with a left turn after landing.

    If it feels as if you've jumped fence A on a straight line and then jumped fence C on the arc of a large circle, you've created the right path. Ride this several times, alternating approaches so you can feel the six-stride and the seven-stride distance.

Lesson #17: Ride a Course

Now you should have all the skills you need to ride a simple course. A good course for schooling is shown in the diagram below, as it incorporates all of the elements usually found in an eight-jump hunter class or a simple equitation round. (The stadium course at a beginner-novice horse trial may be somewhat longer and more complex, and you will have to deal with a cross-country course as well. Cross-country jumping is addressed in chapter 10, "Specializing: Finding the Right Fit.")

The practice diagram shows just six jumps, but you can create several different courses if you build the fences with ground lines on both sides, so they can be jumped from either direction. (Be sure, however, that you always jump an ascending oxer from the correct direction, with the lower bar in front.)

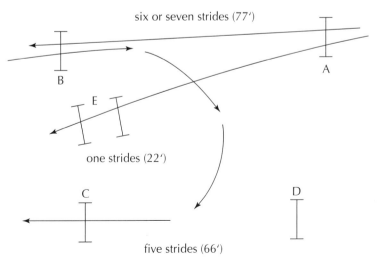

This illustration shows a simple practice course. Note that fences A and B are slightly offset, so they can be jumped at an angle or on a slightly bending line.

You have many options. You can ride this as a quiet hunter round, beginning counterclockwise and taking the direct path over the outside lines of jumps once around (A-B-C-D), turning left to go across the diagonal over the combination at E, and then turning right and finishing up over B and A.

Or you can vary your course by choosing any of these paths:

* Go from A to B on a bending line.
* Turn on a clockwise circle from B to C.
* Go across the diagonal from B to D.
* Jump A from a left turn and go across the diagonal to the combination at E.

As you plan your courses, be sure to think about spacing and paths for turns, and where you might be able to add or remove a stride on a line. Start with a height you're very comfortable with—2' or 2'3" is good—and raise the heights gradually. Pay attention to what courses are used in local competitions, and try to duplicate them at home. (And remember to duplicate the *distances* between jumps, not just the path, height, and appearance of the jumps.)

If you encounter a problem, analyze it. Here are some typical problems you may face (see chapter 11, "Troubleshooting," for more suggestions):

• Are you losing visual focus or turning too sharply? Simplify your path and figure out where your focal point should be for each line.

• Are you having trouble seeing a distance? Go deeper into your corners to create longer bending lines and a waiting distance.

• Is your horse losing impulsion or jumping awkwardly? Lower the height, go back to your gridwork, or try to fix any responsiveness problems on the flat before returning to jumping.

If you're planning to compete, always remember that you should training at home over fences that are 3–6" *higher* than what you'll have to jump in competition. It's difficult enough to manage show-ring nerves, an unfamiliar environment, and crowds of unfamiliar people and horses. You should be able to enter the ring, look at the nice low jumps, and think, "Yes, we can do this. No problem."

And if you or your horse take a vacation or have a layoff, don't expect to simply pick up where you left off. Both of you will need to reestablish your communication, stamina, responsiveness, and balance.

Lesson #18: Get Out of the Arena

Hopefully, during the process of learning to ride and jump, you've been going on trail rides and having fun outside of the arena. If you're not regularly riding outside of your level, safe, enclosed practice ring, please take a break from jumping and go on a few trail rides.

One of the very best ways to develop a strong seat, solid balance, and good communication with your horse is to tackle varied terrain on the trails. Remember that your horse is an equal partner on the trails—you get to choose the path, but he must choose where to place his feet and find his balance. You cannot micromanage his every step the way you might do in your arena. But you can continue your training by doing the following:

1. Find a gentle hill, get into three-point or two-point position, bridge your reins (see page 151), and trot or canter to the top.

2. Come back down the hill *at a walk,* sitting straight in the saddle with heels down, and allowing your reins to slip if necessary. (See the illustration of the "safety position" on page 58.)

3. Go into a forward trot on a straight, open stretch—not downhill—and allow your horse to lengthen stride. Most horses will lengthen willingly, and many will get a little too forward. If this happens, work on regaining control and shortening stride.

4. Be sure your horse is paying attention and staying connected to you. At a walk or balanced trot on a smooth, straight track, try this exercise to improve responsiveness: Leg-yield left for a few steps, straighten, and then leg-yield right for a few steps.

Always ride with a buddy on the trails. And, when you feel secure and comfortable on your trail rides, find a few small, safe jumps to hop over. See chapter 10, "Specializing: Finding the Right Fit," for more on cross-country riding.

Chapter 8

STARTING THE GREEN HORSE
OVER JUMPS

Running and jumping are natural behaviors for horses. And most horses that have a bare minimum of jumping talent even seem to enjoy it. They must enjoy jumping at least a little; otherwise, why would a horse go *over* an obstacle when it's much easier to simply go around?

To learn to carry a rider safely over jumps, a horse needs to be:

- Sound, healthy, mature, and physically capable
- Balanced in his basic flatwork
- Confident and responsive to his rider
- Motivated

And he needs the right trainer to show him the way.

Sound, Healthy, Mature, and Physically Capable

How can you tell if your horse is physically ready to begin jumping? Physical condition, age, and a prior career are three major factors to consider.

PHYSICAL CONDITION

No horse should begin jumping if he's underweight, overweight, unfit, or in generally poor condition. Body condition should be at least a 4, but no more than a 7. (See "Nutrition and Health" in chapter 2 for more information.)

Deworming, vaccinations, and hoof care must all be up-to-date. Your horse should be fit enough for an hour's worth of work each day for several days a week. And he should be sound—not just "serviceably sound," but pain-free and willing to exert himself.

Muscling over the topline is especially important. A strong back and loin are necessary to create thrust and an athletic bascule over a jump. Cavalletti and gridwork will certainly help strengthen the topline, but a horse with a long back and a weak loin will need more careful conditioning than the horse with a naturally strong back and good muscling.

One of the best ways to develop a good topline is with long, slow distance training (for example, gradually increasing work until the horse can trot or canter continuously over five miles or more), and hill-climbing. A horse that has been ridden frequently on the trails will generally be in better shape to begin jumping than one who has spent his life going around in circles in a level arena.

AGE AND GROWTH PLATES

Don't start your horse jumping until he is *at least* 3½. Age 4 is much better and 5 is best, but few trainers or owners feel they can afford to wait until a horse is 5 if they're planning to sell or campaign him as a jumper prospect.

A spectacular jumper brings big money at the young horse sales. However, your strapping big 3-year-old is not ready for serious jumper training just because he free-jumped over a 4' fence at the warmblood sales.

Young horses spend a lot of time being physically unbalanced and weak as a result of natural growth processes. Trainers will often speak knowingly of "waiting until his growth plates close" before starting to ride or jump a youngster. But what does this mean?

All bones (except for the horse's skull) have *growth plates*—the ends of the bones that start as growing cartilage and then produce hard bone as the horse grows. There are no "late-maturing" or "early-maturing" breeds. All horses attain full maturity at about the age of 6 years. Some breeds may *look* mature long before that, but a 3-year-old quarter horse is no more physically mature than a 3-year-old warmblood.

Usually when people talk of "waiting until the growth plates close," they're speaking of the long leg bones just above the knees. These often close (turn to bone) at about 3½ years of age. The bones in the hocks, however, don't close until a horse is 6, 7, or even 8 years old—thus the importance of getting hock X-rays if you're considering the purchase of a young horse who's been started over fences.

Of more serious concern are the growth plates in the horse's vertebra—these don't close until age 6. Young horses that are regularly asked to carry more than 15 percent of their body weight, jump with a rider, or perform collected movements are in danger of having their backs damaged because the ligaments and vertebra weaken, stretch and slip out of position. At the very least, young horses who are asked to carry too much weight, too early, learn to stiffen and brace their backs in an effort to carry a stressful load.

Longeing over cavalletti or cantering over a crossrail isn't likely to cause harm, but serious jumper training with a rider should wait until the horse is 4 or older. And don't even *think* of jumping if your youngster's rump is higher than his withers—he won't be able to balance himself, much less the weight of a rider, and is likely to go tail over tea kettle on a downhill slope or in the descent of a jump.

PRIOR CAREER

If your horse has recently changed careers or riders, or had his feet re-balanced through major changes in shoeing, he'll need time and work to re-balance himself. Off-the-track racehorses, in particular, must go through a lengthy adaptation period before they're mentally and physically ready to tackle a new job. Horses used for western pleasure competition, driving, or any discipline that requires a different balance, responsiveness, or equipment, will also need to learn new skills. Give your horse adequate time and training on the flat to adapt. He'll need to develop new muscles and learn new communication methods.

Balance and Skills on the Flat

Don't start a horse over fences until his flatwork is confirmed. What does "confirmed" mean? As mentioned in chapter 1, many trainers use the requirements of a First Level dressage test to determine a horse's balance and responsiveness before starting to jump. Essentially, this requires a horse to:

- Travel with steady rhythm, relaxation, and connection (on the aids) at walk, trot, and canter
- Perform smooth, prompt transitions between gaits
- Be able to balance and bend correctly on a 15-meter (49') circle at the trot and a 20-meter (66') circle at the canter, on either lead
- Perform a simple change of lead with only one or two trot steps
- Move freely forward on a loose rein without changing rhythm
- Lengthen and shorten stride at trot and canter
- Leg-yield at the walk and trot

How long does it take to develop these skills from when a young horse is first ridden? Perhaps 6 months or a little less, if a mature horse is started under saddle carefully and then ridden 5 or 6 days a week by an accomplished trainer.

For most people, the schedule can be a little more relaxed. If you start your young horse in light work under saddle at 3 or 3½ and spend a year of riding in the arena and out on the trails, then he's probably ready to begin work over small jumps at age 4 or 4½.

Basic dressage training provides an excellent foundation for jumping, especially when it's combined with trail riding. Remember, however, that jumping does require a different balance than higher-level dressage: In jumping, you ask the horse to travel on less contact and require him to change his balance more quickly, from horizontal to vertical and back. The other very large difference is that you ask the horse to take on more responsibility for his own balance and stride length.

That's why riding out of the arena—on trails and hills, through woods and open fields—becomes very important in the development of a safe, smart jumper.

Confidence and Responsiveness

If your horse doesn't trust you and respond willingly, and if he isn't relaxed and confident in his flatwork, then don't begin jumping. You must trust each other to stay safe!

Some problems with confidence and responsiveness can include:

- Balking, bucking, pinning ears, being stubborn or herd-bound, or unwilling to move forward when you use your legs, spurs, or crop

- Cutting corners or diving into the center of the ring when trotting or cantering

- Using "evasion spooks" to refuse to go past an object he's thoroughly familiar with

- Inability to bend or uncomfortable bending in one direction or picking up a lead

- Bolting, rushing, or otherwise ignoring your signals to slow, stop, or shorten stride

Fix these problems on the flat first, *before* you move on to jumping.

Motivation

We've all seen horses playing in a field or paddock, galloping and leaping in what seems to be sheer athletic joy. When running freely, horses may jump an obstacle for any of several reasons. Young horses develop their strength, stamina, and survival skills through jumping, because that's part of their ability to flee from predators. Older horses may find a reward by jumping a fence to join the herd in the next paddock, or run back to the barn at feeding time. A truly panicked horse will attempt to escape by jumping anything in his path.

In training, you must always remember to use effective motivation to keep the horse's responses willing and honest.

When you ask a horse to begin jumping at *your* direction rather than his own, what motivation can you use? You certainly don't want to use fear and the need to escape. A much better motivation is the horse's need to please the leader. An additional motivating factor can be rest. ("Do as I say and we'll take a break.")

So before you can start a horse over fences, you need to have developed a system of requests-and-rewards that both you and your horse understand. In other words, you need a way of saying, "Good boy!" so he knows he's pleased you and he clearly understands how to please you again.

The Right Rider and Trainer

This should be obvious by now, but I'll say it again: Only an experienced, confident trainer should start a green horse in jumping. For safe learning to take place, *someone* has to know what they're doing. And if it isn't the horse, it must be the rider.

The best trainers generally *aren't* the people who are winning all the hunter or jumper classes on the show circuit. Good trainers demonstrate patience instead of competitive spirit. They love to teach, and they concentrate on solving problems instead of winning ribbons. Good trainers know how to develop trust and confidence in their horses, they understand how to condition a horse mentally as well as physically, and they know how to back off if a horse isn't ready for the next skill level.

However, good trainers, like good horses, develop from a combination of natural talent and learned skills. So if you've got a few years' worth of solid experience in jumping—if you're very secure jumping a complex course, if you've tackled a few cross-country courses with confidence, you enjoy solving problems, your seat is very secure, and you've helped train green horses on the flat—then there's no reason why you can't give a young horse a good start over fences.

Begin with the Great Outdoors

Many trainers today seem to be creating hot-house flowers, riders and horses that can perform well in a quiet, well-fenced arena, but can't adapt to changes in their environment or think for themselves. If these fragile horses and insecure riders attempt to leave the safe, level, enclosed arena with its perfect footing and predictable arrangement of obstacles, they lose confidence and become nervous and frightened. That's not true horsemanship.

Riding outside of the arena is a vital part of every horse's training, but especially so with jumpers. Why? Because in jumping you must trust the horse to make good decisions that will keep both rider and horse safe. To jump well, your horse needs to be aware of how he's using his body to balance and move. He's got to be able to shut out distractions, trust his rider, deal with unpredictable situations, and focus on the task at hand.

Trail riding challenges the horse to develop these skills *before* he learns to jump. Every trail ride is a unique training opportunity, because it's a chance for the rider to ask the horse to consider and then make judgments about his environment.

By trail riding, I don't mean just a 20-minute walk around the pasture perimeter at the end of your regular training session. Useful training on the trails includes terrain challenges and unexpected obstacles that will develop your horse's physical and mental skills in a controlled, logical fashion.

So get a couple of safety-conscious riding buddies on dependable horses, strap on your helmet and cell phone, and get out of the arena. Follow these steps to incorporate trail riding into a good training program:

1. *Start with small hills and gentle slopes, at a walk.*

   Use three-point to go up, encouraging a forward effort. Your horse shouldn't rush wildly up the hill, but he shouldn't stall, either. He should tackle it eagerly, with a little extra energy. Encourage him with legs and a stick, if necessary.

   Coming down, keep your seat light and a little forward, with knees in and heels well down. If he's having trouble staying straight, widen your hands so they're low and a foot or more apart, and stay very light on his mouth. Don't drop the reins, however—be ready to check him if he's clumsy and doesn't seem able to apply the brakes.

   Most green horses don't understand how to balance a rider on a downward slope—they let gravity take over and stumble their way into an awkward trot. Be sure your horse is responsive to your requests for half-halts and full halts on level ground, then ask him to come down the hill slowly.

   The balance he needs to carry a rider down a hill is very similar to the balance he needs to maintain in the descent when jumping. If he can't manage his balance carrying you down a small hill at a walk, then he's not going to be comfortable landing over a jump with a rider!

2. *Trot up and down* **gentle** *slopes.*

   Your mother probably told you, as mine did, "Don't let that horse trot down that hill!" But trotting and cantering up and down gentle (5–10 degree) slopes is a great balancing exercise—*when your horse is ready for it.* Find a straight path with good footing and start at a walk. Check your horse's responsiveness when you ask for a halt, then bridge your reins and pick up a slow, controlled trot in a light (three-point seat) or with very low, quiet posting. If your horse starts to get fast and disorganized, shift your seat deeper and ask him to walk, or, if you have room (in a field or large open space), turn so he's heading back uphill, and then walk.

After walking and trotting up and down hills, try a canter. If your horse gets a little keen, just keep your aids quiet and your seat light, and let the hill help your horse learn to be steadier. Even moderate hill work will help a horse strengthen the loins and haunches, which is essential conditioning for jumping. This photo shows a good example of a correctly adjusted running martingale, doing its job as my horse powers up a small slope.

3. **Do large circles and figure eights on a gentle slope.**

   This requires a large open field with good footing—no rocks, holes, or slippery spots. The varied terrain will pose continual rebalancing challenges, while the circles or figure eights will help you keep control. As much as possible, let your horse figure out the balance while you mostly steer and stay in a light seat. Keep the circles large so you don't strain joints and ligaments, especially if your horse isn't truly fit. This is much more tiring than working on level ground or a consistent incline.

   If your horse is managing the trot well, try adding a canter on the uphill parts, then transition back to trot for the down slopes.

4. **Deliberately find a trail with rocks, logs, or tree roots that your horse will have to pick his way through.**

   I don't mean clusters of sharp boulders and sharp slippery shale with holes and huge mud-holes in-between; just a moderately trappy trail with a few easy obstacles so your horse has to devote his full attention to where he's putting his feet.

Encourage your horse to slow down, look down, and step carefully. If he rushes or seems anxious, use your voice and small half-halts to ask him to slow down. Be sure the other horses aren't getting too far ahead and making him feel left behind. If he's still tackling the rough spots too quickly, simply turn him around and ask him to go back and forth over the same spot a few times. See if he'll stop in the middle of the obstacles and stand quietly. If so, praise him for his courage. Whatever you do, don't tense up or hang on the reins or punish him in any way. You've asked him to walk through a rough spot and he's trying to comply, so he needs reassurance for attempting the task, not corrections for failing to do it perfectly.

If you can find a shallow stream or large puddle, walk through that. If the footing is good, and he's comfortable with this task, try trotting through. (Be sure he doesn't stop in the middle and roll with you!)

RICHARD VALCOURT

This photos shows how I can use the trails to develop calm acceptance and good judgment. Pandora is giving this muddy ditch her full attention. I'm staying centered, with eyes up, heels solidly down, and a light contact. I've let the reins slip a little so she can look down and use her neck for balance. If she decides to leap up suddenly out of the ditch, that's okay—I'll grab the mane and go with her.

Safe Trail Riding on a Greenie

- Shying, abrupt halts, imbalance, and sudden moves are all routine behaviors you'll encounter when working with a green horse. *If your skills and confidence aren't up to handling a few spooks and stumbles, you shouldn't be on a green horse.* Ask a more experienced rider to put some mileage on your young horse while you continue to work on your own seat and balance.

- Use your horse's need to "stay with the herd" to your advantage by following an older or more experienced horse through the trappy spots.

- Don't expect or ask your horse to ignore these new experiences, and don't punish him if he looks at things. You *want* him to look, think, and process the new information. To "encourage" is to "enable courage," so go ahead and encourage his curiosity.

- Don't force your young horse through something he's really not ready to deal with. Trail rides with green horses are often very slow events, as an insecure youngster may show concern or fear about every new object. Use the more experienced horses as your lead and praise your greenie for every attempt he makes to do what you ask—even if it's not a complete success.

- *Always* wear protective equipment. This means a helmet, riding pants with good "grip," and boots with a proper heel. Chaps and a protective vest are also good ideas. Your horse needs protective boots, too, and preferably on all four legs. A running martingale can help limit any sudden head-high maneuvers.

- *Never* use a standing martingale if there's even a remote possibility you might be crossing a river. A horse wearing a standing martingale can drown if he falls in the water or is forced to swim. Stop to unfasten a standing martingale before crossing any water more than a few inches deep.

- Practice good trail etiquette and be sure your horse will listen to your aids so he doesn't rush or crowd the other horses. Before you go out on the roads and trails, he should be familiar with traffic, dogs, and bicycles—those are challenges that should be introduced in the arena, at home where your horse feels safest.

- Review your plans with other riders before you go out. Let them know you may need them to go very slowly and make allowances for your green horse. Be sure at least one rider is on a trustworthy, trail-wise horse who will provide a good example for the others.

Free-Jumping in the Arena

One of the best ways to introduce a horse to jumping is through free-jumping, which can help the horse find his balance and striding without having to manage a rider's weight and influence. At any point in his education, jumping without a rider is good exercise to help a horse loosen his muscles and stretch his topline.

FACILITIES

Free-jumping requires specific training facilities and at least two people: the trainer and an assistant. It requires a space large enough for the horse to approach, jump, and land comfortably, but small enough so the trainer and one or two assistants can maintain control over the horse's speed and direction. The best set-up for free-jumping is an indoor arena that measures 70–85' wide and 120–150' long, with solid walls 6' or higher.

Don't use a typical round pen (50–65' diameter) for free-jumping, except perhaps for very basic trot work over a small crossrail. To avoid excessive strain on legs and balance problems, the horse needs room to travel on a straight line while jumping. Ideally, he needs at least 50' before the jump for a straight approach, and 50' beyond the jump to recover his balance and rhythm before having to turn.

Some trainers like to use a *jumping lane,* a straight outdoor track 10–12' wide and up to several hundred feet long. A lane has a high barrier along the sides and jumps set up every few strides along the track. An advantage of a jumping lane is that the horse can't duck out. One disadvantage, however, is that the trainer can't easily control the speed of the horse once he's started down the lane. A lazy horse may lose momentum and simply stop in the middle, or an excitable horse may build up speed and rush over the jumps, especially if he's heading back to the stable.

If you have a suitable facility and want to introduce your horse to free-jumping, be sure he's first comfortable with following your voice, whip, and body cues on the flat, in a round pen, or on a longeline. He should walk, trot, canter, and stop on command, in a relaxed and confident manner.

SETTING UP

To begin free-jumping, set up a single jump with wings along a straight side of your arena. Even if you're using wing standards, it's a good idea to lean an extra rail against the top of the standard to create a chute so the horse can't duck out. Position the jump so your horse will have at least 50' of approach on a straight line and *at least* 50' of straightaway after the landing.

Put protective boots and a snug-fitting halter or longe cavesson on your horse so you can catch and lead him as needed. You may need to put him back on the longeline to regain control.

Place a rail on the ground between the standards, lead your horse up to it, and ask him to step quietly over it. Don't turn him loose until he's thoroughly comfortable with walking between the jump wings and stepping over the rail on a lead-line.

Then position yourself and your helper with longe whips. One person directs the horse toward the jump and moves parallel to the horse as he travels down the line on the approach. The second person should be positioned to help send the horse the rest of the way around the arena after he lands. If the arena is large, you may also need a third person at the far end of the arena to keep the horse traveling along the wall. (See the diagram below.)

Keep the horse moving forward on the track and around the arena, but don't frighten him into a headlong gallop. Keep the jump low enough in the beginning so he can jump it from either a quiet canter or a cautious trot. The goal is to direct his path and focus his attention on the jump, not force him into an escape route or make him jump from fear. Let the horse choose how to approach and handle the obstacle. If he decides to rush madly around, bucking and playing, just keep him going around on the track until he gets rid of the excess energy and settles down.

First Jump

After the horse has trotted or cantered over the ground pole a few times in both directions, build a crossrail. Use four rails: two for the jump, and two as ground rails so the jump can be approached from either side. Don't brace or fix the rails in place; instead, build the jump so it looks solid but can be knocked down if the horse gets into trouble.

Now send him around again. If he brakes and stops in front of the small jump, encourage him a little, and be ready to clip a lead-line to the halter and lead him quietly over at a walk.

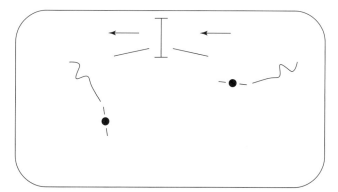

To free-jump your horse, you'll need an arena with high walls, a jump with ground poles and wings (you can place one end of a rail on top of the jump standard), and an assistant.

Tips for Free-Jumping

- Don't yell, wave the whip wildly, run at the horse, or chase him over the jump. You want him to jump from his own decision to go forward, not because he's terrified.

- Try not to let him turn away or duck out. Be ready to walk up and quickly clip on the lead or longe line if he shows signs of avoiding the jump.

- Start with just one rail on the ground, and then advance to a single crossrail. You can also build a second jump on the other long side of the arena, but remember that if your arena is large or wide, you and your helpers must be able to quickly reposition yourselves to keep your horse traveling all the way around near the wall, from one jump to the other. That can be exhausting! Better to focus on one location and allow the horse to re-balance and settle back into a trot or quiet canter as he travels the rest of the way around the arena.

- Don't ask your horse to free-longe over cavalletti spaced for trotting. You can't control his speed with any precision, and if he gallops over ground poles set only 4' or 5' apart, he's likely to bungle his way through and scare himself. Instead, space your cavalletti rails 9'–10' apart. Then he has two choices, both of them safe: he can canter through in a bounce pattern, *or* trot through with two steps between the rails.

- Raise the height of the jump gradually, and be sure to roll out the ground rails a little to encourage a more precise takeoff as the jump gets bigger. Use fillers and extra rails to make the jump substantial looking, but be sure the top rail can always be knocked down.

If the entire process excites him so much that he's unable to respond to your direction, or he manages to escape around the jump standards more than once, put him back on the longe line and spend as much time as you need to quietly regain control. Then try longeing him over single ground poles and cavalletti until he's calm and confident.

If he shows a nice attitude toward jumping the crossrail—straight approach at a trot or canter, good focus and a careful jump, and landing neatly and recovering his stride well—then you can raise the jump a few inches or change it to a vertical.

A ONE-STRIDE COMBINATION

When your horse is comfortable with the added height, add another pair of standards, wings, and a ground rail one stride beyond the first jump.

- An ascending (ramped) oxer is a very good jump to encourage a horse to round his back and jump out as well as up. Just remember a ramped oxer can be jumped safely in only one direction, with the higher bar at the back of the jump.

- *Never* leave empty jump cups on the jump standards. Even the plastic ones can create a nasty bruise if a horse jumps crookedly and catches a leg on a jump cup.

- Allow your horse to make mistakes and learn from them. If he chips in and lands awkwardly, you should encourage more energy on the next approach, so he lands going forward with more momentum. Don't, however, make him rush at the jump. And if he knocks a rail down, fine. He'll learn to pick his toes up and fold his legs better the next time.

- Jumping requires strength as well as agility. If your horse is free-jumping with a high head, a hollow back, and no bascule, then he's not ready for this kind of work. Have a veterinarian check him for lameness or injury, then strengthen his back with flatwork and hills—or let him mature a bit more!

- With a young horse, resist the temptation to "see how high he can go." Keep the sessions short and quit while it's still fun and fairly easy for him. Your horse should enjoy jumping, and you want to preserve that fresh, willing attitude.

Be sure to measure the distance correctly, so the distance fits your horse's baseline canter stride. Don't try to make him shorten or lengthen stride yet! (If you're not sure how long his baseline stride is, send him around at a steady canter and then measure the tracks from one stride, left rear hoofprint to left rear hoofprint.)

A general rule for setting a one-stride distance: If he's approaching the small jump at a trot and landing in canter, put the additional ground rail 16'–18' beyond the jump. If he's going over the small jump in a strong canter, open up the distance to 20'–22'. A big-striding horse may need a 24' distance. When in doubt, go for the slightly shorter distance to encourage him to round over his hocks instead of flattening and reaching over the second jump. You want to encourage a coiled loin and an athletic bascule, not a desperately long, dangerous leap.

RICHARD VALCOURT

This horse is ready to begin longeing over jumps: She wears boots on all four feet, understands voice commands, moves well on a large circle in both directions, and demonstrates a calm, responsive attitude.

When your horse accepts the additional ground pole, and you can see that the distance is correct for his stride, build the second jump into a crossrail to create a one-stride combination that can be jumped from either direction.

You can gradually raise the heights and spreads for both fences, but this is about as far as you can take free-jumping without building a more elaborate facility. And, if your horse is free-jumping in good form at 3' or a little higher, he's probably ready to begin jumping under saddle.

Jumping on the Longe

Because it's easier to control the horse's direction and speed with a longeline than while free-jumping, many people start a young horse jumping on the longe. Longeing over jumps, however, requires a measure of agility and line-handling technique from the trainer.

These points are especially important to keep in mind before you ask your horse to jump on the longe. You must:

- Be sure your horse longes well on the flat, in both directions, at all three gaits, and halts quickly when you ask him to.

- Allow the horse freedom to use his head and neck all the way through the jumping motion, from approach to landing and recovery. This means you must be able to move quickly alongside your horse, or pay out the line rapidly, as he lands and moves away from the jump in a straight line. Be very careful not to pull him off balance immediately after landing!

- Build the jump and handle the longe line in such a way that you won't snag the line on any part of the jump. You'll frighten your horse badly if the longeline gets caught on a rail, a jump standard, or your horse's legs.

LONGE OVER JUMPS IN THE ARENA

Begin by longeing over a single ground rail at a walk and trot. If your horse leaps, rushes, tries to scoot around the rail, or trips over it and frightens himself, then quietly slow him down, lead him up to the rail, and let him investigate it further. Lead him back and forth over the rail a few times until he relaxes.

Then progress to a cavalletti with four or five rails spaced for trotting. The cavalletti can be simple ground poles or they can be raised a few inches off the ground. I like to use heavy round fenceposts or logs as cavalletti—they're too heavy to be easily dislodged, yet light enough to be moved for spacing adjustments. Their solid feel and size encourage a horse to engage his hindquarters and pick his feet up.

You can set the cavalletti in a straight line, or you can position them in a slight "fan" shape so your horse can continue on the path of his circle as he steps over the rails. If you build the cavalletti on a straight track, you must be prepared to move quickly along a parallel track for several feet so you don't pull him off balance as he travels on his straight path. Your longe "circle" must become an oval.

After the horse has accepted the cavalletti and is working well at a trot in both directions, approaching with energy, maintaining a steady rhythm, and beginning to adjust his approach by shortening or lengthening his steps so he doesn't trip over the first rail, then add a pair of jump standards and a single ground rail 10'–12' beyond the last cavalletti rail. Use an extra rail to create a wing for the jump standards. This type of wing will help keep your horse straight on the approach, and if you do get the line caught, it will slide up and over the top of the jump.

Polyethylene jump standards designed for schooling (for example, PolyPro cavalletti, Blocks or the Stacker System) are excellent for this exercise because they're very stable, they're no taller than they need to be, and you're less likely to get the line tangled than if you use post-type jump standards.

After the horse moves calmly over the rail set between standards at a walk and trot, you can remove the cavalletti and ask your horse to canter over the single rail. If the canter worries him or he has trouble with the striding, just let him continue trotting over the single pole.

Then build a small crossrail. If you've left the cavalletti in place, be sure your horse approaches at a steady trot. If you're using just the single jump, either a trot or canter is appropriate. Some green horses are much happier tackling their first jumps at a trot; others are better balanced at the canter. Regardless of whether he trots or canters, aim for a steady rhythm and a slightly increased energy on the approach.

Your horse should land in canter. And you must *move along with him.* Pay out the longe line and take big rapid steps to travel in a path parallel to his, allowing him to stay on the oval track so he can land going straight and forward. Don't startle him by running alongside, but do be ready to keep up with him. After he's recovered with a few strides of canter, you can ease him into a turn. If he's gotten a bit exuberant and you're having trouble keeping up with him, ask him to come back onto a true circle while you reorganize and catch your breath.

LONGE OVER JUMPS OUTSIDE THE ARENA

Many trainers longe over jumps only briefly, using this as a preliminary step to be sure the horse is comfortable jumping by himself over a few small fences before adding a rider. But if your horse is quiet and responsive on the longe, think of how useful this tool can be when introducing a young horse to cross-country jumps.

If your green horse is thoroughly familiar with riding through fields and trails, you can probably introduce him to almost any natural obstacle on a longe line or a long lead rope. Longeing or leading your horse over a small ditch, up a bank, or through a water crossing can be a very effective way for him to gain his balance and confidence without having to worry about a rider.

It's a good idea to ride out on the course first, to assess your young horse's energy and attention levels. Be sure to have an experienced older horse along—both to provide a good example when your horse needs to follow a leader and to act as a "magnet" in case your green horse pulls away from you. Ride up to the obstacle, examine it from several angles, then dismount and prepare your horse for longeing or leading over or through.

Longeing outside the arena carries more safety risks. The environment is less predictable and will probably provide more distractions, your horse may get excited and pull loose, and you may find it harder to keep your own footing on uneven terrain. Proceed cautiously and be ready to change your plans as needed.

Cavalletti help the horse learn rhythm and focus while strengthening the muscles of the back and hind legs. Pandora must work through her hindquarters, flex the joints of her hind legs, and create an uphill balance to push herself through the cavalletti.

Are you training the horse or attempting to sell him? A capable but lazy horse over a small jump may show "loose form," as Pandora exhibits here. A slightly higher jump would be a better test of talent. But the main goal now is to build the horse's confidence, experience, and good judgment, not just "see how high she can go."

Longeing over Jumps

- Use a cavesson or snug-fitting halter, not a bridle, to longe your horse over jumps. You don't need a surcingle or saddle. Don't use side reins or any other device that limits the horse's use of his head and neck. And don't run a chain over his nose for control. He *must* be able to use his head and neck freely, without worrying about being pulled off-balance or hurt.

- Try to position the cavalletti or jump so a natural barrier such as a building, arena wall, or a pasture fence will help turn your horse about 40–50' past the landing spot. Then you won't be tempted to pull him back onto the track with the longe line. Allow him to approach, jump, and land on a straight line. Be prepared to pay out line and move quickly on a parallel path so you don't pull him off balance.

- Be sure jump rails will fall forward and not bounce back toward the horse's hind feet if dislodged by a front foot. Or you can attach the rails securely to the standards so they can't be easily dislodged. Some trainers prefer to longe over solid obstacles, with heavy rails securely attached, so the green horse quickly learns to respect the obstacle and jump clean. (The PVC rails in the photos on pages 161, 164, and 170 are attached to the Stacker bases to create a solid obstacle that still has some "give" to it, so if the horse hits it, he's not likely to hurt himself or get tangled in a flying rail.)

- Ask for and expect your horse to put energy into his effort. Whether he approaches at a trot or canter, he should land going forward into a canter, not stall or "stop and sit" after the jump. Avoid the temptation to raise the jumps "just to see what he can do." You want to build a jump that provides just enough of a challenge so your horse begins learning to judge height and takeoff, and can figure out how to use his body to good advantage. But if you build the jump too high, too soon, you'll risk over-facing and scaring him. Then he'll try to avoid jumping—and you *don't* want him to learn that he can duck out or stop.

- Carefully monitor your horse's attitude. If he shows signs of anxiety—rushing, bolting, ducking out, or skidding to a stop to avoid jumping—stop, calm him, and go back to walking and trotting over ground rails so he can perform a task successfully. Be ready to revise your goals for that training session and *never* punish him for nervousness or fear.

- How many jumps on the longe per session? Ten to fifteen is probably enough for both of you.

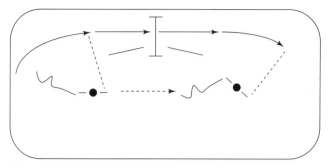

When longeing over a jump, you must be able to reposition yourself quickly and pay out line so your horse can approach and land straight. Agility is required!

Four Signs Your Horse Is *Not* Ready to Jump with a Rider

1. A growth spurt puts him off-balance. If his croup is suddenly higher than his withers, wait and let him even out. He can't be expected to carry a rider safely until he regains an uphill (or at least a level) balance. Be patient.

2. He's developed health problems, shoeing issues, or any sort of injury. Stop jumping. Be patient and take care of the problems.

3. Issues with straightness, balance, or responsiveness have cropped up in his flatwork. Jumping will *not* help resolve these problems; they'll just make them worse. Find a solution on the flat.

4. When free-jumping or jumping on the longe, he frequently balks, trips, refuses to go forward, chips in and lands on the jump, or seems fearful and reluctant to approach the rails or standards. Assuming there are no underlying issues with health or basic balance, go back to the earlier basics. Lead him over ground poles, spend more time on the trails, and work to develop his confidence and trust. You may have to accept the fact that some horses simply don't like to jump.

RICHARD VALCOURT

It's the trainer's responsibility to create a straight, balanced approach on a loose line. Your horse must have full freedom to use his head and neck. Don't pull on the line on takeoff or landing, as the handler is doing here—you'll scare him if you cause him to lose his balance.

Carrying a Rider: Preparing to Jump

By now you should have developed a systematic training program in which your young horse is being schooled several times a week, working two or three times a week under saddle in the arena, once or twice on trails, and perhaps once or twice on the longe or in the free-jumping arena.

Before you ask him to carry a rider over a jump, however, it's a good idea to review several key exercises on the flat.

DEVELOP YOUR HORSE'S BALANCE, RHYTHM, AND TRUST

The rider makes several position changes during jumping, so you must be sure your green horse becomes familiar with your changes in seat and balance, and learns to accept the different movements a rider makes when jumping.

These exercises are very similar to those recommended for novice riders, but the goal is a little different. Instead of strengthening the rider's abilities to stay in balance with the horse, you're now going to ensure that your green horse becomes comfortable with the feel of his rider's changing position and balance.

Green horses are awkward when they're learning to jump. They move abruptly. Occasionally they stumble or stop suddenly. The experienced rider has learned how to "stay with" the green horse, but sometimes the rider's sudden attempts to stay with his horse can frighten the horse at the moment when he's already feeling insecure. So before you tackle any serious over-fences work on your greenie, try these exercises on the flat.

Exercise #1: Change Seat Positions
At a trot, shift from rising to three-point or two-point and back again. At a canter, shift from full seat to three-point and two-point. Be sure your horse continues in the same rhythm, and that you can control his speed, path, and stride length.

Make the changes in your seat position smooth and gradual at first, and then make the changes a little more abrupt. (But don't hurt your horse, catch him in the mouth, or bump on his back.) Be sure he's comfortable with your shifts in balance and that he continues to move forward readily from your legs.

Exercise #2: Rein and Hand Movements.

While in two-point, bridge the reins and lean on his neck for a few strides. Grab the mane and tug on it. Practice an exaggerated *shove release,* where you push the hands forward and loosen the reins suddenly.

Make these moves gently as first and then a little more abruptly. If your horse responds with nervousness, confusion, or hesitancy, then you'll need to spend more time on this so he learns to ignore these moves.

Exercise #3: Emergency Dismount.

Practice your emergency dismount, if you haven't already done this. You may find yourself in a situation where you'll need to bail out, and you'll want to do this safely, without terrifying your horse. A horse that's comfortable with his rider suddenly leaping off is less likely to spook, kick, or buck if you fall. And if you get partially dislodged and end up on his neck over an awkward fence, you'll have a better chance of sliding safely to the ground.

So practice hopping off briskly from either side, first at a walk and trot and then, if you're confident and agile enough, at a canter. Try to land on your feet, facing forward. Reward and reassure your horse, every time, for being patient and putting up with all this silliness.

CAVALLETTI AND GROUND POLES

Jumping without a rider can help your horse learn to manage his own balance and coordination over a jump, but your goal is to develop a horse that jumps well under saddle. Assuming all has gone well, he should be ready to begin riding work over cavalletti and single ground poles after perhaps half a dozen sessions of jumping without a rider.

Use the exercises below to develop your horse's balance, rhythm, and agility.

Exercise #1: Single Rails

Use the "Focus and Release" and "Simple Rails" exercises in Lesson #4 to get your horse accustomed to traveling on a straight path between jump standards and over single ground poles. Move into and out of two-point, use a long crest release so your horse can look down at the rails on the ground, and follow the same routines described in the lesson.

If you've longed or free-jumped him over ground poles and small jumps, this should present no problems for your green horse. The biggest challenge, from his point of view, will be to focus on the obstacles while also managing his rider's changes in balance. Again, if he speeds up, loses impulsion, or has difficulty responding to your aids while you're in two-point, stay with the flatwork and single ground rails before moving to a cavalletti or grid.

1. As you canter your horse over the single ground rails, pay attention to how he's meeting them. Does he try to adjust so his stride "fits over" the rail, with hind feet on one side and front feet on the other, as if it were a jump? If not—if one front or hind foot consistently gets left behind as he puts in an awkward step, stumbles over the rail, or breaks stride— you'll need to help him learn to make some adjustments.

   First, let him canter over three or four random rails in whatever balance and stride length he offers—just focus on rhythm and path. Then offer a little help. Try to see a distance to the next rail, and ask him to shorten stride and find a slightly rounder balance. Keep it subtle. Don't make any radical adjustments to his rhythm or wrestle him into "a frame." Your objective is simply to show him that he will be more comfortable if he re-balances, focuses on the rail, and listens to your suggestions for adjusting his stride.

   Then sit quietly and see if he can figure out the striding to the next few rails on his own, with minimal help from you. You want him to make good decisions on his own, not just blunder along waiting for you to rescue him.

   Placing a single rail on a circle (or two, on opposite sides if you can ride a very large circle) is a good exercise, because you can vary the strides on a bending line more easily than on a straight line.

2. Next, set ground rails at related distances: a three-, four- or five-stride line. Measure accurately, so he'll be able to canter smoothly down the line and put in the expected number of strides. (You should know what your horse's baseline stride length is! If not, review the information in chapter 6, "Understanding Strides, Distances, and Grids.")

Canter these rails quietly, helping him to shorten or lengthen stride a little to meet the first rail in each line smoothly and in balance. Then try adding or removing a stride on a six-stride line to see if he'll listen to your requests to close or open his stride without rushing or hanging back.

If all goes well, you can also set rails to create bending lines on a related distance, similar to the exercises in Lessons #15 and #16, but with ground poles instead of jumps.

Your goal with these ground poles is to create a steady rhythm and calm approach, with the horse thinking and looking but never getting anxious about where he's putting his feet. We refer to the ground-pole exercises as being still "on the flat," but really, they're jumps—reduced to the lowest possible height!

Chapter 9

JUMPING WITH A RIDER

B y now, you'll have a pretty good idea of whether your horse is ready to carry you over a few small jumps. This chapter uses a step-by-step progression to build the skills your horse needs to balance himself with a rider.

You may find that you won't need all of the exercises outlined here. You may be working with an experienced older horse that merely needs a refresher course, or you may need to focus on a specific retraining goal. So rather than setting up specific "lessons" for the trainer of the horse, as I've done for the novice rider in previous chapters, here I approach training by discussing different skills, presenting specific exercises that can be incorporated into your larger training program, and referring to several lessons outlined in previous chapters.

Train with Grids

The basic grid is at the heart of all jumper training, and some form of it should be used in every training session, regardless of how green or experienced your horse is. It serves as both a warm-up for veteran jumpers and a standard exercise for less-experienced horses.

SIMPLE GRIDS

Refer to the illustrations shown on pages 106, 109, and 111 and see the chart in chapter 6, "Distances for Elements in Gymnastic Grids," to be sure you're setting up the grid components correctly.

Exercise #1: Cavalletti to a Crossrail

After your horse is well warmed up on the flat, begin by riding him at a trot over a single rail, and then add a second, third, and fourth rail to create a cavalletti. Be sure you're staying in two-point and using a generous crest release so he can use his neck and back fully. Be sure also that the spacing is correct for your horse to maintain a solid medium trot—don't force him to take bigger, longer, or faster steps. If he's done similar work on the longe line, this exercise should look entirely familiar to him.

Go over the cavalletti several times from both directions, alternating between rising trot, three-point, and two-point, and make sure to shift your positions smoothly and gently so your horse doesn't think he needs to make big adjustments in stride or rhythm.

Then add a small crossrail (12"–18") as shown in the diagram on page 106. Channel poles can be very helpful for a green horse, but be sure to space them far enough apart (10' is good) so he doesn't focus on the channel poles instead of on the rails he must step over.

Trot over the cavalletti, and then use your legs and a cluck to encourage him to actually *jump* over the crossrail and land in a canter. Don't be upset with him, however, if he just takes a big awkward trot step over the jump. And don't punish him if he slows down, stares at it, or stops. Get him to at least walk over it, though you must be ready in case he pops straight up in the air and jumps from a standstill.

Be prepared for *anything*—having a good grip on the mane or jumping strap is a good idea, because your horse may execute a huge leap, land in a tangle, and stop on the other side. Or stumble forward. Or leap into a fast canter.

Many green horses have no trouble managing the approach and takeoff, but can't seem to balance themselves comfortably on landing. And they may express that discomfort with a buck, a swerve, or a head toss. That's why it's very important to have an experienced rider on board, someone who isn't going to be dislodged by all the abrupt, unpredictable movements that a green horse can perform.

If your horse takes it all in stride with a straight, steady approach and a nice little jump, landing in a balanced canter, then congratulate yourself and tell your horse how wonderful he is. This is a good indication that all your preparations have been on track.

Remember, though, that however your green horse gets over his first crossrail, if you both make it over intact, he deserves praise for making a good effort. So reassure him, reestablish the rhythm and control, and keep going.

Exercise #2: Learning to Focus

After your horse is thoroughly comfortable with the cavalletti and crossrail combination, add a ground rail one stride beyond the crossrail, and then build that up into a vertical.

Many horses can handle the cavalletti to crossrail easily, but then become confused when you add another element beyond the crossrail. They don't know where to look or what to focus on, and may trip over the crossrail while staring at the rail beyond. With gridwork, you're training the horse to shift his

Remember to Reward

No matter how much talent your young horse has or how lovely he performs on the flat, learning to jump with a rider requires your horse to work with a new focus, a greater level of physical effort and confidence in his rider, and a whole new set of skills.

He needs his supervisor and teacher—you—to tell him how he's doing. Don't just correct him when he gets it wrong; tell him very clearly when he's done something right.

So whenever he canters over a simple ground rail in good rhythm, travels straight through a grid with nice focus and a steady pace, or accepts your help in finding balance on a turn or a distance to a jump, reward him! Use whatever seems appropriate: your praising voice, a quick pat on the neck, or a small release of the reins.

Keep building a system of positive reinforcement so he'll develop confidence and continue working to please you.

And don't micromanage your young horse. Allow him to make small, safe mistakes so he'll learn from them and gain the confidence to make good decisions.

focus—in essence, to use an equine version of soft eyes and hard eyes to first see the entire pattern of obstacles, and then to focus on what's immediately in front of him.

Remember, too, that your horse's eyesight works differently from yours. He can use either *binocular vision* (eyes working together and looking ahead) or *monocular vision* (eyes working separately in peripheral vision), so he can literally see in two directions at once.

To focus on an object far in front of him, the horse must raise his head. If he's overly restricted by the rider's reins and a too-tight martingale, with his neck over-bent and his chin on his chest, he will *not* be able to see what's in front of him and he *cannot* jump safely.

An object that's directly in front of a horse's nose and closer than 4'—a jump, for instance—is in a blind spot. So he must judge the fence's height and position as he approaches, and then leap just before the fence disappears from his view. (For additional information on this topic, check out the article, "Equine Vision and Its Effect on Behavior," by Dr. Patricia Evans. You should be able to download a copy from the Internet.)

What does this mean for your green horse who is just starting to jump? Learning how to process all this visual information comes with time, practice, and repetition. Don't surprise him. Be honest with him and introduce each new task in a logical way by building on his earlier knowledge.

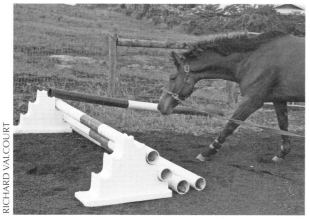

Watch how your green horse uses his eyes as he approaches a new jump. Here Pandora stares intently at the obstacle, trying to gauge its size and position as she decides what sort of effort is required. She gets very close . . .

. . . yet still manages to jump competently. However, if your novice horse is approaching all his jumps like this, he needs more practice without a rider so he can more easily judge height, jump with confidence, and look beyond the jump.

With more experience, Pandora shows a much better balance, greater confidence, and a "looking ahead" focus on her approach.

Build Your Horse's Confidence over Fences

Change only one thing about the jump at a time: its appearance, height, placement in the arena, or its relationship to other jumps. Don't move the jump, raise the jump, and add flowers to it all at the same time!

Think in terms of comparison, not contrast. (Comparisons find similarities, contrasts point out differences.) This means you want your horse to find something familiar about a new jump, so he can look at it and think, "That's new, but it looks very similar to the other one I've already jumped," instead of "Wow! That's different! I've never seen *anything* like that before! What do I do??!!"

Stay with low, easy jumps until your horse has gone over every possible configuration of strange-looking, weirdly placed fences. When he becomes slightly bored jumping 2' fences adorned with foam pool noodles, a duck pond with rubber duckies, balloons, boogie boards, palm fronds, and a checkered tablecloth, *then* you can raise the height and widen the spread.

If your horse seems to lose confidence, then simplify. Lower the height, remove an element or slow to a trot.

Use substantial-looking jump materials that won't fool the horse into thinking he can push through them. Use multiple rails and fillers, not airy-looking single rails. Use true ground lines on *every* jump for a green horse.

Consider shadows and available light. Most horses have good night vision, but a deep shadow may look like a black hole in the ground. Some horses are very nervous about jumping into or out of shadows, and will need extra patience and practice to learn how to judge their jumps if there's strong contrast between light and shadow.

Be sure your jump elements provide visual contrast, especially for a novice horse. Don't use gray or medium-green rails in a grass arena, or natural rails in an arena with neutral-colored footing.

Exercise #3: Build Out the Grid

Use the diagrams in Lessons #8 and #9 to add elements to your basic grid, building from cavalletti to crossrail to small vertical to oxer.

Keep the cavalletti in place and stick to a trot approach until your horse is consistently meeting his fences comfortably, without rushing. Then remove the cavalletti, widen the distances for a canter approach (see the "Distances for Elements in Gymnastic Grids" chart in chapter 6), and quietly canter through the grid. Keep the first crossrail low, so even if he gets a little deep or a little long to the first takeoff, the crossrail will help him correct his striding for the rest of the grid.

Then you can set up a series of raised cavalletti or small crossrails, set 9-10' apart, to create a bounce grid as explained in Lesson #10, and canter through.

The grids and bounce exercises from Lesson #10 are designed to help your horse develop both his physical strength and his judgment, so he can:

- See what different arrangements look like and decide how to handle them.
- Feel what it's like to meet his jumps from the right distance.
- Develop the power and agility to jump easily out of a rhythmic stride.

Exercise #4: Add Single Fences

Next, you'll use the exercises outlined in Lesson #10 to set up a related distance, with measured strides from your grid to a single jump.

When your horse is comfortably cantering down the line to find a good distance to the single fence, you can begin adjusting the distances and strides, and begin incorporating large, gradual turns into your training sessions. Depending on your horse's talent and attitude, and your own skills, it may take him four weeks or four months, or even more, to get to this point. Work to keep everything balanced, steady, and predictable for your horse so he builds confidence.

Keep this work fun for your horse and don't drill him, but *do* use repetition to confirm the patterns of responsiveness and good judgment that you're looking for. And don't rush to raise the fences; it's very hard to rebuild a horse's confidence after a bad mishap.

Exercise #5: Simple Courses

After a few months of work with grids and longer lines with related distances, your horse should be ready to jump simple courses at 2'3" or 2'6"—and perhaps higher, depending on his age and talent, your own skill level, and the discipline you're working in.

However, you should still be using simple hunter-style courses to focus on rhythm, balance, and adjustability. Don't over-face him with tight turns off a corner, rollbacks, jumping in counter-canter, or tricky angles. Keep it simple and be very sensitive to how he responds to new challenges. The course shown on page 141 is a good course for a novice horse as well as a novice rider.

With a young and still green horse, you'll want to use lines with no surprises—those that require steady distances, gradual turns, and logical lead changes. It's critical, however, to *have a plan* and know your course. Unless you are very clear about the route, you'll confuse your horse.

When you feel he's ready to move on to greater challenges, construct a course of jumps that will test his responsiveness and your ability to plan and execute your ride. Set up a course similar to the one shown on page 174. Then ride this sequence:

1. Begin with a large right-hand circle to establish your canter, and jump the bending line from A to B in seven steady (or eight quiet) strides. Hold the right lead and make a large sweeping right turn after you land over B and head toward E.

2. On the long line to E, if you know the 24' one-stride and the oxer will require a little extra effort, then ask for more impulsion and open up the canter a little so your horse lands a little deeper into the combination. (If his approach is a little too quiet and he doesn't land very deep into the combination, he'll have to really reach and struggle to make it out over the oxer. Help him get it right!)

3. Continue your right turn after E and find your approach to the diagonal line F-D. Be sure you ride straight to the oxer at F so you don't force your horse to make more of an effort than necessary. Ask for a change of lead over D and shift into a left turn after D.

4. Ride almost a complete left-hand circle and line up your approach to A, in the opposite direction from which you first jumped it. This gives you an introduction to a large rollback—something you can tighten and refine later, as your horse's skills and balance increase. Ride a quiet rhythm to A, because you'll . . .

5. Ask for a change to the right lead over A, and turn right. If your arena is long enough to permit a smooth turn to F, open up the canter a little and ride the line F to G in three smooth, bending strides. If you don't have room to do this safely, continue around F and finish by jumping G as your final fence.

6. Complete your round with a quiet canter circle and a smooth downward transition, just as if you were in the show ring.

If your horse isn't putting together a steady round for you, try to analyze the problems and check chapter 11, "Troubleshooting" for suggested solutions.

Standard Distances

There may be one more element you need to put into place before you head down the road to a local schooling show. If you've been schooling your young horse at anything other than the standard distances (usually multiples of 12'), now it's time to ensure that you're meeting the standards for the type of event you'll expect to compete in. If you're riding a small horse and you've been schooling with a baseline stride of 11', you can always add a stride on a line

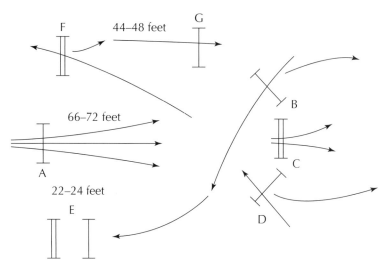

This figure shows a useful schooling set-up that doesn't require many jumps but can be used to create many different courses for different skill levels. (The arrows show several possibilities, not a single course.) You can make the turns smooth and gradual (a bending line from A to B or E, for example) or a little more challenging (D to F or B to E). And a rollback from F to A will truly test your ability to guide and your horse's ability to respond on a snug turn.

of jumps that are set three strides or more apart, but you cannot add a stride in a one-stride or two-stride combination without losing rhythm, jumping awkwardly, and being marked down for it. For a low-hunter class, for example, you'll be expected to ride a 24' in-and-out in one stride and make it look smooth.

So be sure you're able to ride those distances and courses correctly at home—preferably at heights that are 3"–6" higher than what you'll find in competition.

Then, instead of raising the jumps and making the courses more complicated in your home arena, it's time to move to a few different venues and confirm the skills your horse has already learned.

You should now be able to put some "traveling miles" on your not-so-green horse: Go to schooling shows, visit a neighboring stable, ride in a hunter pace, find new trails to ride on, or make a date to ride over a new cross-country course with small, inviting schooling jumps.

Jumping outside the Arena

Jumping obstacles on a trail or a low-level cross-country course is an invaluable experience for a green horse. Logs and walls, banks, ditches, barrels, drop jumps, and water crossings all present different challenges that can

Riding a Schooling Course

You must ride accurately and be absolutely clear about your course plan. A good method for planning a schooling course is to first measure the distances, then walk the course and view the lines from the ground. Next, get on your horse and *walk* him along your intended path, looking for visual focal points, noting where there might be tight corners, uneven footing, distractions, or other obstacles. After you've developed a clear plan, you can jump the course at the correct pace.

When you have a choice of lines to follow, don't assume your horse knows where to go. And *don't* let him choose which jump to take next! You share the navigation duties, but *you* are the pilot. Be clear and plan your approach well in advance of every jump.

Plan for contingencies. What if he lands on the wrong lead? Will you drop to a trot and ask for a simple change of lead, push for a flying change, or continue on the wrong lead? Your decision should be based on your horse's level of training and the requirements of the course—if he's not comfortable with flying changes, don't ask for one. If there's no room to change leads or you're planning to compete in hunter or equitation classes, it's better to continue on the wrong lead than to break gait. If, however, your goal is to help him balance around the next turn, you may want to do a simple change.

Is there a new jump on the course that might cause a problem? Don't risk a run-out by trying to jump at an angle, and don't fly at it as fast as possible in the hopes your horse will go over because he can't stop. Instead, try to give him extra time and room to balance, turn, and look so that he can process the information. Then ride the approach in a round, controlled canter with plenty of impulsion.

Ride the horse, not the jumps. In other words, focus on your horse's path, balance, and rhythm. Let your horse do the jumping.

greatly help to build his confidence and judgment. And the very solid nature of natural jumps will remind a green horse to pick up his toes and judge his efforts correctly.

Just remember the following tips:

- Go with a friend, preferably on a quiet horse who can give you a lead if your horse hesitates.

- Pick your fences carefully, so you can be absolutely certain of the footing and the terrain.

- Ride every jump several times as a single problem before you try to put a course together or attempt to jump anything at cross-country speeds. Galloping is the *last* element to be added to cross-country riding, not the first!

- Choose jumps that are a few inches *lower* than what you've been jumping in the arena. Logs don't fall down if your horse makes a mistake and hangs a leg, so you'll want him to jump carefully and not have to struggle with the height.

- Look for the small jumps that are set on a slight upslope, on a straightaway, and with an open field of vision. Don't tackle any serious terrain questions—drops, *pimple jumps* (set at the top of a hill, with an upsloping approach and a down-sloping landing), any obstacles set on a side slope or a tight turn—until your horse has developed excellent balance and confidence on level ground with a straight approach and landing.

- Don't jump anything with a false ground line (for example, a log with space underneath or a spread that's offset the wrong way, with the higher element in the front).

- Consider trotting the approach to every new fence *except* a bank. (See the "Banks" section, below.) Trotting the approaches will give your green horse time to look, think, and judge, and you don't have to worry about getting the striding correct.

- A running martingale and galloping or splint boots are always a good idea on a green horse. Be sure to wear your protective gear and chaps or grippy breeches!

LOGS AND WALLS

Simple, straightforward jumps over logs or walls shouldn't present any problems on the approach, but be careful about what happens *after* each jump. An exuberant young horse jumping in an open field for the first time may give you a focused, controlled approach, put in a big effort over a small log, and land in a flat-out run, bucking for the sheer excitement of it all.

You mustn't punish him, because he *did* jump, but you need to regain control quickly. One good method is to have your experienced friend on her steady, experienced horse jump first. Ask her to trot over the jump and then halt and stand out of the way about 100' beyond the jump. This will give your horse something familiar to focus on and a point to ride to.

Hopefully, your green horse will follow the other horse's example, including the part after the jump where he slows down and comes to a quiet halt next to his buddy.

BANKS

Hopping up a bank seems simple—it's just the "up" part of a jump, without the "down." But many green horses have trouble with banks on their first try, especially if the bank is additionally supported with a log or small palisade so it looks like a jump. The problem is that his front feet will land on the bank before his hind legs have finished folding and unfolding, so he may lose momentum and scramble. It can feel as if he's trying to drag himself up with his front end, which is essentially what's happening.

Jumping up a bank requires more energy than this. Pandora has dropped to a cautious trot, losing momentum. With her hind legs not pushing together, she must pull herself up with her front end—not an easy task. The approach to a bank, even a small one, must be from a round, vigorous canter so the horse can push off energetically with both hind legs, both on the takeoff and in the first stride after the landing.

In the next stride, Pandora registers her displeasure. I should have applied my legs firmly to send her forward. And a running martingale would help me steady her.

To jump up a bank safely, the horse must learn to exert more effort than seems necessary. He can't just canter up and over, as he might do over a jump of similar height. He needs to be quick and strong with his hind end, pushing sharply off the ground and then getting the "landing gear" (hind legs) up onto the bank rapidly, before the front end falters.

You need to help him. Remember that his engine is in the rear, so you've got to engage it with a forward, energetic approach, but don't let him get strung out. Don't trot a bank; canter it. The hind legs have a much better chance of simultaneously planting and pushing at the canter than at the trot, and you'll have more forward momentum at the canter. Add a vigorous leg aid or a touch of your crop one stride before the bank, and keep him *going forward* with his hind legs engaged.

Becoming comfortable with jumping a bank requires experience. After a few attempts, he should figure out that it's easier to get up the bank if he expends some serious effort and brings those hind legs up quickly.

DITCHES

Find a ditch or depression about 2'–3' wide and shallow enough for your horse to step down into and clamber through if he needs to. Following your lead horse, go back and forth at a walk, letting your horse find his way through however he wants to. Be prepared for anything: a gigantic leap, a cautious slide down and lurch up, or a sudden decision to depart the scene entirely. Keep your hands wide to channel him, look where you want to go, and sit deep and anchored with your heels down.

After your horse has made his way through or over the ditch a few times at a walk, ask your friend to lead you over at a trot. Chances are, your horse will hop over the depression rather than have to deal with stepping down and then up again. But if he trots down through it instead of jumping over, that's okay at this stage of his training. Later, you can introduce him to larger ditches that he won't be able to climb down into.

You can also encourage him to jump instead of trot through the ditch by placing a jump rail or heavy tree branch on each lip of the ditch to delineate its edges. Now when you approach at a trot, he should jump the ditch, poles and all.

BARRELS

Some cross-country courses include a jump made from plastic barrels, and many hunter courses include rolltops, which look somewhat like barrels. I'm not entirely sure why, but many novice riders and green horses have problems with barrels. It's actually very easy to introduce your green horse to a low jump made from barrels, and it's a good trust-building exercise.

Ride up, dismount, and let your horse investigate the barrels thoroughly. Then have your helper hold your horse while you remove one or two of the middle barrels. Be sure your horse is watching from a safe distance, so he can see that the barrels might move but aren't going to threaten him. (If he shows concern about the barrels moving, take a few minutes to roll one *away* from him and ask him to follow. From the horse's point of view, if it were a dangerous predator, the barrel would chase him, wouldn't it? Predators don't move away, so it can't be a predator.)

Then lead him up to and through the gap in the middle of the jump. If he needs to examine the barrels again, let him. Next, mount and ride back and forth through the gap, following your lead horse if necessary.

Now trot through the gap, and perhaps even canter through if he feels confident and you've left a fairly wide gap.

Finally, close up the gap, be sure the barrels are firmly fixed in place so they won't roll, let your horse examine it again if he wants to, then follow your lead horse and ride over the barrels at an energetic trot. The first jump will probably be awkward—just keep encouraging your horse and trot back and forth over the barrels until the exercise becomes almost boring.

It's not possible to dismantle all the jumps you'll ever meet, but this technique of creating a gap and then moving the elements closer together also works well with flower boxes, coops, and brush boxes that are built in two sections.

Pandora is learning how to get comfortable with barrels. Examine . . .

. . . walk through the gap . . .

. . . and trot over the barrels. (Note: For safety, use plastic barrels.)

179

DROP JUMPS

Don't tackle a drop jump until your horse can balance well up and down hills and he's had plenty of practice jumping small fences on level ground, both in and outside of the arena. The challenges presented by a drop can frighten a green horse and threaten your safety.

To prepare for riding a drop, practice riding down moderately steep slopes. Be sure your horse is able and willing to "sit down" and put the brakes on, as shown in the pictures on pages 58 and 73.

Your horse's first drop jump should be small, 18" or less, and solidly built with secure, level footing for takeoff and landing. There should be nothing slippery that might slide under his feet.

Approach a drop *slowly,* preferably at a walk. Let the reins slip a little and give your horse a chance to look down and locate his landing spot. (You, of course, must look up!) Stay in a light seat, specifically a modified safety position with your heels well down.

Pandora is approaching this drop in good balance at a nicely balanced short trot—a walk would also be appropriate for a green horse.

She drops down close to the base of the log—much safer than flying outward in a long leap, especially if the landing has a slope to it—and lands straight. Compare our balance and position in this picture to the one on page 122, where the log is on level ground.

Encourage him forward but don't rush him. What you want is for him to just pop down cautiously and land in a few strides of trot or canter. What you *don't* want is a *space shot,* which is a huge leap forward, outward, and downward that will upset your horse's balance and possibly dislodge you.

As your horse drops down, keep your seat deep but light, with weight in your heels. Let your hands give and slip the reins a little more if necessary. Be prepared to gather up the reins again as your horse lands and goes forward into canter, but be careful not to snatch the reins sharply. It's normal for a green horse to sort of lurch back into the canter as his downward trajectory changes back into forward impulsion. (And some horses will register their unhappiness with a buck on landing. See the chapter 11, "Troubleshooting," to create better balance on landing.)

Perhaps more than any other type of jump, riding a drop jump on a green horse requires you and your horse to trust each other. You must trust to let him have his head, and then allow the entire front end of the horse to disappear downward while you stay centered and balanced. And your horse must trust you to stay centered and balanced, so he can overcome gravity and keep you both safe.

WATER CROSSINGS

You've probably crossed streams and puddles on your trail rides, but crossing water on a cross-country course is a little more challenging.

First, find a shallow pond or stream with excellent footing that you can walk, trot, and canter through. Ideally, you'll have access to a cross-country course with a water splash (a jumping complex created from a shallow pond). The footing should be solid and secure with the water no more than 12" deep, and there should be several options for entering and leaving the water: an area with gradually sloping sides, a bank that can be jumped on the way in or out, and possibly a jump set in the middle of the water crossing.

As you did on your earlier trail rides, encourage your horse to investigate and become thoroughly comfortable with walking through the water. Use a lead horse to show him the way, but be prepared to hop off and lead him through the water yourself if he's hesitant. Most horses enjoy splashing in water once they've learned to trust their footing (and their riders), but be sure not to let him stop and roll.

If you plan to compete your horse in combined training (see chapter 10), you'll need to practice trotting and cantering through the water as well. At anything faster than a walk, you'll need to consider how the drag of the water will affect your horse's effort and movement. If the water is only a few inches deep, there's not much drag, but if the depth is more than 6", you'll quickly notice the extra effort he has to put into his steps.

Your approach to a water crossing should be at a walk, a strong trot, or a balanced, round canter. Don't let your horse sprawl forward in a long frame on a loose rein, because the drag of the water will slow down his front end while his hindquarters are still pushing forward—and that has the makings of a somersault. Practice trotting and eventually cantering through in three-point position to let your horse use his back and hindquarters more effectively.

Don't attempt jumping into, out of, or in the middle of a water splash until you and your horse have had plenty of practice walking, trotting, and *cantering* through shallow streams and splashes.

After you've given your horse a solid all-around education in and out of the arena, you can begin to specialize in your jumping and consider the additional skills you'll both need for various types of competition.

Chapter 10

SPECIALIZING:
FINDING THE RIGHT FIT

Many riders enjoy partnering with their "all-around" horses in a variety of activities: participating in a hunter pace one weekend, a low-level combined test a week later, and trail riding in between. Perhaps your horse also works part-time as a lesson horse, carrying different riders at different skill levels, at Pony Club rallies or at local schooling shows.

All the training outlined in the previous chapters of this book is designed for this "generalist" approach to riding and jumping, with the belief that every horse and rider can benefit from experiencing a wide variety of activities as part of basic training.

But to do really well in any type of competitive jumping, you'll need to specialize, because each discipline requires a higher level of particular skills. This chapter addresses the specific demands of these different disciplines and explains how to develop the resources you'll need to reach beyond the "generalist" approach to jumping.

Competition horses generally fall into one of four types:

1. Show-ring hunters

2. Equitation mounts

3. Jumpers

4. Eventers

Other less-competitive jumping activities include hunter paces and field hunting. Depending on your skills, you and your horse may be able to cross-train successfully for some of these disciplines. Show-ring hunters, for example, often make good equitation horses. Eventers may be bold field hunters or lower-level show jumpers. The demands of these different disciplines are explained in this chapter.

A Critical Component: Your Coach

When you began riding, you needed full-time supervision to stay safe and learn the basic skills. So, riding probably meant paying for instruction. If you're like most riders, you began learning to ride at a local multipurpose stable or possibly as part of a camp or school program. Your first instructor was probably a generalist, someone who could give you sound basics on the flat, lead you out on the trails, and perhaps help you understand how to ride over small jumps.

But as your skills improved—and especially if you've been fortunate enough to own or lease your own horse—you've probably spent several periods in your life when you've ridden without any instruction. You may have decided you could get by without professional coaching, or the costs of horse ownership may have forced you to decide between paying the farrier's bill and signing up for instruction.

But the bottom line is that you owe it to yourself and to your horse to continue learning and improving your skills. Even the top coaches take instruction from their peers. They participate in clinics, watch other riders, critique their own performances, read books, and watch DVDs to hone their riding skills.

And if you really want to succeed in a specific riding discipline, you'll need a coach who excels in that field. At this level, your instructor is not simply a good teacher; she's also a topnotch manager who will help you make decisions about everything from conditioning and shoeing to selecting a new saddle or choosing a show schedule. She'll even help you set goals and recover from setbacks.

CHOOSING A COACH

When you began riding, you didn't care whether your teacher was a jumper rider or a three-day eventer. You probably chose that instructor (or your parents chose the instructor for you) because the stable was near your house or your friends rode there, and the price was reasonable.

Now, however, as you begin to specialize and think about more serious competitions, you need to choose a specialist, someone who can help guide you down a specific path to your particular goals.

Think about the following considerations before hiring a coach:

1. First, decide what's important to you. What are your goals? Which discipline? Will you try to compete with your present horse, or will you want your trainer to help you find a new horse? How far are you hoping to go?

2. Next, be straightforward about the cost. How much can you afford to spend and what does that money pay for? How important is it for you to ride at a prestigious facility? Do you need access to schoolmaster horses or are you primarily interested in riding your own horse? Will the lessons be private or in a group?

3. Then ask lots of questions. Get recommendations from riders whom you admire. Then ask questions about an instructor's methods, her emphasis on safety, and whether she treats her students and horses with respect. Will this person communicate openly with you and can you trust her?

4. And finally, how flexible will this instructor-student relationship be? Will you be tied into a rigid schedule, or can it be on an as-needed basis? Many riders work with a regular instructor and also attend clinics with other trainers to gain a fresh approach to problem-solving. Will your regular instructor support your going to clinics, or will she feel threatened?

Ultimately, you need to be utterly comfortable with your instructor, you need to believe you're getting good value for the money you're spending, and you need to feel safe, so you can concentrate on your riding.

If regular coaching is impossible because of time, distance, or budget, a dedicated rider with a good foundation can learn a lot by watching top-notch riders and trainers, and studying instructional books and DVDs. (See the "References" section at the back of this book for a list of recommended reading.) When you're trying to troubleshoot a particular problem or special situation, however, there's no substitute for hands-on education. Try to spend at least a couple of hours each month under a top trainer's eye to be sure you're heading in the right direction with your horse.

Making Sense of the Competitive Scene

In the United States, the competitive riding world is amazingly complex. We have USEF, FEI, USHJA, USEA, and USET. Then there's Pony Club and the breed organizations, plus state, regional, and local riding clubs.

Each organization promotes a specific aspect of the horse industry and recognizes different levels of competition, depending on the focus of its members. Here's a quick summary of the best-known organizations:

- **U.S. Equestrian Federation (USEF):** This is the national governing body for equestrian sport in the U.S. It regulates and oversees most *equestrian competitions* in the U.S., helps set industry regulations and standards, and serves as the national member of the Fédération Equestre Internationale (FEI). The USEF rule book is the "bible" for many competitions at the local as well as national level. Web site: www.usef.org.

- **Fédération Equestre Internationale (FEI):** The international governing body for all Olympic equestrian disciplines (dressage, eventing, jumping) and FEI World Equestrian Games (dressage, driving, endurance, eventing, jumping, reining, vaulting). Web site: www.horsesport.org.

- **U.S. Hunter Jumper Association (USHJA):** An affiliate of the USET, the USHJA promotes the sport of hunter and jumper competitions. Major programs include trainer certification and young-rider development programs. Web site: www.ushja.org.

- **U.S. Eventing Association (USEA):** This organization promotes education, training, competition, and organizer support in the sport of combined training or eventing, also called the *horse triathlon.* Eventing requires excellence in the three disciplines of dressage, cross-country jumping, and stadium jumping. Web site: www.useventing.com.

- **U.S. Equestrian Team Foundation (USET):** Provides fund-raising and support for the training, coaching, and mentoring programs for U.S. team members in the seven high-performance international disciplines of dressage, jumping, eventing, driving, endurance, vaulting, para-equestrian sports, and reining. Web site: www.uset.org.

- **U.S. Pony Clubs:** Originating in England, this international organization promotes education and skills development for young riders in thirty countries. Programs vary by location, but usually involve dressage, eventing, show jumping, knowledge quizzes and stable management, and may also include mounted games, tetrathlon, quizzes, vaulting, foxhunting, and polocrosse (a combination of polo and lacrosse on horseback). Web site: www.ponyclub.org.

- **American Quarter Horse Association (AQHA):** The largest breed organization in the U.S., the AQHA has expanded in recent decades from its original western-riding orientation to embrace hunter and jumper competitions. AQHA rules often differ from the USEF format. Web site: www.aqha.org.

When you're considering competitive venues, it's important to be sure you're thoroughly familiar with the rules, regulations, and expectations of the governing organization. Be sure to join the association that governs your discipline and take advantage of the educational resources available.

And be sure to read the rule book! Rule books contain far more than just information on how not to get eliminated. Heights of fences for different divisions, class formats and protocols, judging criteria, and notes on equipment and expected attire are all in there.

What Can You and Your Horse Accomplish?

Nearly any horse-and-rider team with solid basic training and a good coach should, with practice, be able to jump adequately around a low-hunter course at a local show or safely canter around a beginner-novice cross-country course.

But if you want to succeed in a highly competitive jumping discipline, you'll need the right horse. Your horse will need not only the ability but also the temperament and the willingness to partner with you. First, review the discussion about conformation, temperament, and suitability in chapter 2, "Finding Talented Horses," and then cast a critical eye over your own horse. Is he suitable for what you have in mind?

If you're absolutely determined to tackle the junior jumper division and your horse is more of a solid-citizen Pony Club guy, capable over 3'3" but not much more, then you're going to have to make some hard decisions. Can you afford a second horse? Will you lease or sell the one you own?

THE SHOW-RING HUNTER

Although few show-ring hunters today are actually ridden in the hunting field, judges are still looking for the horse that they would choose to ride on a long foxhunt. The judging of hunters is entirely subjective.

Winning show-ring hunters are beautiful and stylish. They must display consistently excellent jumping form, flawless balance, and a willing attitude. Only the horse is judged, not the rider, but a good rider knows how to show-case his horse's ability and responsiveness by riding very quietly with subtle aids. Over the jumps, the rider should show off his horse with a slightly loose rein in the crest release, as proof that the horse will jump with little direction from the rider.

Any breed of horse can compete as a hunter in *open* (non–breed-oriented) shows, but the winners tend to be thoroughbreds or warmbloods, 16 to 17 hands in height.

Specific training goals should focus on improving your horse's responsiveness, his movement and balance on the flat, and his form over fences. To be competitive, he'll need to have:

- *Excellent form over fences.* Style counts a lot. Your horse should jump from a correct and consistent distance, tuck his legs up evenly, and create a round bascule to follow the arc of the jump.

- *Excellent balance and movement on the flat.* His gaits should be forward and fluid but never rushed, and relaxed but alert and confident. His stride should be long and low with minimal knee and hock action. He travels straight with a pleasant expression, his neck and back are stretched and relaxed, his head is down with slight flexion at the poll, and his face is in front of the vertical. He should hold a steady rhythm with only very light contact and direction from the rider.

- *Smooth, relaxed, and balanced lead changes.* Your horse should perform prompt flying changes on the flat or over fences, without changing late, cross-cantering, or resisting (no pinned ears, swishing tail, tense back, or bucking).

- *Scope.* Hunter courses have become more technical and challenging in the last several years, so your horse should be scopey enough to make the distance in a combination and agile enough to handle a rollback.

Show-Ring Style: Courtesy Circles

Each hunter or hunt seat equitation round should include an opening, or courtesy, circle and may (but doesn't have to) include a closing circle after you jump the last fence on the course. These circles are important transition times for the horse and rider. The *opening circle* establishes the rhythm and pace, while the *closing circle* creates a smooth and safe transition back to a walk before the horse exits the arena. Experienced riders know that these circles can also be used to show off a horse's gaits and responsiveness.

The rules allow you to make just one opening circle, so make good use of the room that's available to you. The circle doesn't have to be perfectly round, but it should have no sharp turns and your horse should not be counter-bent or trying to drift back toward the in-gate.

Know where you can and can't make your opening circle—be sure you don't cross over the dotted line marked on the course diagram, if there is one.

Make your circle in the same direction as the first part of the course—for example, make a clockwise circle if you're required to pick up the right lead and proceed clockwise to start the course. The goal is to establish a smooth, steady canter well before you approach the first fence.

If your horse has a lovely canter but not a wonderful trot, you can move right from walk into canter, and then canter your entire opening circle. If your horse has a nice fluid trot, you might want to show that off for a few strides before picking up the canter.

When you finish your round, a closing circle is a good idea if the last jump has you heading straight for the gate. You'll want to transition smoothly back to a walk, and the closing circle gives you room to do that. If the last jump on the course has you heading away from the gate, you probably have plenty of room to transition quietly to a trot and then a walk before arriving at the gate. The goal is to finish smoothly and in obvious control, showing your horse's steadiness and responsiveness every moment that you're in the ring.

To save time, many shows now require riders to perform two or more rounds in fairly quick succession in a "rotation" format. Brush up on your memorization skills, include an opening and perhaps a closing circle in your course strategy, and don't assume the rider who went just before you is riding the same course that you'll need to do next.

- *Perfect manners in company.* He should ignore the other horses in the flat class, moving steadily regardless of what happens around him. He should transition smoothly from a walk to a canter with no trot steps, and from a canter to a balanced hand gallop to a quiet halt.

Years ago, outside courses were popular at many shows. Outside courses demanded a big, forward stride—a true "hunting pace"—and the distance for an in-and-out was often set at 26"–28". Today, because of time and space limitations, most hunter courses are in a standard arena, so the distance for a one-stride in-and-out is usually set at 24".

Horses showing in a regular hunter division will be expected to jump 4'–4'6". First-year green hunters generally compete at 3'6", junior hunters at 3'3"–3'6", and adult amateur hunters at 2'9"–3'.

HUNT SEAT EQUITATION

Good equitation is the basis for all effective riding. Equitation emphasizes a rider's form, control, effectiveness, and judgment, whether on the flat or over fences. The judging is subjective and, theoretically, the horse's performance should not count in scoring. But in reality a good horse can make a mediocre rider look good and a poor horse can cause an excellent rider to look ineffective.

In a hunter class, the horse is supposed to look as if he's performing beautifully with almost no direction from the rider. In equitation, the rider provides more direction and therefore rides with more contact.

A good equitation horse is expected to travel in a slightly more compressed frame than a hunter and be a little quicker to respond to the aids. He gives a prompt response to a request for stride adjustments and transitions. His flying changes are prompt and correct, and he can manage tight turns with good balance and impulsion.

CYNTHIA DEMETER

Good equitation requires good planning, so Rachel looks for the turn while in the air over the first fence, but doesn't begin her turn until she knows her path. Nani is jumping straight and square as Rachel asks her to change and land on her right lead. This is a nice example of a well-executed strategy.

Riding a Rollback

Jumper, advanced equitation, and even hunter courses may require a rollback, which is a tight U-turn from one jump to another. In a jumper class, you'll want to get as quickly as possible from one jump to the next, but in an equitation or hunter class, a rollback is designed to test your ability to shorten stride, plan a path, make a prompt, balanced turn, and find a distance to a single fence. (See the diagram on page 174: The turn from Fence F to Fence A is a rollback.)

To perform a rollback in an equitation or hunter class:

1. Ride the first jump straight through the center.

2. In the air over the first fence, use your eyes to locate your turn to the second jump. Ask for the correct lead, but be sure your horse lands straight over the first fence.

3. Keep your eyes on your path as you shorten stride and slow the pace for the turn to the second fence. Keep the pace slow but the impulsion strong.

4. Establish a new straight line to the second jump and reestablish your baseline stride and pace, as you look for a distance to the second jump.

How tightly you turn in the rollback depends on two key factors:

How much can you safely shorten your horse's stride for a tight turn? If you slow the pace and shorten the stride to make the turn, you *must* increase the impulsion or he'll "stall" on the approach to the second jump. If you're not sure about your ability to keep his engine engaged, use more room for the turn and keep the pace forward.

If, however, you're confident about making a balanced turn—say it's a rollback to the left and your horse prefers his left lead—you can show off your talent a bit by making quite a snug turn.

How clearly can you see the path to the second jump? Both you and your horse need to see where you're going. If anything is obstructing your view, wait and give yourselves more room to turn.

Basic equitation classes are often divided by age and competition experience. These lower-level classes feature simple courses with standardized striding and large, smooth turns.

The most advanced equitation classes for juniors are the U.S. Equestrian Federation (USEF) Medal, the American Association for the Prevention of Cruelty to Animals (ASPCA) Maclay, the Professional Horsemen's Association (PHA) Medal, and the USEF Talent Search classes, in which riders earn points to qualify for national championships. In USEF, PHA, and Maclay classes, the jumps are 3'6" high with 4' spreads (up to 5' spreads for triple bars). In the USEF Talent Search classes, judges are looking for the next generation of show-jumping riders, so the jumps are set from 3'6" to 3'9" with spreads up to 5'. The courses include combinations, changes of direction, roll-backs, and "skinny" fences. At this level, riders should manage the tight turns, stride adjustments, and lead changes with ease and control.

JUMPERS

Jumper classes are highly competitive crowd-pleasers and the showcase events at any show. At the highest (Grand Prix) levels, these classes attract sponsors and award substantial prize money. Successful competitors may become eligible for Olympic team consideration. Even at the lowest levels—such as local shows and Pony Club rallies—the jumper classes draw the most enthusiastic spectators.

Jumpers are judged objectively on their ability to clear high jumps at speed. Form doesn't count, as long as the jumps stay up and the rider stays on. Faults include disobediences, rails knocked down, and exceeding the time allowed. In some competitions, *touches* (touching a rail without knocking it down) may also incur penalties.

The USEF designates different levels of classes, which define how high and wide the jumps can be. Level 1, for example, has jumps up to 3' in height and 3'6" in width. The height for each level increases by 3" up to Level 9, which has jumps up to 5' and spreads to 5'6". Jumpers can be of any breed or size, as long as they're strong, agile, fast, and scopey. The best jumpers are bold but careful, demonstrating excellent natural balance and a desire to jump cleanly. Necessary skills for the horse and rider include the ability to:

- Jump at an angle or turn in the air.
- Rapidly adjust speed and shorten or lengthen stride.
- Make very tight turns.
- Jump from a very long or very short spot.

Walking the course: Check terrain, turns, focal points, and line of sight, then visualize everything you're going to do correctly.

Tips: Walking a Course in the Arena

Whatever your discipline, make it a habit to walk a course whenever you're given the opportunity. And be sure to analyze what you're seeing. Bring your coach, the course diagram, and a pen to make notes. As you walk, look for the following:

1. *Courtesy circle.* Where will you do this? Be sure not to cross the dotted line (if there is one) shown on the course diagram.

2. *Line to the first fence.* How much room do you have to establish your pace? Are you heading toward or away from the in-gate, and how will this affect your horse's stride and rhythm?

3. *Distances in combinations.* Pace out the distance and decide how you'll ride it. If a combination consists of a vertical to a vertical at 24' on a slight upslope, and you're riding a horse with an 11' baseline stride, then you're going to have to power *forward* all the way to make it through safely in one big stride.

4. *Distances on longer lines.* Look beyond the last fence in the line, see where you'll want to go next, and decide what path to follow. If it's a bending line, will you be conservative, add a stride. and jump both fences straight? Or take the direct route and angle the jumps?

5. *Terrain and footing.* Is there a slight slope that will cause your horse to lengthen stride going downhill? Is the footing hard, soft, muddy, or inconsistent? How will this affect your plan to ride a turn or angle a fence?

Jumper courses often include both a double and a triple combination, with varied striding to test your horse's scope and strength. Half the jumps may be *spreads*—wide oxers or triple bars. Before entering a jumper class, be sure you're schooling over jumps that are slightly higher and wider than what you'll find at the show, and be sure to practice riding *doubles* and *triples* (combinations of two and three jumps) set at competition distances. You must be sure your horse has plenty of scope to make the distances between jumps. Many small horses with limited scope can jump a single big jump in good form, but can't manage the 24'–26' distance to the next big jump in a double or triple combination.

Also, be sure you understand and can gauge the speed you'll need. A jumper course must be ridden in the "time allowed," commonly set at 382 yards per minute. That's faster than what an equitation or hunter round requires. Use a surveyor's measuring wheel to mark out a course. Practice galloping at that speed, or a little faster, and then practice jumping at that pace.

6. *Line of sight.* Pick out a focal point for each line of jumps. Is anything obstructing your view as you approach the line? How long will it take you to find the focus? Can you shorten or lengthen the approach to find a better line of sight?

7. *The nature of the jumps.* Which jumps are verticals, which are oxers? How will you ride a "tight" distance to an oxer or an "open" distance to a vertical? Are there skinny jumps that require dead-center accuracy?

8. *New obstacles.* Is there anything you haven't seen or jumped before that bothers you or might give your horse pause? Figure out a way to ride that jump by comparing it to something you've both jumped successfully before. Can you address this by jumping something similar in the warm-up area?

9. *Distractions.* These might include judges' stands, flapping flags, vehicles, or the loudspeaker. Figure out a plan to keep yourself and your horse calm and focused.

10. *The jump-off.* If it's a jumper class, note the jump-off sequence on your diagram, and walk this separately. You won't get a second chance.

If you have trouble remembering courses, then you will need to work at developing visualization skills. Look at the diagram, look at the actual fences, and then close your eyes and visualize the course.

Practice walking a course whenever you have a chance, whether you're in that class or not! (But don't get in the way of the actual competitors. They always have priority.)

FIELD HUNTERS

Field hunters carry their riders for many miles over the countryside, following hounds on a foxhunt or a *drag hunt* (in which artificial scent is laid; no live quarry is chased). Field hunters need strength, stamina, and the ability to remain calm in the company of many other horses and a pack of hounds. The best field hunters tend to be sturdier and less elegant than their show-ring cousins. They can be any breed, color, or size.

Many field hunters are talented jumpers, capable of safely jumping 4' or higher fences in rough terrain. Other horses (or their riders) may only be comfortable over a 2' wall. Many hunts allow riders to *hilltop*, which means to stay at the back of the field and away from the main galloping and jumping action. *Hilltoppers* are often riders on green horses, small children on ponies, and other folks who wish to participate on a limited basis without jumping high fences.

Different Jumps, Different Distances

The width of a jump affects a horse's take-off point. Horses tend to get *deep* (close) to a vertical on take-off. And when they take off close with a steep angle of ascent, then they also tend to land closer on the far side. These horses tend to stand back on takeoff and land farther out from an oxer. So each type of fence must be ridden slightly differently, especially if it's in a combination. For example, you'd have a slightly different plan for each combination even if the distances were all set at 24' (measured from center to center of the jumps). Here's a list of combinations and suggestions for how to ride them:

- *Vertical to vertical:* Ride this in a steady one stride and prepare to open up his stride in the middle if he lands too close to the first fence.

- *Oxer to vertical:* Prepare to sit up and shorten the stride in the middle of the in-and-out, because your horse will land deep into the combination after jumping the oxer and his next stride may put him close to the vertical.

- *Vertical to oxer:* Open up the middle stride, especially if takeoff to the first fence is tight. Help him make the distance to the oxer by riding *forward*.

- *Oxer to oxer:* The first oxer can encourage him to make such a big effort that he lands too deep into the middle and then has to back himself off from the second oxer. Keep the approach and the middle stride round and bouncy, not forward and flat.

Remember that other factors can affect your horse's stride length. A horse tends to lengthen stride when he speeds up, goes down a slope, sees a wide open space, heads back toward the barn, or feels fresh. His strides will tend to shorten in a high-walled arena, when he's tired, or when the footing isn't ideal.

Field hunters must be excellent trail horses, sure-footed, and smart about managing un-level ground, water, mud, and rocks. They must be able to gallop strongly, and then stop and wait quietly without fussing while the hounds find a scent. Horses that excel in the cross-country phase of eventing can also make good field hunters, but field hunters must display an extra dose of calmness and good manners in company—virtues that aren't required of eventers.

Many riders who enjoy foxhunting also like to ride in hunter trials and hunter paces. *Hunter trials* are judged competitions that feature hunt teams (usually three riders riding together) and individuals who ride at hunting pace over an outside course.

Hunter paces are competitions held over longer courses, usually 6 to 10 miles. Teams of two or three riders travel together through fields and trails, negotiating obstacles and jumping fences that are normally found in hunt country. It's not a race; instead, riders attempt to match an optimal time for the ride, which tests their ability to judge hunting pace and rate their horses based on the varied terrain. The winning team is the one that completes the course closest to the optimal time.

CYNTHIA DEMETER

EVENTERS

Originally referred to as the "military," *three-phase eventing* (also called horse trials, combined training, or the horse triathlon) evolved from cavalry training programs that emphasized the total development of athletic horses and riders through dressage (obedience, balance, and precision), cross-country jumping

Eventing means cross-training. At the lower levels, the horse who wins the dressage generally wins the event. Wile E Coyote, a Quarter Horse/Hanoverian cross who excels in dressage, doesn't exhibit the tight front end of a classic hunter, but he presents a very athletic bascule and a great attitude for Greta in a novice-level event.

(endurance and ability to travel at speed over solid obstacles and natural terrain challenges), and stadium jumping (handiness, precision, and agility over jumps in the arena).

Event riders embrace the concept of *cross-training,* using the skills learned in one phase of the sport to improve performance in the other two. They thoroughly enjoy the neverending process of learning and tend to be strong self-learners—because not many riders can afford three coaches for the three different phases!

Good event horses can be any breed or size, as long as they're strong, bold, honest, and confident. They need good natural balance and must love to gallop and jump, yet also be compliant and responsive in order to perform well in dressage. At the lower levels (Beginner Novice, Novice, and Training), the horse that wins in dressage is also likely to win the event, because the jumping tests are fairly straightforward and many competitors will go clean in cross-country and stadium (in a ring or arena) jumping.

HAMILTON AHLO, JR.

A big bank on a cross-country course requires a big effort with plenty of impulsion. Emma has brought her horse in at a good forward pace and is staying well forward to stay off his back and allow the hind legs to get up quickly.

CHANDRA CHOWANEC

Prepare yourself and your horse to deal with distractions and surprises on a cross-country course, such as people, vehicles, and strange-looking fences. Try to simulate the situations you know you'll face when competing.

Cross-country is at the heart of eventing. The courses at the lower levels are often around 2,000 meters (1.25 miles) long and they include a variety of natural obstacles such as logs, walls, ditches, water crossings, and banks. The terrain may be flat or hilly. Cross-country requires speeds of 300 mpm (meters per minute) for Beginner Novice riders to 470 mpm for Training level. Novice-level cross-country courses require horses to jump fences that are up to 2'11" high and up to 4'11" wide at the base; Beginner Novice jumps are no higher than 2'7" and up to 4' wide. Jumper riders tend to think of these as "baby" jumps, until they gain respect for the length of the courses and the difficulties of the terrain.

Stadium jumping courses are simply jumper courses, often with a few extra twists and turns to demonstrate handiness, but without the extra speed or the raised fences of a jump-off. Horses at the lower levels need to jump at speeds of 300–325 mpm. That's not especially fast when compared to an open jumper round, but if your horse is tired after your cross-country ride, he's likely to drop a few rails and incur jumping penalties during the stadium jumping phase.

To do well in eventing, you and your horse must be well-conditioned and well-prepared for all three phases. You'll also need to gain experience and learn certain skills that are unique to cross-country jumping. Here are some training recommendations:

- *Practice jumping very narrow fences.* At the lower levels, cross-country jumps are simple and straightforward, and they're not very high. So, to create more of a challenge, designers have begun incorporating narrow fences into many courses. (For a useful exercise jumping narrow fences, see the "Disobediences (Refusals)" section in chapter 11.)

- *Practice jumping banks, drops, and ditches.* Jump into and out of water. Jump bounces at a canter. (Set the distance to 12'–13', a little longer than what you used in the practice grids, and approach at a strong canter.)

- *Get comfortable trotting and galloping up and down hills.* Practice slowing and shortening your horse's stride to jump on a downhill slope. Use your safety position and know when and how to slip your reins.

- *Practice jumping corner fences and angled fences on a bending line.* To practice jumping a corner fence, set two jumps at a 45-degree angle, touching each other at one end to create a corner. The support for the rails where the two jumps meet should not protrude above the height of the rails; you can use a barrel or Stacker System standard to replace a regular post-standard. Then practice jumping this corner fence on a very precise line, centering your approach on a spot about 3' in from the corner.

- *Consider additional equipment needs.* A breast collar or overgirth will help keep your saddle from slipping. A protective vest is required. If you use a running martingale, be sure it's long enough to give your horse freedom of his head and neck when landing off a steep drop.

- *Schedule time for conditioning.* You and your horse must both be fit enough to gallop for a mile and a half, without becoming winded. Practice holding your two-point position for 2-, 3-, 4- and eventually 5-minute gallop intervals, on gentle hills as well as flat terrain.

- *Be able to pace yourself for cross-country and stadium jumping.* Novice eventers are required to travel at 300 mpm (meters per minute) on cross-country—barely more than a brisk canter. However, if the course is trappy and muddy, and you must frequently slow down to a trot, then you'll have to go faster in the straightaways to make up time. (And remember that if you go too fast, you may be penalized with speed faults.) Buy a good stopwatch, mark out a set distance in a field or on a galloping track, and time your gallops so you can develop a feel for the pace.

Strategies for a Successful Round

No matter what your discipline, if your planning and practice are thorough, then you can ride a successful round over fences.

Remember these key points:

1. *Prepare yourself and your horse before you go.* Every show is a learning experience, but you should try to be prepared and learn as much as

Walking a Cross-Country Course

You can walk a stadium or show-jumping course in 15 minutes, but to properly walk a mile-long novice cross-country course you must allocate an hour or more. Walking a cross-country course is a safety issue, not just a performance concern. Riders at the higher levels often walk the entire course two or three times, and then go back to analyze the more challenging sections a third or fourth time. No matter what your level of competition, if the event offers a scheduled course walk with one of the event officials, be sure to attend!

Many novice-level event riders don't have a coach handy at the competition, but it's a good idea to walk the course with a friend—a fellow competitor, your groom, or a riding buddy. It's easy to miss key items such as flags and directional markers when you're on your own, especially if the course is marked for several different levels of competition.

Many of the crucial factors on a cross-country course are similar to what you'll find in an arena—the nature of the jumps themselves, any related distances, options for turns—but there are several challenges here that you won't find in the arena.

Be sure to bring your course diagram. Many riders also bring the rule book, a tape measure, and a camera to help them measure what they're seeing and also to create a record of the jumps so they can build similar obstacles for schooling at home.

Things to look for:

1. *Start, finish, directional markers, and jump flags for your level.* Know the course. Know which course is yours, as several levels may share the same path and even the same jumps. Note if two jumps are

possible before you spend money to compete. Try to minimize surprises. Don't enter a 4' jumper class if you've only been jumping 3'6" at home. Don't show in critical new equipment (boots, saddle, horseshoes, bit) that you haven't fitted, tested, and practiced with at home.

2. *Know the rules for this class, in this division, at this show.* Really know the rules so you won't be eliminated on a technicality such as jumping a fence the wrong way in the warm-up area, carrying a crop that's too long, or leaving the bell boots on your horse when you ride your hunter round.

3. *Organize your support team.* You'll need at least one friend along to help you memorize a course or hold your horse while you walk the course. Besides, it's more fun with friends.

labeled A and B, or have separate numbers, so if you have a refusal you'll know whether you need to re-jump both or just the one.

2. *Surprises and distractions.* Green horses can be very distracted at the sight of spectators in the woods or jump judges sitting in lawn chairs. Where are these distractions likely to be? How can you keep your horse and yourself focused?

3. *Condition of the ground.* If your round is late in the day and the approach to a jump becomes a deep mud-hole, what are your options? What's on the landing side? Should you jump dead center or take a different option?

4. *Straight approaches.* You've walked the course but your horse has not. Create a precise route to each jump that will bring your horse in straight—this is especially important with narrow jumps, which are tremendously popular with course designers. Find a focal point for each jump.

5. *Know where you can circle if you need to.* You're allowed to circle between jumps on a cross-country course as long as you're not on a direct approach to a jump. Check the rule book.

6. *Look for what you should do.* There are so many variables on a cross-country course that it becomes easy to see how many things can go wrong. Don't focus on the mistakes you might make; instead, visualize where to go and how to do everything well. And don't look at the jumps you don't have to jump! You can always come back later and watch the higher-level rides—after your ride is finished.

4. *Plan your warm up.* Spend most of your time warming up on the flat, concentrating on balance and responsiveness. Jump a couple of low jumps, then jump two or three that are just a little higher than what you'll face in competition. Then, if you've timed it right, you'll be able to leave the warm-up area and begin your round while your horse is fresh.

5. *Visualize success.* Plan how you will ride, not how you won't ride. (And have a Plan B in mind in case your horse doesn't like Plan A.) Pat your horse, tell him he's wonderful, and go prove it.

6. *Focus. Breathe. Enjoy.*

Competitive success shouldn't be your only goal in riding, but it can serve as a solid validation for lessons well taught and learned.

Chapter 11

TROUBLESHOOTING

I f you're running into problems with your jumping, ask your coach or a knowledgeable friend to help you figure out what's happening and figure out what corrections might be needed. Video and photographs can be very useful when you're trying to analyze a problem.

Trainers often categorize problems as either rider problems or horse problems. The solutions, however, are always the rider's responsibility.

Rider Problems

DUCKING, DIVING, OR OVER-JUMPING

Riders who "duck and dive" over every jump often think they're helping the horse jump. But a rider who makes a big move or ducks in midair distracts the horse and disrupts his balance. The horse then has to shift his own weight suddenly to compensate for the rider's motion. As a result, many horses will develop evasive or protective behavior: cutting down on the arc of the jump to get back on the ground more quickly, twisting the head or neck to rebalance, or protesting by bucking on landing, which only worsens the balance problems. More tolerant horses may manage to compensate for the rider's sudden shift in balance, but they're still likely to drop a shoulder or knock down a fence in mid-air, because the rider is unbalanced.

Causes

1. A rider who spends a lot of time on a green, hesitant, or sluggish horse often develops the habit of sitting back a bit on the approach to a jump so she can use her legs strongly to keep the horse going, and then over-jumping or throwing her body forward to "catch up" after takeoff.

2. A novice rider may also feel she has to time the takeoff and lurches forward to avoid being left behind, instead of holding her position and waiting for the jumping motion to close her hip angles. This is also called *jumping for the horse.*

3. When a rider begins jumping higher fences, she may also get nervous about the height and drop her eyes, lie on her horse's neck, and look down.

4. If the horse gets too close to the base of a big vertical and the ascent angle is very steep, the rider may have no choice but to throw herself forward.

Solutions

If your legs get behind your center of gravity because your horse lacks impulsion, causing you to squeeze or kick hard on the approach, you'll lurch forward over the jump.

PATRICK O'LEARY

It's hard for a rider not to over-jump when the jumps get high and her horse gets very deep to a big vertical with the ground rail set directly underneath. The angle of the ascent is so steep here that Lily has thrown herself forward in a big effort to stay with Waiwi's motion. But by being this far forward, Lily is making it tougher for Waiwi to get off the ground. Nevertheless, Lily's legs are solid and she's giving her horse free rein to get airborne.

First, go back to flatwork exercises and remind your horse to go forward in response to a light request from your legs. Keep your weight securely in your heels, keep your calves on your horse to signal "forward," but don't grip with the lower legs. Instead of gripping with your calves and kicking hard with your heels, carry a stick and use it (touch, tap, or swat his barrel, just behind your leg) to remind him to go when you say so, and keep going.

Then, practice jumping lots of low fences with light leg contact and without holding on with your hands—reins knotted, arms out to the side—so you can practice staying balanced over your stirrups and waiting for the horse's effort to close your hip angle.

If your horse is consistently taking off too deep to the fences—jumping sharply up instead of up and out—move the ground rails out a little more from the base of your verticals, and then practice grids and combinations with slightly longer distances. Use oxer-to-oxer combinations to encourage him to stand back a bit more.

GETTING LEFT BEHIND

This is the worst fault in jumping. *Getting left behind* means your balance is unintentionally behind the horse's balance as he jumps, so you're probably thumping down on his back or jerking him in the mouth—not very pleasant for either of you, and a guaranteed way to convince a horse that jumping is not fun.

Staying slightly behind the motion, as you do when riding in a safety position, is not the same as getting left behind. A horse generally doesn't mind if the rider is a little behind, as long as the rider's hands give forward and the rider's deep seat doesn't interfere with the effort of the horse's back, loins, and hind legs. But getting left behind on every jump, sitting heavily on the horse's back and snatching the bit is one of the quickest ways to create a *stopper:* the horse simply won't want to jump because he's being punished every time he does. If the rider's seat is heavy in the saddle over a jump, then the horse can't round his back up into a bascule and he's likely to catch a rail with his hind legs.

If you jam your heels forward, as this rider is doing, your lower legs won't be under your center of gravity and you'll be behind the motion in jumping. Keep your feet under you.

To follow the motion over a jump, a rider must have good balance, secure seat and legs, independent use of all the parts of her body (especially the hands and arms), and the confidence to trust her horse and move with the jumping effort. If any of these components is missing, there will be problems.

Causes

1. Loss of balance, generally caused by insecure or improperly positioned legs and feet, can cause a rider to get left behind. When your balance is fragile, you tend to pull your legs up and grab with your hands, which is not the response your horse needs from you.

2. Lack of confidence can also make a rider approach a jump in a stiff, upright, and defensive posture. She may be afraid to follow the motion and commit to the jump.

3. Lack of skills development; no independent hands or release. Some riders can keep their seats secure in the middle of the saddle, but haven't learned how to release adequately with their hands and arms to follow

the horse's head and neck. From the horse's point of view, this is still "getting left behind."

4. Physical stiffness and inability to "fold and go." Older riders may find that the mobility in their hips, knees, shoulders, and elbows just isn't what it used to be.

5. An instructor's insistence to "get the heels down." A rider may swing her lower legs forward in an effort to jam the heels down. Then her lower legs can't support her because her stirrups are in front of her center of gravity. The photo on page 203 shows an example of this.

PATRICK O'LEARY

A modified form of "left behind," in which the rider's hands are following but her seat is not. Experienced riders learn to ride behind the motion when necessary, but it mustn't become a habit. This rider needs to stop gripping with her lower legs, put weight in her heels, flatten her back, and lighten (lift) her seat so she is balanced over her horse's center of gravity. (She may be in this strong, "defensive driving" position because her horse has threatened to refuse; his sour expression indicates he's not a happy jumper in this photo.)

Solutions

To improve balance and leg position, ride without stirrups on the flat in rising trot, two-point, and three-point. Lessons on the longe can be especially beneficial, as the rider can ride without reins as she moves from rising trot to two-point and back again, with and without stirrups.

To improve the "give and release" with hands and arms, practice a long crest release over single ground rails and small crossrails. Use a jumping strap to help your hands stay forward and off your horse's mouth. See Lessons #8 through 10 for skill-building exercises using jumping grids.

Confidence should improve with balance, but be sure you're not overfacing yourself by trying to jump too high, too soon. Continue trotting over cavalletti and small crossrails until you're very certain you're ready to move up. Keep everything simple and safe!

If physical stiffness and mobility issues are a problem, work with your physician to design a program of exercise and physical therapy to keep your joints limber as well as strong. Flexibility through the hips is especially important in all aspects of riding.

If you're riding a horse who has become reluctant to jump because he can't trust his rider's hands to follow and stay soft, you may be able to restore his confidence by switching temporarily to a gentle hackamore or Dr. Cook's Bitless Bridle.

OVERRIDING

Are you an overly aggressive rider? Assertive people often feel they can't just sit quietly—they must *do something* all the time. Good riding means quiet riding, and that requires doing as little as possible to get the results you're looking for.

Overriding confuses, distracts, and frightens a sensitive horse, and it will teach a duller horse to ignore subtle signals—thus requiring even more aggressive riding in the future.

Experienced riders can get in the habit of overriding when they ride problem horses, or green horses that may not be ready for the work they're being asked to do. This can lead to a habit of riding behind the motion with overly aggressive aids.

Causes

1. Experienced riders may override because they're working with "problem horses" that have learned to evade and ignore the rider's aids. These riders tend to anticipate and attack problems aggressively to get an immediate response from a balky or tentative horse.

2. Novice riders may develop the habit of overriding because they've become accustomed to riding sluggish or sour school horses. They may believe that every horse needs continuous, vigorous application of stick and spurs just to keep the canter going. Or they've seen more experienced riders pushing their horses hard in a very competitive environment. Or, sadly, they may have a coach who overreacts or pushes the riders and horses too hard.

Solutions

Whatever the cause, the solution is the same. First, analyze why you seem to be riding so aggressively. It can be helpful to videotape a ride and ask an independent instructor or experienced friend to help you see what's happening.

Second, get the help of a coach whose riders are known for their quiet, effective riding. If the instructor feels you're secure enough in your basic abilities, ask to ride a more sensitive horse so you can work on keeping your aids subtle and precise. Work on the flat to refine your aids, and don't jump at all until you have rebuilt your system of requests and rewards so you gain a new understanding of how to ask, what it feels like when the horse responds correctly, and how to reward the response. This is where cross-training can really help. The ideal coach would be a dressage trainer known for her ability to help jumper riders.

Next, you'll need to ride over fences on horses that are willing, uncomplicated, and not dead to the aids. And you'll probably have to re-school your own horse to be sure he responds promptly to your newer and quieter riding style.

UNDER-RIDING

Under-riding occurs when the rider does too little. The very passive rider doesn't help the horse at all because she's dropped the lines of communication. A sensitive, well-trained horse may be quite comfortable with a non-assertive rider, while a sluggish horse will simply quit working. A green horse, on the other hand, will become confused, unpredictable, and often fearful when he receives no direction from his rider.

Causes

1. Fear. The rider may be anxious about doing something wrong, and so does nothing at all. Or she may be afraid of falling, and therefore directs all her energy to simply staying on. Show-ring nervousness or stress from other areas of her life can also play a part in creating a passive rider.

2. Too much experience riding overly sensitive or overly aggressive horses. A few rides on a horse that overreacts to the smallest stimulus can quickly create a too-quiet rider. The under-riding technique may work on this type of horse, but the rider can't adapt to any other horse she might need to ride.

3. Trying too hard to be elegant and pretty. The instructor is probably at fault. A coach who neglects the functional aspects of good form can create a photogenic but ineffective rider.

Solutions

If anxieties are causing you to "freeze," focus on the negative aspects of your riding, or forget how to ride effectively, then try to analyze your concerns and go back to the basics of good position and effective use of your aids. Try to remember why you ride—for the joy, the sense of partnership with your horse, the feeling of accomplishment and confidence when you learn something new.

You can also ease your fears by expanding your overall equestrian skills and participating in other aspects of riding and competition. Sharpen your ground-handling techniques, or help someone else train her horse to longe. Instead of competing, go to a show as a groom. Walk the courses, help set jumps in warm-up, and observe the other riders to decide whom you admire and would like to emulate.

If you're riding an overly sensitive or aggressive horse, ask your coach to put you on something a little less responsive so you'll have to work a little harder. Try to gain experience riding many different (but trustworthy) horses. Meanwhile, ask a more assertive (but still tactful) rider or instructor to work with your sensitive horse. Sometimes a horse and rider simply aren't a good match—the horse's anxieties worsen the rider's fears and vice versa.

And if you're that very stylish rider posing for a picture, remember that form follows function, so good riding must be effective riding. A beautiful position is desirable because it works, not because it's pretty. Get some experience riding horses that require you to really ride, not just go along for the ride.

UNABLE TO SEE A DISTANCE

It's happened to everyone at some time or other: You come off a turn, look down the long side to a single fence, and you can't decide what to do to get to a good take-off spot. Do you shorten stride, lengthen stride, or what? That's called "not seeing a distance." So you clutch and fuss with your horse's stride, and yes, just as you feared, he chips in and pops awkwardly over— thus confirming your negative belief that you cannot see a distance.

Causes

1. The rider doesn't have enough experience regulating strides, speed, and the path to a jump. She may generally lack experience riding over a wide variety of jumps.

2. Anxiety can also cause a rider to become distracted and lose the feel for a distance.

3. The horse is irregular in his striding or responsiveness to the rider. This is a common problem with green horses if they've been pushed to jump before they can easily adjust strides on the flat.

When you can't see a distance, focus on what you can do: establish your focal point, keep a straight path, and maintain rhythm and impulsion. If you can do those things, your horse will figure out where to take off.

Solutions

The solutions to all three problems should be obvious. First, get more experience riding the exercises that will produce the feel for strides. Practice Lessons #11–13 again, because you need to review the skills that will help you make decisions about adjusting strides and paths.

Second, remember to trust your horse. You and he have practiced all the exercises together, but he's the one actually doing the jumping. So if you can't see a distance, just find your visual focus, keep a good rhythm and a straight path, and let him make the call.

Third, if you're riding a horse that you can't trust to hold a steady rhythm or respond reliably to your aids, then you need to go back to the basics and help him learn to be steadier and more responsive on the flat.

LOSING A STIRRUP, LOSING BALANCE, OR FALLING

It's true—you do sometimes lose your balance and part company with your horse. But there are a few things you can do to minimize these experiences.

Causes

1. Your saddle or stiffup pads may be slick and slippery. New saddles are notorious for shine but no friction.

2. Your stirrups may be too long.

3. You haven't had enough practice in the basics. Your legs may be weak or you may lack general fitness or coordination.

4. If you fall often, you may be riding "more horse" than you're ready for.

Solutions

Be sure your saddle supports you with good balance, the right fit, and a non-slippery surface. Replace those worn stirrup pads with a pair that will offer more friction. Wear leather-seat breeches or chaps while schooling, but also ride in the gear you'll wear during competition. Don't introduce yourself to a new saddle in competition.

Be sure your stirrups are the right length, and check them often because leather stirrups often stretch gradually without the rider realizing it. If you find yourself reaching for them or losing them often, then shorten them a notch. As you ride, practice dropping and then picking up a stirrup without looking down. Your balance should be so secure that simply losing a stirrup should not cause you to fall off.

Work more without stirrups, in two-point and three-point. Jump through simple grids without reins. Ride bareback. Participate in a regular exercise program to strengthen your core muscles, flexibility, and balance. (Pilates and yoga are both excellent programs for riders.)

Riding bareback can help with your balance and feel. Emma's back is slightly roached here—a common result of having no stirrups for support—but she demonstrates a lovely following hand, relaxed lower legs, and a secure seat.

If you're riding an athletic horse with a lot of bascule in his jump, or one that's fast and sensitve, and you find you're falling off when the horse isn't doing anything wrong, you need more experience on a quieter, less-athletic jumper. Also work on learning to fall. Practice an emergency dismount and get your horse familiar with it. Take a few tumbling lessons and learn a forward roll. If you know of someone who teaches vaulting on a reliable horse, take a few lessons. You'll be much more comfortable when you have some control over a hasty dismount.

Horse Problems

Disobediences (Refusals)

Only a confident, focused, responsive, and comfortable horse will be willing to jump. The horse must trust his rider as well as his own ability to balance himself as he judges height, speed, and distance.

There are many, many reasons for a horse to say "no" to a jump. It's the rider's job to figure out the underlying causes and not simply assume the horse is misbehaving or "won't jump for me because he doesn't like me."

Causes

1. Pain or fatigue. He's unsound, his back hurts, the saddle or bridle pinches, or those spurs hurt. Or he's just plain tired.

2. Remembered or anticipated pain. The last time he jumped well, the rider yanked on his mouth or thumped on his back. Or he's willing to take off, but he knows that landing on hard ground may hurt his feet or back.

3. Lack of confidence or training. He's never seen that jump or combination before, and he needs time to figure it out. He doesn't trust his rider to give him good direction. He doesn't trust his own balance or skills. He's had a bad fall.

4. Over-facing an inexperienced horse, or asking an older horse to jump beyond his present ability. Young, old, and unfit horses may not be able to do what their riders think they can.

5. Distractions and excitement. Flags are flying, other horses are milling around, there are loud noises, and he doesn't know what to look at first, so he forgets to look at the jump.

6. Poor line of sight. He couldn't see the jump until he was on top of it.

7. Rider errors. His rider steered him crookedly or pulled him off balance or didn't ask for enough impulsion. His rider was too passive, too aggressive, lost focus, hung on his mouth, or sent contradictory signals.

8. He just doesn't like jumping. No matter how talented a horse is, if he doesn't like his job, he's not going to do well at it. He may just not be suited for jumping—perhaps he's clumsy or has poor vision.

Solutions

You may be able to correct an unexpected refusal in competition by creating a better approach and using your driving aids more vigorously, but you've got to fix the underlying causes at home, not during a competition.

First, be sure your horse is sound and pain-free. Check the fit of his saddle, bridle, and bit. Have his teeth inspected and floated if necessary.

Next, be sure your basic riding skills are solid. If you're losing your balance, giving conflicting signals, or transmitting your anxieties to your horse, then he's likely to choose the prudent option and simply not jump.

Be sure you've used progressive training to give him the skills he needs. Sometimes a talented young horse gives the impression that he can advance very rapidly, but you mustn't skip any steps in the training or he can easily lose confidence. Go back to cavalletti and grids, use channel poles on the ground to help him find a straight approach, and don't over-face him with angled jumps or tight turns until he's truly confident with straight, steady approaches to all his fences.

Increase a young horse's confidence by introducing him to many new experiences before you ask him to perform under pressure. Take him to different venues and let him look at everything. Ride different trails and jump many small jumps with odd appearances. Ride near flags, picnic tables, and lots of other horses, dogs, traffic, noise, and construction projects. Use "spook-proofing" methods to increase his confidence in you, at all levels, so when he needs to ignore distractions and focus on jumping, he can do that.

Then, if your horse still can't give you an honest, reliable ride over jumps you're both familiar with and you know you can both manage, you may have to face the fact that this horse simply doesn't want to jump. Jumping requires willingness and trust between two partners, so if he's not willing and can't trust, he may need a change of career.

When things go wrong, figure out what's missing and address that in your training. A crooked approach, no focal point, and a lack of impulsion all contributed to this pony saying, "No, I don't feel good about this."

WRONG LEADS OR UNEVEN KNEES IN THE AIR

These two problems are listed together because they often have the same causes and solutions. A horse that favors one lead over the other will often jump with the knee of the non-leading leg dropped down, ready to land first. So if he favors his left lead, he's likely to consistently drop his right knee in the air. This is a form fault in hunters, because it can be unsafe.

If the dropped-knee problem is severe, he may also be dropping his shoulder or twisting to one side in the air. He's probably also difficult to turn to his "stiff" side on the flat *and* over fences.

Causes
1. Unsoundness or injury.
2. Weakness through the back and loin.
3. Uneven or unbalanced riding, for which the horse tries to compensate.

HAMILTON AHLO, JR.

PATRICK O'LEARY

By dropping his right knee early—or not picking it up as high as the left—this horse is already preparing to land on his right front foot, which will put him onto his left lead. Note that his right shoulder is also down and his right hind has pushed off before his left. He's tilting to the right with an unbalanced effort, though his rider looks straight and focused. Compare this to the picture of the mare in the next photo.

This mare is absolutely straight, absolutely square, and thoroughly focused. Waiwi is snapping up both knees to the same height, and both hind legs are pushing off at the same moment to maximize her jumping effort. Lily is looking to the right and probably preparing for a right turn, but she can easily ask her horse to land on either lead.

Solutions

It's important to first rule out physical issues for this problem, such as a sore back, shoulder, or leg; or teeth that need floating. A sore mouth or bad teeth can cause a horse to tilt or twist his head, which can create an imbalance throughout his body.

If your horse favors the left lead—as many do—you can help straighten out the imbalance by doing everything from the right that you normally do from the left: leading, turning, saddling, and even mounting. (Think about it: If you always get on from the left, you're pulling your horse's withers to the left at least once every time you ride. At the very least, you should use a mounting block whenever possible, and it doesn't hurt to get on from the right side occasionally.)

Use longe work, flatwork, and stretching exercises to make the weak side stronger and more flexible. Leg-yielding in both directions will help strengthen your horse's back and increase his ability to step underneath

Raise one side of a jump to help correct a horse that hangs a knee and favors one lead. This jump is built to help bring up the right knee: Approach in right-lead canter, hold the lead over the jump, and turn right after landing. Be sure to jump in the center of the obstacle.

himself more equally, with both hind legs. Trotting over raised cavalletti and jumping through low grids with snug distances will also help strengthen his back and loin coupling.

Be sure your own riding isn't at fault. Check your stirrups and saddle to be sure everything is absolutely even. Work to keep your shoulders square; don't dive, duck, or tip to one side.

Then work on maintaining and changing leads over small jumps, keeping your horse well between your legs and hands. Practice Lessons #14 and #15 to help you hold or change leads.

Finally, build several jumps as shown in the illustration on this page, in which you've raised the rail on the side of the "hanging" knee. Approach this in canter on his less-favorite lead, and hold the lead as you jump through the center, land, and turn in the more difficult direction (toward the high side of the jump).

Another good jump to practice over is a *high cross jump,* in which the center is only 2' high but the poles are resting against the standards at the 4' level so the horse must bring both front feet up evenly or risk rubbing a pole.

RUSHING OR PULLING

A horse that gets excited and rushes or pulls while jumping is neither pleasant nor safe to ride.

Causes

1. Pain. A horse in pain will tense up and try to get away, often rushing around the course to get it over with. He'll then make mistakes and hit fences, thus causing himself more pain.

2. Fear. A horse that's been forced to jump when he lacks the necessary skills or confidence will often rush from a fear of being punished.

3. Overriding or restriction by the rider. Horses who aren't allowed to balance themselves or jump freely sometimes feel their only solution is to grab the reins and run.

4. General excitability and exuberance. A horse who's been allowed to run and buck when he's feeling fresh is likely to use the activity of jumping as a way of blowing off excess energy.

Solutions

As with most other problems on this list, you should first resolve any pain and discomfort issues. Then take your horse back a few steps in his training, and be sure the basics are covered. Repeat the exercises that are easy and a bit boring, but be sure he does them correctly.

If he is physically fit, then try to identify the source of his anxiety. Is he over-faced? Does a particular type of course or jump make him nervous? Don't go to a harsher bit—that will just increase his tension. If possible, switch to a milder one. A hackamore or bitless bridle might lessen his anxiety but still give you sufficient control.

See how he goes with a different rider or coach. If you tend to ride aggressively, or your balance isn't what it should be, get some help from a coach or rider whose horses are known for going quietly.

Work to reduce the horse's anxiety and anticipation, and increase his responsiveness to you. Be patient and ride a lot in trot and canter, jumping single small jumps at random. Ride circles and ring figures in front of the jumps, occasionally go over a jump, and then continue working on the flat.

If he's just plain fresh, turn him out more, reduce his feed, give him longer warm-ups on the flat before you begin jumping, and work on long, slow distance rides. Then develop greater responsiveness over small fences, and stay with the simple exercises until the work becomes a little bit boring. Mix an occasional jump in with lots of flatwork. Don't jump an entire course until he's calm and responsive with all the other exercises.

JUMPING "LONG"

Jumping "long" is different from merely being scopey. The scopey horse will put in an occasional long distance when he's got to stretch to reach a reasonable take-off spot. The occasional long distance is not a cause for worry; consistently jumping "long," however, is.

This is the horse that regularly leaves out a stride, takes off well before his rider is ready, and produces the catch-your-breath "space shot" leap that threatens to land them both on top of the jump. He brings down rails with his hind legs and often leaves even good riders behind with his unexpected take-offs. This is unsafe jumping that needs fixing.

Causes

1. Lack of impulsion with a trailing hind end.

2. Former training as a steeplechaser, or any horse that's been encouraged to jump at high speed with very long takeoff spots.

Solutions

It sounds strange, but the horse that strolls up to a jump in a lazy, disconnected canter is the one most likely to take off dangerously early. This sort of horse has a "whenever" kind of approach to the fence. Instead of bringing his hind end underneath so he can rock back to shorten or push to lengthen the last few strides, he just completes a stride somewhere in front of the jump and heaves himself off the ground.

Aside from leaving his rider badly behind, the danger is that this horse will miscalculate the effort needed to clear the fence and crash. The irony is that if the horse put more effort into his canter, he could put less effort into the bone-jarring leap.

The horse that produces a long distance from a lazy canter has so little impulsion that he may just stop entirely after he lands. (One friend has a large pony mare who specializes in this. The mare never refuses to jump, but two steps after landing from one of her long-distance leaps, she stops to bury her nose in the grass. This produces some interesting cross-country rounds.)

Another problem is the horse that's been trained to stand well back and jump at speed from a huge stride. A steeplechaser traveling at racing speed can produce a leap that may cover 30' in a single jumping stride. When you try to slow him down, he still thinks he can take off from 12' in front of the jump.

For both horses, the solutions are similar.

It's vital to keep the haunches engaged. Work on the flat to create a bouncy, round, short canter; lengthen it, then shorten it again. Use leg-yielding at walk and trot to help the hindquarters engage. When the quality of the basic canter has improved, work through grids set at snug distances, and be sure to ride your horse on contact. Hold him between legs and hands on the approach; insist on a round, balanced canter; and try to bring him to the base of the jump.

Push the lazy horse all the way through the arc of the jump and keep riding after landing.

When you move to single jumps, use two ground lines, one close to the jump on the take-off side and one on the landing side rolled out a bit more than usual—perhaps 2'6" for a 2' jump. Place a ground rail 9'–10' feet in front of the jump to regulate the last canter stride, and another ground rail 10'–12' beyond the jump so the horse will pay attention to where he's going to land.

Don't be a passive rider with the horse that leaves out strides. You'll need to provide assistance so he can find his balance, keep his impulsion, canter to the base of the jump, jump and land safely.

CHIPPING IN

The horse that consistently takes off too close to a jump is in danger of hitting a rail with his front legs. He loses impulsion over his jumps because he must jump upward at a steep angle to clear the fence, instead of jumping forward as well as up.

Causes

1. Either the rider or horse is misjudging the takeoff. This may be a more serious problem with verticals, as it's harder to judge your distance to a vertical than to an oxer.

2. The rider is restricting the horse too much and driving him too deeply to the base of the jump. The horse must have the room and freedom to stretch his head and neck forward as his jump begins.

3. The rider can't see a distance, and tries to make the horse "wait" until he can see one. They get too close to the base of the jump, and then it's too late.

RICHARD VALCOURT

Be sure you're supporting, but not restricting, your horse on landing. A green horse in particular needs a very balanced rider who can stay centered to help the horse find his own balance.

Solutions

In schooling, always use ground lines with your verticals. Roll the ground line on the takeoff side out to a point at least equal to the height of the jump so you both have a reference point for judging the takeoff.

Ride through grids and combinations with ground poles set to establish the take-off points. Use Exercise #3, "Lengthen Strides on a Four-Stride Line" in Lesson #12 to help you find a slightly longer stride and be comfortable with a longer takeoff spot.

Be sure you're not riding with a too-tight martingale or restrictive hands; work to soften your release and follow-through. Try to "allow and go" instead of micromanaging the approach. Forget about finding the perfect take-off spot and just focus on the path, the speed, and the rhythm. Let your horse jump the jump.

BUCKING, SWERVING, OR BOLTING ON LANDING

Many horses and riders manage the approach quite well, but run into major balance issues on landing. Something unexpected happens, the rider loses her balance and puts the horse off-balance, and then the horse has to make a sudden move or he delivers a protest on landing. And two strides after the jump, the rider falls off.

Causes

1. Unbalanced horse or unbalanced rider, which causes an unbalanced horse.
2. Fresh, playful horse who's having fun and taking advantage of the rider's insecurity on landing.

Solutions

To produce a safe, balanced jump, the horse must be confident in his skills and ability. A green horse needs an experienced rider to help him balance. A novice rider needs a reliable, experienced horse who can compensate for the rider's small mistakes and insecurities.

Every green horse puts in an awkward jump from time to time. And, in an effort to recover his balance from a disorganized landing, he may fling his head up, scoot sideways, or buck. If this happens more than just occasionally, a tactful rider will go back to the cavalletti and low gridwork, or return to longeing or free-jumping the horse if necessary. (This is especially important if your horse is under the age of 6 and still growing; his balance may change so that he literally cannot jump safely for a while.)

The experienced horse that begins to buck or bolt after landing over a jump has a different problem. He's issuing a protest that something isn't right. Common causes for problems on landing include a too-tight martingale, or a rider who gets left behind, restricts his head, or catches him in the mouth.

Or, he may simply be having a little fun, because he's learned that it's fun to gallop and jump, and the moment after a landing is a good time to cut up because his rider hasn't quite re-established control. If this sounds like your horse, give him plenty of turnout in a pasture or paddock and a long warm-up on the flat to help him focus and prepare for work.

Try to analyze what's happening in the air and when you land. Although you might want to respond by holding the contact tighter, try to ride with a lighter hand over the jump and on landing. Jump on a slight bending line, using a soft opening rein to direct your horse into the turn instead of a backwards pull. Practice jumping uphill and up small banks with a good crest release, so neither of you has to worry so much about the descent part of the landing.

Work through grids set for your horse's comfortable baseline stride. Place a ground rail 9'–10' beyond the last fence to encourage your horse to organize his landing and recovery better by rounding back up into his balanced canter.

And reward him for every good jump and every good landing. There's joy for both of you, when it's done right.

Afterthoughts

One of my greatest delights has always been to teach riders and horses how to become confident, happy partners, who are secure in their athletic abilities. Teaching, training, and riding are all part of the same tapestry; jumping just adds another dimension of fun and satisfaction to the pure pleasure of the partnership. There's nothing quite so thrilling as completing a successful round on a horse you've trained yourself or watching a student turn in a brilliant ride on her own young horse.

I hope that everyone who reads this book will have many such moments, and will find as much joy in riding and jumping as I do.

REFERENCES

Bennett, Deb, Ph.D. "Timing and Rate of Skeletal Maturation in Horses, with Comments on Starting Colts and the State of the Industry." http://equinestudies.org/knowledge_base/ranger.html (accessed March 22, 2007).

Harris, Susan E. and The United States Pony Club. *The United States Pony Club Manual of Horsemanship.* New York: Wiley Publishing, 1995.

Hugo-Vidal, Holly with Sue M. Copeland. *Build Confidence over Fences.* Gaithersburg, Maryland: PRIMEDIA Equine Network, 2005.

Mailer, Carol. *Jumping Problems Solved: Gridwork: The Secret to Success.* North Pomfret, Vermont: Trafalgar Square Publishing, 2005.

Micklem, William. *Complete Horse Riding Manual.* New York: DK Publishing, Inc., 2003.

Teall, Geoff with Ami Hendrickson. *Geoff Teall on Riding Hunters, Jumpers and Equitation: Develop a Winning Style.* North Pomfret, Vermont: Trafalgar Square Publishing, 2006.

White-Mullin, Anna Jane. *Judging Hunters and Hunter Seat Equitation*, Revised Edition. North Pomfret, Vermont: Trafalgar Square Publishing, 2003.

INDEX

hands. *See also* release
  carry position, 69
  crop carriage, 69–70, 72–73
  developing independent, 70, 73
hanging a leg, 10
head, conformation of, 20
health, assessing, 30–32
heel, as anchor point, 62
heel lifts, 75, 76
height of jump
  length of jumping stride and, 6–7
  raising, 156
helmet, 49
high cross jump, 213
hills and slopes
  cantering, 151
  circles and figure eights, 151
  trotting, 150
  walking, 150
hilltoppers, 193
hindquarters, conformation of, 20–21
hock
  conformation, 21, 24–25
  growth plates of, 146
hollow, 10
horse, finding talented
  breed, 25–26
  conformation, 17, 19–25
  evaluating yearlings and two-year-
    olds, 36–38
  experience and judgment, 35–36
  fitness level, 33–34
  inherited characteristics, 17, 18–30
  nutrition and health, 30–32
  parentage, 26
  partnership development, 18, 34–36
  physical development, 18, 30–34
  responsiveness, 35
  size, 22–24
  skills training, 32–33
  temperament, 26–30
  trust and confidence, 34–35
horseshoes, 31, 49
hunter class
  body condition, 30
  hack class, 91
  horse size for, 22–23, 24

horses suited for, 189
  rollback in, 190
  stride for, 25
  temperament for, 28
hunter paces, 195
hunter trials, 194–195
hunt seat equitation. *See also* equitation
  forward seat, 41
  horses suited for, 189
  position differences from
    dressage, 55
  standing martingale, 43
hyaluronic acid, 31

impulsion, 37
interfering, 24

joint supplements, 31
judgment, 35–36
jump cups, 112, 113, 157
jumper class
  courses, 192
  horses suited for, 191, 192
  judging, 191
  levels of classes, 191
  popularity, 191
jumping ahead of the motion, 121
jumping bat, 50–51
jumping behind of the motion, 121
jumping lane, 37, 154
jumping line, 103
jumping long, 214–215
jumping strap, 46, 75
jumping stride, 5–7, 90–95
jump-off sequence, 193
jumps
  changing aspects of, 171
  combination, 102, 194
  constructing safe, 112–113
  longing over, 158–164
  natural, 174–182
  related distance and, 118, 119
  setting up, 154–155
  single, 118–123
  skinny (narrow), 103
  types of, 102–103
jump standards, 112, 159

ABOUT THE AUTHOR

SARAH BLANCHARD is a trainer and riding instructor with forty-plus years of teaching experience. She began riding "too far back to remember" at her family's boarding stable in Stamford, Connecticut. Her mother provided early riding lessons on a series of challenging ponies, while her father, a dairy farmer, taught her to hitch and handle driving horses.

As a teenager, Sarah polished her skills in hunt seat equitation under the eye of well-known trainer Victor Hugo-Vidal, Jr., and competed in AHSA Medal and Maclay hunt seat equitation classes. After her family farm was sold, Sarah spent several summers teaching riding and jumping at camps in New Hampshire and New York.

At the University of Connecticut, Sarah earned her bachelor's degree with a major in English literature and a minor in animal science. She rode at Hal Vita's Shallowbrook Stables and was a member of the UConn Intercollegiate Horse Judging Team, which placed second at the national finals in 1971. She won the hunt seat equitation championship at UConn for three consecutive years.

After college, Sarah established a small stable in northeastern Connecticut. During this time, Sarah developed an interest in dressage and combined training, and successfully competed her homebred and home-trained horses in hunters, dressage and eventing, qualifying for the Area I Training Level eventing championship in 1990.

Sarah is a licensed instructor in Massachusetts, where she lived for several years. As an advisor to the Eye of the Storm Equine Rescue Center in Stow, Massachusetts, she helped evaluate and rehabilitate neglected and abused horses. A popular trainer, clinician, and judge, Sarah has managed and judged local shows in New York, Connecticut, Massachusetts, Rhode Island, Vermont, and Hawaii, where she now lives with her husband, Rich Valcourt. She serves on the board of directors for the Hawaii Isle Dressage and Combined Training Association

Sarah, who also earned an MBA from Nichols College in Massachusetts, teaches horsemanship, business, and marketing courses at the University of Hawaii-Hilo.